T4-AKQ-442

The Cultural Labyrinth
of María de Zayas

The
Cultural Labyrinth
of María de Zayas

Marina S. Brownlee

CABRINI COLLEGE LIBRARY
610 KING OF PRUSSIA ROAD
RADNOR, PA 19087

PENN

University of Pennsylvania Press

Philadelphia

#42708168

Copyright © 2000 University of Pennsylvania Press
All rights reserved
Printed in the United States of America on acid-free paper

10 9 8 7 6 5 4 3 2 1

Published by
University of Pennsylvania Press
Philadelphia, Pennsylvania 19104-4011

Library of Congress Cataloging-in-Publication Data

Brownlee, Marina S.
   The cultural labyrinth of María de Zayas / Marina S. Brownlee.
      p. cm.
   Includes bibliographical references and index.
   ISBN 0-8122-3537-1 (alk. paper)
      1. Zayas y Sotomayor, María de, 1590–1650 Novelas amorosas y
ejemplares.   2. Zayas y Sotomayor, María de, 1590–1650—Literary
style.   3. Paradox in literature.   I. Title.
PQ6498.Z5 N6833   2000
863'.3—dc21
                                                      99-054377

For Kevin, Madeleine, and Nico

Contents

Acknowledgments

It is a pleasure to acknowledge here several special people and organizations to whom I am indebted.

The Class of 1963 College of Women, which has endowed the chair that I am honored to occupy, has provided me not only with valuable research funds, but also with some very impressive female role models. The Guggenheim Foundation granted me a crucially important leave year, without which the writing of this book would have taken substantially longer.

My thanks to Eric Halpern, director of the University of Pennsylvania Press, and to Jerome Singerman, its Acquisitions Editor, for their guidance in the production of this book. Andrew Frisardi, Noreen O'Connor, and Alison Anderson have offered meticulous and intelligent editing of the book manuscript. I wish to thank John O'Neill, Curator of Manuscripts and Rare Books of the Hispanic Society of America, for his generous assistance in this project.

I thank Ed Friedman for his insightful reading of the manuscript, and Israel Burshatin, María Eugenia Lacarra, Amy Williamsen, Margreta de Grazia, Peter Stallybrass, José Regueiro, and Lance Donaldson-Evans for their valuable remarks. John D. Lyons and Valeria Finucci, exemplary friends and colleagues, I thank for their inspiration and encouragement in my work on Early Modern Spain.

Finally, I thank Ann Chahbandour for her invaluable friendship.

Preface

In recent years the perils of periodization have attracted considerable attention—a logical outgrowth of the rethinking of the politics and arbitrariness of canon formation, as various interest groups attempt to determine which works should or should not be considered canonical. Thought-provoking studies on the ill effects of periodization—such as those by Margreta de Grazia, William Kerrigan, and Gordon Braden, which critique Titus Burckhardt's idea of the Renaissance—are revising key aspects of early modern studies.[1] At the same time, we can not escape the need to organize cultures, their production and evolution, with notions of periods. The wealth of writing on postmodernism is an obvious and timely case in point. And it is particularly instructive to consider in studying the seventeenth-century Baroque, with which it shares many affinities.

Postmodernism acknowledges that all cultural practices have an ideological subtext that determines the parameters of their meaning production. It may be seen, in part, as a corrective to the belief in textual autonomy that dominated literary studies in the 1960s and 1970s. It is, by all accounts, a self-reflexive attitude that interrogates our institutions, intellectual as well as aesthetic—the media, the university, museums, and so forth. As a consequence of this relentless interrogation, the postmodern condition in which we currently find ourselves has been aptly termed a "crisis of legitimation."

In terms of literary production, postmodernism concerns itself very centrally with the power and constraints of mimesis. It is committed to metafictional self-reflexivity in order to address extratextual issues of politics and history. García Márquez's *Cien años de soledad* is often evoked as a paradigm of the contradictory features that define postmodern fiction. As Larry McCaffrey observes that the book "has become a kind of model for the contemporary writer, being self-conscious about its literary heritage and about the limits of mimesis . . . but yet managing to reconnect its readers to the world outside the page."[2]

Another feature of this trend is specified by Linda Hutcheon, namely that postmodern literature is "an art of shifting perspective [inscribing narrators who are] either disconcertingly multiple and hard to locate or resolutely provisional and limited."[3] Rosalind Krauss posits a third defining feature of the postmodern text by coining the neologism "paraliterary"—a type of text that challenges "both the 'work of art' and the separation of that concept from the domain of the academic critical establishment: the paraliterary space is the space of debate, quotation, partisanship, betrayal, reconciliation; but it is not the space of unity, coherence, or resolution that we think of as constituting the work of art." This is the space of the postmodern—"the paradoxes of continuity and disconnection, of totalizing interpretation and the impossibility of final meaning."[4]

Such descriptions of postmodern discourse bear a striking resemblance to the literary Baroque of the seventeenth century. Far from signaling an unprecedented moment in Western culture, the postmodern shares notable affinities. Like the Baroque, postmodernism is both a chronological and a theoretical construct—both historical and typological in conception, both a period and an assembly of transhistorical features. In an unintentionally provocative remark, Ihab Hassan juxtaposes postmodern and Baroque, stating that postmodernism is "an ongoing cultural process or activity," one that eludes definition "except as a shifting matrix of ideas, a moot consensus, which may or may not harden some day into a term like 'baroque.'"[5] Yet it would be just as dangerous to view the Baroque as a homogeneous cultural movement as to misrepresent the polymorphous nature of the postmodern. Moreover, this configuration of shared features—far from being a unique phenomenon—recurs periodically in literary history. Articulating this recurrence, Nietzsche, for instance, recognizes "a baroque stage after the Renaissance, which he . . . conceives also as a recurrent phenomenon in history, occurring always at the decadence of great art as a decline into rhetoric and theatricality."[6]

Like the Baroque, postmodernism is the cultural expression of a society that critically reappraises the myths of the preceding era which viewed itself as paradigmatically "modern." Both movements undermine a humanist vision, be it Erasmian humanism or secular humanism. Both movements likewise discredit utopian cultural structures, be they imperial or Marxist. In other words, both demythologize—and that is what the "crisis of legitimacy" is all about. Postmodernism, like the Baroque, is much more form-conscious than the age that preceded it and to which it is responding. Both exploit the same literary figures: antithesis, oxymoron, catachresis, hyperbole, example, and (of particular importance for Zayas) paradox.

Paradox is at the root of Zayas's work—from the opening words of her global prologue to the end of the epilogue and all twenty tales in between. Readers looking for predictable events, characterizations, and values are likely to find frustration at the end of their journey. Instead the collection illustrates the complexity, ambiguity, and unresolved tension that characterizes Zayas's literary self-portrait and, indeed, her representation of both sexes throughout her novella collection. Her narratives reveal her to be torn between the needs of sexuality and individual fulfillment on the one hand, and, on the other, the firmly established demands of the code of honor. The *sarao*, an evening party or soirée, during which the stories are all recounted is very revealing of this tension. Speaking of the privileged, unstable environment represented by Zayas's literary soirée, William Clamurro observes, "The social space and social moment of the *sarao* are simultaneously apart from and critical of the aristocratic world of its participants, and yet are subtly indicative of the temporary, limited liberties made possible by an aristocracy's material power and idleness."[7]

The simultaneous condemnation of aristocratic abuses and the affirmation of them is paradoxical, to say the least. In fact, at the conclusion of part II of her stories, while the hostess of the *sarao* (Lisis) withdraws to a utopistically conceived convent in the company of several other women partygoers who are equally convinced of the need to escape the dangers of men, Zayas simultaneously calls for a return to the exemplary era of gender relations, as she perceives it, the reign of Ferdinand and Isabella, when men esteemed and protected women, fathers protected daughters, brothers protected sisters, husbands protected wives, and lovers protected their beloveds.[8]

This conservative social context, with its imperial overtones, seriously complicates any essentialist reading of the *Novelas*. Zayas is an outspoken defender of the cause of women, and therefore, a harsh critic of male abuses, but she is at the same time rich and contradictory in her portrayal of each.

If we turn to her prologue to follow the shifts in her self-presentation, we note that Zayas places herself first among those whose prose will fare very favorably in the "publication crucible," thereafter indicating that her "scribbles" shouldn't be condemned, out of common courtesy. She then shifts from this image of inferiority to one of equality with men, explaining that no matter what we are made of "es una misma la sangre," and, in addition, "las almas ni son hombres ni mujeres" (I, p. 21) [our blood is the same . . . our souls the same, for souls are neither male nor female (1)].

She concludes by saying that the only reason for the disparity that exists in the learnedness of men by comparison with the lesser degree of learning in women is not biological, but rather the result of social conditioning: "Si en nuestra crianza como nos ponen el cambray, en las almohadillas y los dibuxos en el bastidor, nos dieran libros y preceptores, fuéramos tan aptas para los puestos y para las cátedras como los hombres" (I, p. 22) [When our parents bring us up if, instead of putting cambric on our sewing cushions and patterns in our embroidery frames, they gave us books and teachers, we would be as fit as men for any job or university professorship (1)].

From this outspoken declaration of equality in terms of intellectual potential, Zayas then moves on to say that, in fact, women may surpass men in this domain, basing her argument on the venerable theory of the humors: "Quizá [somos] más agudas por ser de natural más frío, por consistir en humedad el entendimiento" (I, p. 22) [We might even be sharper because we're of a colder humor, and intelligence partakes of the damp humor" (1–2)].[9]

What strikes the reader is the level of disparity contained in this array of conflicting perspectives, whereby in a brief space she presents herself, and more broadly, womankind as being first truly creative, then inferior to men, thereafter equal and finally superior to them. By this concatenation of contradictory appraisals, the aim and effect is both to amaze and amuse. But without pausing to explain this kaleidoscopic presentation, she swiftly turns from issues of biology to examples taken from history. The illustrious Lucan admits that his wife helped him revise the *Pharsalia*, as well as having written many poems which he passed off as his own. Themistoclea, Diotima, Eudoxa, Xenobia, and Cornelia are singled out as other eminent and venerable examples who prove the intellectual equality of women to men. Many more could be enumerated from antiquity and from the present as well, but Zayas chooses to end her list there so as not to be guilty of the proverbial female vice—prolixity.

We see Zayas overtly toying again with her intellectual status, speaking now of her "ignorance," but at the same time deflating the ego of her male readers who should, of course, be familiar with "infinite numbers of women from antiquity and from our own times" whom she will not mention even if the male readers are uneducated. Clearly, no one wishes to be labeled "uneducated," and, in addition, it is logically impossible, no matter what the educational level of the reader, to have in mind the "unnamed multitudes" of female role models whom Zayas has in mind. This jibe at her reader, its logical absurdity, no doubt elicited laughter from her audience of readers, just as Cervantes's playfully pejorative initial address to his "idle" (rather than dear, kind, or subtle reader) did.

Given the plethora of role models, Zayas argues, it is clear that women, particularly those who are bookish by nature, are capable of tremendous learning. Speaking of herself not just intellectually, but in the physical terms of a reader, she explains, "En viendo cualquier [libro] nuevo o antiguo, dexo la almohadilla y no sosiego hasta que le paso. Desta inclinación nació la noticia, de la noticia el buen gusto; y de todo hacer versos, hasta escribir estas novelas, o por ser asunto más fácil o más apetitoso" (I, pp. 22–23) [The moment I see a book, new or old, I drop my sewing and can't rest until I've read it. From this inclination came information, and from the information good taste, and from this the writing of poetry, and then the writing of these novellas, perhaps because they seemed easier or more interesting to write (2)]. In this way, she figures herself as both reader and writer, the first activity resulting in the second, disclosing also her identity as poet.[10]

This detail (like others in the prologue) has its Cervantine reminiscence, recalling Cervantes' celebrated physical self-presentation as a writer, but, in his case, as a writer in a state of verbal paralysis: "suspenso, con el papel delante, la pluma en la oreja, el codo en el bufete y la mano en la mejilla" (20) [in this quandary, with the paper before me, my pen in my ear, my elbow on my desk, and my hand on my cheek (26)]. At the beginning of his magnum opus Cervantes' narrator finds himself tongue-tied because he claims to lack the obligatory laudatory sonnets, Latin quotations, endnotes, and so on, with which other authors (especially Lope de Vega) fill the pages of their prologues. By contrast, Zayas gives us the impression that her writing abilities come much more naturally than Cervantes's. This is a playful and audacious rewriting indeed, given that Cervantes was not only a male author, but by all accounts a brilliant one.

She concludes the prologue with a great degree of cagey playfulness, claiming woman's invulnerability for a variety of (conflicting) reasons: that it would be discourteous, and as we know, men are obliged to treat women courteously; that to insult a woman is like being ungrateful to your own mother; that readers should refrain from adverse criticism if they judge the novellas to be inferior since they were written by a woman (2).

With this unanticipated climax to her prologue we see Zayas's articulate, yet at the same time, deftly contradictory and calculatedly paradoxical presentation of herself in terms of female authorship, the female intellect, and womankind in general. The complex presentation of these themes in the prologue serves as an opening signal that alerts the reader to her nonlinear, indeed, labyrinthine discourse. And it is no accident, I think, that near the end of both the last tale in part I and the last tale in part II we find the repeated locution "tan intricados laberintos" [such intricate labyrinths], referring to many different kinds of labyrinths—physical, psychological, judicial, erotic, illusory.[11] As analysis of her tales and their inherent contradictions will reveal in the pages to follow, the labyrinth represents both the writing subject and the reading subject in the Zayesque enterprise.

1
Spectacle and Surveillance: A Writing Woman in Seventeenth-Century Spain

What King and Queen are these [Ferdinand and Isabella]
who would send into exile those
through such chimeric schemes
—based on secret counsel—
who scarcely offend them? . . .
What new mode of scrutiny and
legal system have we here?
Why are trials now held in secret?

—*Lope de Vega,* El niño inocente de la Guardia

A Web of Words

The distance separating early modern Europe from previous ages, in Michel Foucault's intriguing analogy, is that between the public spectacle characteristic of premodern cultures and the dominance of private surveillance in the modern world.[1] With the coming of modernity, the focus shifted from public life and the community to private individuals and their relation to the state. This new fascination with private life and the complex subjectivity that it entails derives both from the desire to articulate new kinds of knowledge (scientific, sexual, social, psychological) and from new forms of regulation (stemming from more centralized forms of government). To illustrate these regulatory innovations Foucault details, for example, the highly efficient elimination of lepers and plague victims in seventeenth-century French cities.

During the same historical period, the Spanish state expressed its regulatory obsessions not so much by focusing on the efficient control of social diseases, as by its projects for social engineering represented by the Inquisition, and by the honor code with its commitment to blood purity— *limpieza de sangre*. While blood purity and religious practices might not necessarily seem analogous, they were so in terms of their consequences for seventeenth-century Spain, as J. H. Elliott explains: "The effect of the statutes of *limpieza* was in many ways comparable to that of the activities of the Inquisition. They fostered the general sense of insecurity, encouraged the blackmailer and the informer, and prompted desperate attempts at deception."[2] María de Zayas y Sotomayor's two-part *Novelas amorosas y ejemplares* (1637, 1647) explores the physical and psychological effects of these social institutions on the private citizen with a degree of obsessiveness and fascination that is hard to equal in that or any other period.[3]

Private life, especially the surveillance and gossiping about the lives of others, was a long-standing threat to the individual in what has been termed Spain's Golden Age, that period sometimes construed as lasting either from the reign of the Catholic monarchs, Ferdinand and Isabella (1474–1504), or more frequently regarded as continuing from the ascendancy of Charles V (1517) until the death of Calderón de la Barca (1681).[4] As a result of Spain's multicultural population, the potential threat of religious heterology—being a crypto-Jew or crypto-Muslim, a witch or sorcerer—led to commentary, in one form or another, by all major authors during this period. Of this unfortunate practice the internationally renowned thinker Antonio de Guevara offers a cultural parable he attributes to Cretan society, yet whose immediate relevance for Spain could not be clearer:

Among the inhabitants of Crete it was customary, even obligatory, not to dare ask any visitor from a foreign land who he was, what he wanted, and from where he had come, under penalty of being whipped or sent into exile. And the purpose involved in promulgating such laws was to rid men of the temptation to be curious, that is to say, to want to know other people's lives and not to pay attention to their own. For what men seem to devote most of their time to is asking and investigating what their neighbors are doing.[5]

The purveying of gossip—the (invariably malicious) delving into other people's lives, *saber vidas ajenas*—became a veritable cultural obsession in sixteenth- and seventeenth-century Spain. The fixation with purity of blood, the privileging of the so-called old Christian peasant as opposed to the urban, potentially new Christian blood of the aristocrat, is a literary staple of the time. Voicing this established view in order to deplore it, Guevara goes on to explain that "one solitary blemish will dishonor an entire generation. A stain on the lineage of some country bumpkin affects no one beyond him, but a stain on an hidalgo's blood affects his entire family, because it sullies the reputation of his forbears, it serves to disinter his ancestors, it leads to the investigation of his living relatives, and it corrupts the blood of those yet to be born" (441–42).[6]

This type of dangerous rumor-mill was then—as it is today, yet even more intensely—a discourse that evoked fear, but also fascination. It is inextricably linked, to some degree, with the titillation elicited by pornography; it is voyeuristic at its core. Even for those who object to it on principle, gossip exerts an irresistible power. As Patricia Spacks observes, moreover, its fascination is related to the effects of pornography. "Gossip, even when it avoids the sexual, bears about it a faint flavor of the erotic. . . . The atmosphere of erotic titillation suggests gossip's implicit voyeurism . . . we thrill to the glamour and the power of secret knowledge, partly detoxified but also heightened by being shared."[7]

While it may not at first appear to be the case, the act of reading and gossip are also closely related. When we read intimate details of even fictional characters, we feel a sense of power over them. This effect was surely savored all the more fully in seventeenth-century Spain by an audience which was constantly subjected to the overbearing surveillance of the *malsín*—the person who secretly warns the authorities of the transgressions of others with the dual motives of potentially malicious intent and self-interest. Yet, the act of reading literary gossip, especially of the sort of urban, domestic strife that Zayas provides, can also at times have the salutary effect of psychological self-healing, according to Spacks: "we perform verbal acts as well as other acts . . . in order to extend our control over a world that is not naturally disposed to serve our interests" (11).

In other words, our surveillance of fictional characters can provide us with a greater understanding of our own real-life complications. The pleasure of reading gossip—even if we admit that it is fiction—ranges from titillation, on the one hand, to power that turns the customarily powerless victim of surveillance into the powerful manipulator of surveillance, on the other, to even a third possibility, as a source of constructive self-analysis. The Spanish word that designates the writing of novellas —*novelar* (from the Italian *novellare*) means to "disclose news"—usually salacious or transgressive in nature. And in her collection of twenty novellas Zayas is acutely aware of all three of these dimensions of gossip. In the voices of her global narrator, the individually inscribed partygoing narrators, as well as the inscribed characters whose lives they disclose, she exploits each of these possibilities intensely throughout the hundreds of pages of her cultural microcosm, evoking both fear and fascination in her reader.[8]

Framing the first of her first ten narratives of deceit, desire, and betrayal is a group of five male and five female narrators, storytellers who take turns telling their stories over the course of five lavish Christmas soirées (*saraos*) designed for the entertainment of the convalescing Lisis. Augmenting the myriad intrigues contained within the pages of the stories they tell is the further complication that the narrators themselves are embroiled in a network of affective psychodramas. While fulfilling the role of recuperating hostess, Lisis is at the same time involved in a love quadrangle along with Diego, Lisarda, and Juan. Their power plays and suspense-filled intrigues spoke clearly to the seventeenth-century reader looking for escape and voyeurism by which he or she could intrude upon the private lives of other contemporary citizens. This desire to intrude on the privacy of others is obviously a cultural constant, analogous to the attraction exerted by the tangled webs of deceit and desire that define the tremendous popularity of the modern-day soap opera.

The second gathering of part I is prompted by Lisis's convalescence from the rejection of her suitor, Juan, who has left her for Lisarda instead. Lisis finally resigns herself to this loss, and to the prospect of marrying another of the partygoers, Diego. Although the second ten tales are planned for a New Year's celebration of Lisis's marriage to Don Diego, they are postponed for more than a year.

When the group reconvenes, things are markedly different. The structural repetition of the first ten stories narrated by characters from the original frame story remains; however, Lisis redefines the rules in thematic terms as well as in terms of gender with a radical shift. The year that has elapsed since part I has obviously been one of personal turmoil for her. As a result, unlike part I, where both men and women recounted tales of adventures replete with perilous human deceptions of all kinds, the ten novellas of part II are narrated only by women members of the party, who must, in addition, tell only true stories that expose the intolerable cruelty of men.

Lisis ultimately rejects Diego (who dies in battle), Juan goes mad (dying soon thereafter), and she enters a convent. The fact that Lisis orders as the theme for her engagement party stories of abuse and cruelty by men against women, especially husbands against wives, is clearly very strange. Why consider marrying at all if that is the way she views men and the institution of marriage? This basic frame situation is indicative of the calculated tension, suspicion, and fear of surveillance that Zayas builds into her text, of the competing, unresolved discourses she stages.

The twenty narratives that comprise Zayas's collection are presented as historically true—hence personally compromising—accounts. These stories detail intimate secrets and transgressions of various Spanish citizens that are so dangerous as to necessitate changing the names of the individuals involved to protect whatever shred of propriety they or their families may still possess. These *novelas* are excitingly transgressive because they recount a wealth of forbidden acts—murder, rape, torture, adultery, black magic, and so on—committed by members of the seemingly respectable aristocracy. And they are as compelling for the inscribed drawing-room audience as they are for each of us—the extradiegetic, private reader. This prolonged act of narration reveals repeated instances of malicious gossips who wield lethal power.

The threat posed by gossip for the individual as perceived by others is expressed by *el qué dirán* (what others will say), a ubiquitous feature of the early Spanish *mentalité* which has been studied in both its literary and historical implications.[9] The terrifying sway often exerted by gossip and also its link to women is confirmed by Guido Ruggiero in a discussion of Italian inquisitorial records. As he explains: "*Fama* was constantly evaluated in late Renaissance life by means of public evaluation and gossip. Significantly, women played a central role in this theory, as gossip was widely recognized as a woman's prerogative. . . . The world of gossip evaluation had the ability to create crucial realities: honor, reputation, and, of course, at times even husbands, wives, and witches."[10] Acknowledging this formidable mode of discursive power, Zayas presents her reader with women empowered to create or destroy the lives of others by their discourse.

Finally, though paradoxically, the third potential effect of gossip—the self-analytical and healing dimension—is also crucial to the *Novelas*. Entertainment aside, Zayas's cultural indictment exposes the brutal repression and hypocrisy of the zealously cultivated code of honor. The general air of inquisitorial suspicion and surveillance that is instrumental to its regulation calls for a rethinking of society's collective values, gesturing toward an improved model, while also serving as a form of consolation for wives who do not suffer an equally repressive domestic environment. The ongoing discussions of the inscribed partygoers, as well as the extradiegetic authorial voice, serve this pedagogical, therapeutic purpose, as the discussions to follow will illustrate.

The Writing Woman

Recent interest in the construction of female authority, authorship, and, more broadly, the exploration of female experience has resulted in a renewed interest in María de Zayas and her literary production.[11] Yet this recuperation is by no means a modern-day reconstruction of a marginal voice, an archival discovery of a largely unknown author. To the contrary, during the first half of the seventeenth century not only was she the most successful female author in Spain by far; her book sales were surpassed only by Cervantes, Quevedo, and Alemán.[12] Given the paucity of female writers in the Spain of her day and, moreover, the undisputed brilliance of these three male authors, her publication profile is quite extraordinary. Outside Spain, she was also tremendously influential, as the long list of translations into other languages attests. A further, frequently un-acknowledged impact of her writings in the rest of Europe can be seen in the number of her tales that were appropriated by other writers without attribution.[13]

Attestations to her fame and great success abound, as we find laudatory remarks in prose and poetry made by the most influential male authors of her day. That a woman should rank so high is particularly impressive in light of the miniscule number of active women writers at the time, and the additional impediment to respectability that was common for the professional woman writer. Zayas, however, enjoyed a privileged status long before the publication of either of her novella collections.[14] A full sixteen years before the appearance of her *Novelas*, Lope de Vega identifies her in his *Laurel de Apolo* (1621) as "la inmortal María de Zayas" on the basis of her poetry, theater, and impressive performance in the literary salons of Madrid, the *tertulias*.[15] Alonso de Castillo Solórzano in *La garduña de Sevilla* (1642) writes of her (including her novelistic accomplishments) with similarly unqualified praise:

En estos tiempos luce y campea con felices lauros el ingenio de doña María de Zayas y Sotomayor, que con justo título ha merecido el nombre de Sibila de Madrid, adquirido por sus admirables versos, por su felice ingenio y gran prudencia, habiendo sacado de la estampa un libro de diez novelas que son diez asombros para los que escriben deste género, pues la meditada prosa, el artificio dellas y los versos que interpola, es todo tan admirable, que acobarda las más valientes plumas de nuestra España.[16]

[In these times the wit of Doña María de Zayas y Sotomayor sparkles and shines with happy laurels. She has justly deserved the name of Sibyl of Madrid, acquired thanks to her admirable verses, her felicitous mind, and great prudence, having published a book of ten novellas (the first part of her collection) which are ten wonders for those who write in this genre, since the meditated prose, the artifice, and the verses that she interpolates are all so admirable that they intimidate the most valiant pens of our Spain.] (my translation)

In keeping with the literary fashions of the seventeenth-century book trade, Zayas's *Novelas* are prefaced by a series of equally laudatory endorsements taking the form of sonnets penned in her honor by other prominent writers. Yet, while it may be argued that promotional material of this sort was the order of the day, the repeated evocations of her as a "tenth Muse" and "sibyl" gesture toward a particular appreciation of her by her contemporaries—namely, of her extraliterary effects.

Each of these mythical ascriptions provides a revealing perspective not only on Zayas's literary project, but also on the wide-ranging possibilities that such female paradigms entail. The sibyl has traditionally been depicted as a laconic female prophet with an ability to see beyond the civic chaos of a given historical era, and a corresponding desire to offer guidance leading to the restoration of social order. Thought to live in oracular caves, the sibyls were ten in number, their most illustrious representative being Deiphobe, the Cumean sibyl who is credited with such genealogical feats as guiding the Trojan Aeneas through the underworld so that he could visit with his father, Anchises. Since she had asked of Apollo that she live for as many years as there were grains of sand in her hand, she had clearly acquired the wisdom of age.

Zayas is referred to repeatedly as a "sibyl" because her short stories disclose the decay of the Spanish Empire through the male-female relations of her day. In the prologues, epilogues, and incidental remarks she makes in the stories, as well as the commentaries with which she endows her storytellers, Zayas acquires a decidedly sybelline persona. While often laconic, she is consumed with a desire to expose excesses and abuses so as to edify society and lead to its improvement. Her voicing of "official discourse" relating to nationalism, gender, class, and race relations is critical of its imperfect, corrupt practitioners—the populace that does not measure up to society's hallowed principles of virtue, honor, and related family values. While her pedagogical project is undeniable, Zayas at the same time is a shrewd marketing strategist who exploits these values for the purpose of selling books.[17] As such, she functions as a novel, self-interested sibyl.

In spite of the few personal biographical details we have, namely, that she was born about 1590, lived in Madrid, and died about 1660, her literary biographical details are telling, indeed. Her fiction, for example, reflects her impressive level of education; her profound knowledge of the European novella tradition (Boccaccio, Bandello, Salernitano, Sercambi,

Marguerite de Navarre, Cervantes, among others) is evident in the creative rewriting of these canonical figures she offers. This learnedness was, no doubt, an important factor in the high regard in which Zayas was held both in the Spain of her time and abroad.

One of the most compelling aspects of her *Novelas* is its relentless focus on issues of sex, gender, and domestic violence. And it is the often grotesque depiction of familial (especially marital) relations which makes her work as compelling to present-day readers as it was to her contemporaries.

In a suggestive observation in *Discipline and Punish*, Foucault speculates on the institution of the family, on its evolution, and on the history of its regulatory functions: "One day we should show how intra-familial relations, essentially in the parents-children cell, have become 'disciplined,' absorbing since the classical age external schemata, first educational and military, then medical, psychiatric, psychological, which have made the family the privileged locus of emergence for the disciplinary question of the normal and the abnormal." [18] It is precisely these dynamics of the family—especially their destructive potential in attempting to conform to the dictates of state doctrine—that Zayas thematizes in her work. The increasingly complex appreciation of human subjectivity resulting from the individual's more regulated relationship to the state, and of gender relations as they pertain to the private life of a couple evident in the early modern period, find passionate exploration in Zayas's narratives, offering a wealth of cultural commentary and criticism.

If we consider Zayas's treatment of gender in even a preliminary manner, we become aware of its inherent complexities. Explorations of the "fictional nature of gender," as Judith Butler terms it—that is, its identity as an unstable, socially constructed phenomenon (from one culture and/or historical moment to another)—characterizes much recent work by and on women and their representation.

One of the most interesting effects of this rethinking has been its consequences for feminist theory—specifically for feminist politics construed as a politics of inclusion. A substantial body of early feminist thought and scholarship originating in the 1970s attempted to construe women of all nations and historical periods as being essentially the same. Writing from a lesbian perspective in order to question universalizing feminist formulations founded on heterosexual models (yet her point holds regardless of sexual orientation), Butler writes: "The effort to identify the enemy as singular in form is a reverse-discourse that uncritically mimics the strategy of the oppressor instead of offering a different set of terms."[19]

This is evident in Zayas criticism, much of which until recently has attempted to cast her in terms of a kind of first-stage feminism, as opposed to current feminist thought, which acknowledges the inescapable diversity that distinguishes female response from one geographical, historical, or social environment to another.[20] Zayas, while bold in her indictment of misogyny, is a subtle and contradictory—eminently Baroque—writer, with a strikingly modern appreciation of subjectivity.

With remarkable perceptiveness, this appreciation of the instability of gender and sex, currently at the forefront of gender studies, was understood and problematized by Zayas in her twenty short stories. She has been recuperated lately because of the interest in early modern women writers, and especially because of the preponderance of sex-related violence against women her work describes. She has been interpreted in recent years primarily as an outspoken critic of the patriarchy and its abuses—of a (rather homogeneously conceived) masculinist signifying economy which preys relentlessly upon an equally homogeneously hence rather artificially conceived female population of wives, sisters, and daughters.[21]

Zayas's literary project is ultimately problematic (unresolved) in terms of gender. As her stories reveal, her portrayal of Spanish society is considerably rich and nuanced. In a suggestive remark, Melveena McKendrick perceptively observes: "Melodramatic as her stories are [Zayas's] views are balanced. She does not denounce men and she offers no practical suggestions for the improvement of women's lot."[22] I would modify this statement by saying that she does indeed denounce men, but she also denounces women, both diegetically and even extradiegetically in the frame narrative into which her stories are embedded. And this conflicting representation of gender persists to the very end of her *Novelas*. In the final pages of her text, as countless atrocities have been perpetrated upon usually guiltless women more often than not by men, we see Zayas calling for a return to the "golden age" of gender relations, which she situates in the period of the Catholic kings, while the principal frame character (Lisis, with whom Zayas is frequently—and erroneously—identified) advocates a definitive withdrawal to the convent as the only viable defense for women (usually wives) against the insolubly unjust male order.

In a related observation, Paul Julian Smith astutely identifies a multiple, unintegrated subject in Zayas on the basis of her contradictory rhetoric: "Zayas' feminist 'message' is severely restricted by the very literary artifice of which she claims herself to be innocent. Her stories could hardly be taken as the 'natural' recreation of historical incident or lived experience even at the time when they were written."[23] Smith speaks somewhat cautiously of either her "inability (or refusal)" to offer an integrated female narrative. I maintain that her unintegrated stance results not from "inability" but from calculated refusal. As Valerie Traub, M. Lindsay Kaplan, and Dympna Callaghan observe in speaking about the evolution of female subjectivity in early modern Europe, "the absence of investment in a fully articulated, coherent subject, may have allowed for the establishment of subcommunities, pockets of resistance, and alliances between subordinated groups."[24]

While the representation of sex and gender lies squarely at the center of the Zayesque enterprise, it does not conform, as analysis reveals, to an unambiguous causal relationship of female misfortune with the abuses of a predatory androcentric society. In fact, the social history of the period—corroborated by criminal law records—reveals that violence against women (particularly uxoricide) was rare in seventeenth-century Spain.[25] For this reason, historical evidence does not authorize us to construe Zayas's writing (or Calderón's gory revenge tragedies, either) as pure mimesis of history. She does not fit neatly into the transhistorical theories about women and writing that were influential in the 1970s and 1980s.

We must also bear in mind that literature—like life itself—is always open to interpretation; that, for instance, fantasy can involve the pleasure of undermining a fixed subject position just as much as it can involve its valorization.[26] To construe Zayas as a gender manifesto, while at times tempting, is to diminish the complexities she offers, and to reduce her readers to one-track minds. Women readers are not necessarily going to identify with exalted heroines—they might be mor intrigued by women and men who stray from the unidimensional categories of predictably virtuous behavior. Regardless of chronological specificity, literature does not function as a clinical or sociological document; it is infinitely more complex, and Zayas understands this manifold complexity.

At the same time, there is a compelling reason for her lack of one consistent integrated female stance, which has a historical basis: namely that the lack of fully integrated, uniform presentation of the female subject was, among other things, a survival strategy. As Traub, Kaplan, and Callaghan explain, "the condition of a fragmented, diffuse subject makes possible certain challenges to the dominant culture that would otherwise be impossible" (6). It is this strategy which enables Zayas to write such a stern indictment of society while managing to elude the literary censors.

Extratextual evidence further corroborates this claim to polysemy. If she is as programmatically subversive of the patriarchy as many recent critics allege, how do we account for Zayas's status as a best-selling author? This question becomes all the more compelling given the low female literacy rates in the Spain of her time.[27] Returning to the issue of surveillance, how do we explain the fact that Zayas's work remained uncensored by the zealous literary expurgators of the Inquisition?[28] Within the text itself, how do we reconcile her contradictory self-presentation as author in her *Novelas*—on the one hand reviling the abuses perpetrated by men, advocating escape to the convent in the voice of her principal female character, declaring, on the other hand (not only in her epilogue, but throughout her text), the recuperability of men (if they read her stories properly), calling for a return to the idealized gender relations she situates in the era of the Catholic kings?

Those illustrious monarchs were by all accounts emblematic of Spain's imperial grandeur, yet also emblematic of Spain's cultural repression and decline, as a consequence of their founding of the Inquisition. As Elizabeth Perry and Anne Cruz put it, "the Catholic Kings set into motion a machinery that would quickly expand beyond investigations of apostasy and heresy. The Spanish Inquisition established tribunals in major towns and cities, developed a large bureaucracy to carry out investigations in most communities of the realm, and permeated all areas of human life, both private and public."[29] And, while Zayas does not explicitly allude to the Inquisition's regulatory zeal in religious terms (extending to racial repression as well), its effects on nationalism, race, and even religion are always a central focus of her writing. So is the question of class, for while reviling the abuses of the aristocracy—its hypocrisy and unfairness toward lesser castes—she belongs to it and does not wish to abandon it. She is, as the pages to follow will reveal, self-consciously and insolubly problematic in her discourse—writing very critically about the wisdom of the official discourses with which she identifies personally.[30]

Within the tales themselves, what do we make of the at times shockingly cruel exploitation of women (and men) by other women? Finally, why do a number of her tales verge on the pornographic if, indeed, her only ambition is to illustrate the blamelessness of her sex? Reflecting on the emergence of pornography during the early modern period and on Foucault's theory of discourses, Lynn Hunt writes: "As with medicine, madness, the prison and sexuality, pornography should be understood as the product of new forms of regulation and new desires for knowledge."[31] In her writing, Zayas is concerned both with new, emerging forms of writing, and with a desire to expose the social conditions which produced them.

A fundamental component of her profile as a writer is, of course, her sex, her identity as a writing woman. Critics of such diverse perspectives as Luce Irigaray and Walter Ong have argued that women writers frequently, indeed necessarily, provide experimental, revisionist readings of culture itself. In *Orality and Literacy: The Technologizing of the Word*, Ong recognizes the significant role played by women in the evolution of the novel, a contribution which he links directly to their lack of education regarding the rhetorical traditions in which their male counterparts were very well versed.[32] Unencumbered by the academic baggage their male counterparts disseminated, women were creative because they lacked literary paradigms they would feel compelled either to emulate or reject. Hence their high level of creativity in the realm of the novel.

By contrast, in *Speculum de l'autre femme* (Speculum), Irigaray posits women's novelistic creativity not as the result of a lack (gendered or otherwise), but instead of an informed, gendered awareness of female marginality in a dominant male social and linguistic order.[33] And it is the novel's identity as the prime oppositional discourse, rebelling against all established institutional forms, which historically has made it so powerfully attractive to women. Zayas, as her prologue proclaims, is keenly aware of both the biological and cultural arguments that have for centuries shaped so much of the debate over the nature and function of woman, and in her writing she exploits each to great advantage.

In the sixteenth and seventeenth centuries, it was both socially and ethically controversial to be a professional woman writer of nonreligious literature. In writing of Aphra Behn, England's first professional woman writer (who may have read Zayas either in the original or in English translation), Catherine Gallagher explains that "the seventeenth century ear heard the word 'public' in 'publication' very distinctly, and hence a woman's publication automatically implied a public woman. The woman who shared the contents of her mind instead of reserving them for one man was literally, not metaphorically, trading in her *sexual* property."[34] The possibility of a *public* mind and a *private* body posed a threat to the integral nature of woman as she had been socially constructed for centuries. A woman can only be a unified, integral subject if she gives herself away to her husband. Gallagher concludes incisively of this lingering paradox that "self-possession . . . and self-alienation are just two sides of the same coin; the alienation verifies the possession" (28). That Aphra Behn was married only briefly and that Zayas in all probability never married appear to corroborate this unfortunate precept.[35]

Writing women were socially tainted in the seventeenth century not simply as divided, unintegral human beings, but also as whores, potentially monstrous. If we consider the reaction to Mary Wroth's publication of *Urania* in 1621, we find the following derogatory judgment contained in the verse epistle addressed to her by Lord Denny: "Hermaphrodite in show, in deed a monster/As by thy works and words all men may conster/Thy wrathful spite conceived an Idell book/Brought forth a foole which like the damme doth look./ . . . leave idle books alone/For wise and worthyer women have written none."[36]

María de Zayas was all too aware of this commonplace attitude, of the dangerous enterprise constituted by female authorship, that women are not suited to the writing of books (either because it compromises their chastity or simply because their gender makes them incapable of the intellect needed to write a good book). As a result, she begins her global prologue to the reader in the following outspoken manner:

Quien duda, lector mío, que te causará admiración que una mujer tenga despejo, no sólo para escribir un libro, sino para darle a la estampa, que es el crisol donde se averigua la pureza de los ingenios; porque hasta que los escritos se rozan en las letras de plomo, no tienen valor cierto, por ser tan fáciles de engañar los sentidos, que la fragilidad de la vista suele pasar por oro macizo lo que a la luz del fuego es solamente un pedazo de bronce afeitado. Quien duda, digo otra vez, que habrá muchos que atribuyan a locura esta virtuosa osadía de sacar a luz mis borrones, siendo mujer, que, en opinión de algunos necios, es lo mismo que una cosa incapaz. (21)

[Oh, my reader, no doubt it will amaze you that a woman has the nerve, not only to write a book but actually to publish it, for publication is the crucible in which the purity of genius is tested; until writing is set in letters of lead, it has no real value. Our senses are so deceived that fragile sight often sees as pure gold what, by the light of the fire, is simply a piece of polished brass. Who can doubt, I repeat, that there will be many who will attribute to folly my audacity in publishing my scribbles because I'm a woman, and women, in the opinion of some fools, are unfit beings.] [37]

Like the sentiments expressed by Denny and others in seventeenth-century England, the "amazement" of the reader at the female author's "nerve" alluded to here appears to reflect a similar disapproval in Zayas's contemporary Spain. Her reference to her writing as "scribbles" serves a parallel function, reflecting society's general skepticism regarding the writing of good literature by women. Yet Zayas not only registers this sexist attitude, she defies it, welcoming the public nature of her writing, saying that only published words are of any real value. Her boldness is matched by her daring juxtaposition of the traditional dualism of gold and lead—speaking of her words as being "set in lead" (rather than gold), which of course is the metal from which type is actually forged. So confident is she of the value of her words that she can speak of them in the same breath as both "genius" and "leaden."

At the end of the first paragraph, however, she suddenly assumes a much more humble attitude toward her prose: "Cualquiera, como sea no más de buen cortesano, no lo tendrá por novedad ni lo murmurará por desatino" (21) [If only out of common courtesy, however, people shouldn't take my book as an oddity or condemn it as foolish (1)]. Zayas here reflects the conflicting, contradictory discourse that necessarily characterizes early modern women writers.

In considering the writings of Louise Labé and Veronica Franco, Ann R. Jones lucidly explains the reason for their inescapably contradictory rhetoric: "It is a transgressive rhetoric in two senses: they refuse injunctions to chastity and silence, and they speak to and for women in ways that shift the man-woman focus of love poetry to new concerns and positions. But theirs is also a rhetoric shaped and contained by the constant presence of men as the ultimate critics—of women's beauty, of their merits as poets, of their present and future reputations."[38] Zayas is aware of the inescapably divided discourse by which the woman writer must speak. And given the enduring conservative humanist perspective on woman's place and woman's education operative not only in Spain but throughout Europe (exemplified by influential writings by authors like Juan Luis Vives), the danger inherent in Zayas's publishing venture as an outspoken female voice is all the more striking.[39]

Mariana de Carvajal, Zayas's contemporary, also a writer of novellas, resorts to the humility topos, likewise belittling her own literary production in the author's prologue, denigrating her book to the extent of referring to it not as an intellectual "offspring," a traditional association, but instead by the surprisingly grotesque image of an "aborted fetus": "Este pequeño libro te ofrezco, aborto inútil de mi corto ingenio" [I offer you this little book, the useless abortion of my meager wit].[40] By this dramatic (indeed repulsive) depiction of her book Carvajal is presumably taking desperate measures to distance herself from the predictably (intellectually impoverishing) function by which women are depicted exclusively as childbearers—or less frequently as intellects, almost never as a combination of the two. At the same time, Carvajal offers an amusing calque on Cervantes' reference to Don Quijote alternately as his "child," "stepchild," or "lean shrivelled, whimsical child."[41]

To a certain extent, however, this deprecatory tone must also be attributed to the time-worn *captatio benevolentiae* strategy by which male authors similarly belittle their literary production, speaking disparagingly about their work in the hopes that readers will look more favorably upon it. A well-known example of this authorial pose can be found in Cervantes, a contemporary of Zayas, and one upon whom she modeled some of her stories as well. Speaking in similarly disparaging terms of his magnum opus, *Don Quijote*, Cervantes' prologue opens in an unpromising and self-deprecatory manner:

Desocupado lector: sin juramento me podrás creer que quisiera que este libro, como hijo del entendimiento, fuera el más hermoso, el más gallardo y más discreto que pudiera imaginarse. Pero no he podido yo contravenir al orden de naturaleza; que en ella cada cosa engendra su semejante. Y así, ¿qué podrá engendrar el estéril y mal cultivado ingenio mío sino la historia de un hijo seco, avellanado, antojadizo y lleno de pensamientos varios y nunca imaginados de otro alguno, bien como quien se engendró en una cárcel, donde toda incomodidad tiene su asiento y donde todo triste ruido hace su habitación? (19).

[Idle reader, you can believe without any oath of mine that I would wish this book, as the child of my brain, to be the most beautiful, the liveliest and the cleverest imaginable. But I have been unable to transgress the order of nature, by which like gives birth to like. And so, what could my sterile and ill-cultivated genius beget but the story of a lean, shrivelled, whimsical child, full of varied fancies that no one else has ever imagined—much like one engendering in prison, where every discomfort has its seat and every dismal sound its habitation? (25)]

Zayas, while an ardent female apologist, is firmly rooted in the relationships of author, text, and reader that define the Spanish Baroque—with all the intricacies and contradictions the aesthetics of this period entail. She resembles Cervantes, for example, in her use of "slippery," unreliable narrator figures who interrogate the very act of reading and the status of the literary text as object. Likewise, we find Cervantine traces in certain stories that she adapts from the *Quijote* and the *Novelas ejemplares*. Of even greater implications, however, is the fact that Zayas was as committed as Cervantes to the representation of modern appreciations of subjectivity—of the possibilities for multiple, fragmented, even contradictory subjects, of human subjectivity in all its complexity. While I do not wish to diminish her commitment to exposing the unwarranted social inequality of women in society, she was in fact a product of the intellectual climate in which she lived—a time consumed with a desire to explore perspectivism, contradiction, and the unresolved tensions that define the Baroque ethos.[42]

Modern Readers

Recent critics have labored to account for the undeniable paradox of Zayas's writing; namely the degree of scandal she generates by her choice of topics and her claim to be writing exemplary fiction in her *Novelas amorosas y ejemplares*. What is the lesson to be gleaned from her salacious prose? Although untraditional in its nature, we will see that exemplarity in the *Novelas* is invoked for the serious purpose of exposing gender, class, and race relations in seventeenth-century Spain (including explicit advice on how to improve them), but also for an unrelated motive—that is, as a means of disguising her titillation of the reader. It is in this difficult, unexpected combination of features that her art lies.

A brief enumeration of the subjects contained within the pages of the *Novelas* reveals their clearly sensationalist intent: torture, rape, dismemberment, murder, male and female cross-dressing, lesbian desire, controversial treatments of race and nationalism, as well as male homosexuality figure among the topics treated. In addition to victimized females (usually chaste wives), we find also libidinous females who abuse their lovers or husbands. Sensationalism is generated also by the extensive treatment given to magic and the supernatural, including witchcraft and even voodoo dolls. Indeed, Zayas's sensationalism is frequently sadistic, verging on the pornographic. It is no accident that the nineteenth-century novelist Juan Valera includes in one of his novels a spinster who locks herself in her bedroom in order to savor the forbidden, exciting stories written by Zayas that no respectable lady would read.[43] In so doing, Zayas, as we shall see, exploits exemplarity in a wholly original manner in the history of Spanish novella composition. She writes cultural criticism that is both ethically informed and aware of a new readership with a taste for scandal.

Modern interpretations of her work tend to view Zayas according to one of three broad interpretive categories. The first interpretation, represented by such critics as Agustín de Amezúa and Eduardo Rincón, considers Zayas to be a writer of realist fiction, a more or less accurate portrayal of life in seventeenth-century Spain. Such a view, however, is undermined not only by contemporary legal records, but also by the abundance of excessively grotesque behavior and at times the obtrusive presence of supernatural phenomena that pervade her prose. The presence of violent details and perverse couplings provoked the eminent German critic Ludwig Pfandl to remark in 1929: "Can there be anything more gross and obscene, more nonaesthetic and repulsive, than a woman who writes lascivious, dirty, sadistic, and morally corrupt stories?"[44]

Whether or not we agree with Pfandl's appraisal of the subject matter befitting the woman writer, we recognize that by the depiction of this type of grisly brutality, not to mention necromancers, ghosts, and even multiple appearances by the devil himself, it is clear that Zayas is not interested in replicating on paper a realistic slice-of-life depiction of everyday Spain. As Matthew Stroud notes about the theme of wife-murder in the Spanish Golden Age *comedia*, on the basis of legal archival research: "The number of wife murders was so small as to make the events remarkable because of their rarity. Those cases that were adjudicated and that indicated the husband's punishments noted that some penalty was always extracted from the husband."[45] That Zayas outdid her male colleagues by the level of violence in her *novelas*, especially violence done to women, is frequently noted. Yet this view is based largely on Cervantes' comparatively nonviolent *Novelas ejemplares*, which have become the paradigm of the genre. Other short-story writers (almost exclusively male) are committed to an equal degree to exposing the hypocrisies and brutality of society by often resorting to similarly graphic violence.

The reason for her excessiveness, especially in part II, has been explained in a number of ways. One view sees her fascination with goriness as an expression of the Baroque ethos so evident in the plastic arts as well as on the stage. Of this excess in violent representation, Maravall writes that it is a means by which the government controls the masses: "There is no doubt that the spectacle of violence, pain, blood, and death—a spectacle that was popularly supported and displayed before the masses—was used by the rulers and their collaborators to terrify people and in this way to succeed more efficiently in subjecting them to their place within the order."[46] Although it is undeniable that violence frequently does serve as an institutional control mechanism, Maravall assumes that Zayas is a spokeswoman for the State—which she is not.

We must bear in mind also that at the time during which Zayas wrote, indeed for the whole preceding century, not only tabloid literature but martyrologies were tremendously popular. Exploited as propaganda by Protestants and Catholics alike, the grisly accounts of martyrs were more popular even than devotional texts.[47] Thus a readership of long standing had a taste for the graphic representation of mutilation and death which Zayas understood. The literature of martyrs was construed as literal fact, whereas Zayas insightfully transposed its shock value to the realm of non-religious fiction—claiming all the while that her accounts are historically verifiable as well.

A different view seeks to account for her tremendous popularity in terms of the violence construed as domestic cautionary tale, as an intimidation technique by which husbands seek to control the behavior of their wives and daughters. Namely, if Zayas were really as subversive of the patriarchal order as numerous critics allege, why would heads of households allow such threatening literature to enter their houses? Allesandra Melloni offers a novel explanation, claiming that husbands wanted their wives and daughters to read such grisly tales because they would thereafter reflect on their own domestic situations, considering themselves fortunate for an existence which, by comparison, seems blissful.[48]

As we now admit, all interpretations are political—based on partisan, specific a prioristic values. In Amezúa's case it is his reverence for "realism" as the highest form of art that leads him to classify Zayas's *Novelas* as such, despite their profusion of unrealistic details. And this interpretation is not the product a gendered reading. Alicia Yllera similarly construes the brutality against women portrayed in the *Novelas* realistically, and Zayas's response as one of two possible courses of action: "Cervantes and Lope de Vega advocate indulgence and pardon of the dishonored woman instead of bloody vengeance. María de Zayas opts for the intransigent posture, in the manner of Calderón."[49] But axiological plurality or instability is what emerges from a reading of Zayas's work, not intransigence.

By contrast, the gory and demonic aspects of her prose has led some critics to regard Zayas instead as the precursor of the gothic novel.[50] Origi-

nating in the late eighteenth century, this novelistic form is characterized by the portrayal of innocence in the clutches of absolute villany, a
fascination for the occult and supernatural, and the creation of a new
aesthetic category identified by German scholars as *Schauerromantik*—
the romanticism of terror. In her stories, Zayas exploits all of the features
that became hallmarks of the gothic novel. It is important to note, however, that whereas the gothic novel locates its narrative in historically remote epochs, typically the Middle Ages, Zayas writes of her contemporary Spain, situating her tales in all the major urban centers of her day.
She depicts terror at home, especially within the home, thereby creating a
"literature of immediacy," with all the psychological power that this contemporary form entails.[51]

Establishing whether or not Zayas is protogothic is of less importance
than the recognition of her fascinating polyvalence, as reflected in the
striking lack of consensus whereby some critics portray Zayas as the author of exemplary narratives designed to celebrate establishment values
(the sanctity of female chastity, the incompatability of love and honor,
and the status quo of Christian marriage), while others view her as offering a scathing indictment of the system. Yllera's view that Zayas opts for
Calderonian rigidity in defending the status quo of the honor code is a
case in point. In this context it is useful to note as Patsy Boyer does that:
"Zayas' novellas are in no way unorthodox and were lauded as exemplary
by the censors, yet they treat moral issues and present material (rape, bat-
tering, murder) with a frankness that seems shocking to us." We read—
necessarily from our twentieth-century aesthetic and moral perspective,
and the collection does at times strive to illustrate the value of fidelity in
wholesome wedlock. But at the same time, as Boyer lucidly illustrates,
other stories depict the unwarranted brutality of husbands toward faithful wives, thereby jeopardizing any clear ideological reading of her texts.[52]

Most recently, Zayas has been read from the perspective of feminist
thought. In the nineteenth and early twentieth centuries, particularly in a
country like Spain, to call someone a "feminist" was a way of summarily
dismissing her from serious consideration. Such is no longer the case and,
indeed, Zayas's literary output is now a topic of considerable interest from
the optic of gender theory.[53] This makes sense given her outspoken defense of the intellectual merits of women, already analyzed in her pro-

logue. The notably greater violence suffered by women at the hands of men in part II further authorizes a critical inquiry based on a gendered perspective.

Beyond this self-consciously feminist stance articulated by these features of her text, several of her twenty storytellers often deliver equally pointed gendered discourses. Yet, on several occasions their words conflict with the characters' personalities. Even more blatant is the fact that they themselves will sometimes disavow in an unambiguous way the validity of their own feminist message. When Lisis instructs the women to speak ill of men in part II, some of them object strenuously. As a preface to her narration of *La más infame venganza* (*Most Infamous Revenge*), Lisarda says, for instance, that she had never been disenchanted or deceived by men (69). She explicitly says one thing—coerced by Lisis' command to speak disenchantingly about men—while believing another; concluding her argument as an apologist for men.[54]

Several other female soirée members likewise problematize the straightforward gendered reading that Lisis imposes. This is a consistent feature of the text which has received insufficient critical comment, yet it is in keeping with Zayas's contradictory, eminently nonlinear discourse. It is, moreover, supremely Baroque in its conception. Speaking in general terms of the unique, contradictory nature constituted by Baroque discourse and the mentality it represents, Brian Turner explains: "Baroque reason is essentially a 'theatricalization of existence' which mobilizes the notions of ambivalence and difference . . . which permits us to see the modern world from within."[55]

In diegetic terms it is equally important to qualify an essentialist reading. It is, after all, not a man but a woman—a malicious gossip—who sets in motion the martyrdom that Elena suffers in *Tarde llega el desengaño* (*Too Late Undeceived*). Likewise, the six-year torture endured by Ines in *La inocencia castigada* (*Innocence Punished*) stems from the greed of another female—a procuress.

We find wicked females along with virtuous ones. Beyond these contradictions, Lisis herself offers perhaps the most incriminating evidence that calls into question the validity of her unambiguous defense of women. While she pointedly defends the cause of women at every turn, showing how they are victimized by men, the story she herself narrates,

Estragos que causa el vicio (*The Ravages of Vice*) (II, 10), centers about a perfidious female, a malicious gossip (Florentina) who cruelly mistreats another woman. If, as the storyteller claims, this tale is intended to instruct women on how to defend themselves from cruelty, then it is female cruelty that is at issue here. The fact that this story is the very last of the twenty tales emphasizes Zayas's polysemy even further.

Putting aside the contradiction that lies at the core of this example, Lisis, in "real life" shows herself to be operating according to motives that are equally questionable in terms of her professed championing of women. That is, in the course of the frame narrative she manipulates Diego (a devoted suitor) in order to take revenge on Juan (who has rejected her). As a result, she emerges as the proverbial cunning female, a victimizer of men. Indeed, having been jilted by Juan for her cousin, she vowed to marry Diego not out of love but vengeance. Clearly this is an undesirable prospect that leaves Lisis in a difficult situation. Her rather Machiavellian strategy to extricate herself from the relationship— the need to deny all men—is astutely perceived by Susan Paun de García, who explains that: "By the beginning of [part II], we see that she is looking for a way out of the relationship. She must find a solution that will be beyond question and beyond reproach. The entire pretext of the *sarao* and the relation of the tales is an elaborate and intellectual way to extricate herself from the fix in which she finds herself."[56]

This revenge motif, spread out among the many hundreds of pages of the *Novelas*, serves to further undermine the ideological purity of her discourse. Details such as these function to remind the reader that one must proceed with caution; that the gap separating *histoire* and *discours*— for women as for men—may be considerable. The presence of exemplary feminist narrators in tandem with unexemplary, hypocritcal ones complicates interpretation substantially. As Hans-Robert Jauss remarked on a somewhat different but related topic, "one puts a princess in a fairy tale next to a princess in a novella, and one notices the difference."[57]

It is not Zayas's desire to invalidate the feminist perspective professed by several of her narrators (and this includes occasional males as well). In attempting to account for the evident contradictions in Zayas's text, Susan Griswold advances the interpretation that her feminism is "a topos which responds to an established literary tradition," one that is, moreover, "balanced by an equally vigorous use of the topos of anti-feminism".[58] From this observation Griswold reasons that the two discourses, the feminist and the misogynist, cancel each other out—being reduced to the status of "pure rhetoric" with no transcendent value. Yet the simultaneous presence of both discourses in conflict can be meaningful indeed. In the context of Zayas's work, I would suggest the appropriateness of Julia Kristeva's relational definition of feminism—that is, the study of "that which is marginalized by the patriarchal symbolic order"—a relational feminism which is, as Toril Moi explains, "as shifting as the various forms of patriarchy itself, a definition which can argue that men can also be constructed as marginal by the symbolic order."[59]

The validity of this perspective is borne out by the fact that Zayas offers several examples of such oppressed male subjectivity, at the hands of male and female oppressors alike. *El prevenido engañado* is a case in point, in which a black slave is relentlessly exploited as sex object by a beautiful European woman of "vicious" sexual appetites. Clearly, this narrative does not offer an exemplary perspective on gender, race, or class. By contrast, many other of Zayas's narratives do. How, then, are we to account for this glaring discrepancy? Zayas is committed to exploring perspectivism in all its complexity—biological, racial, social, and intellectual—with a degree of intensity that is hard to equal. Her project is as calculatedly perspectival as that of Cervantes. Once Zayas's text is understood in this light, the necessary contradictions become the vehicle for her discursive tour de force.

This project does not diminish her keenly gendered reading of society. Instead of an exclusive focus on the gender of the speaker or the character, she undertakes an analysis of the many discourses (of sexuality and gender and socioeconomic status as well as racial and national identity) whose conflicting imperatives collectively define the unstable boundaries of the individual subject in Baroque culture.

Zayas calls attention to the power of language, to its complex performative function, and to the equally complex subjectivity of its users. She presents a variety of potentially exemplary, totalizing discourses—feminist and masculinist, among others—in their power both to represent legitimately and to manipulate illegitimately. And by this conflicting representation of the most venerable cultural institutions—marriage, honor, religion, and the justice system—Zayas reveals her commitment to cultural commentary and her obsessive focus on human subjectivity with all its potential for contradiction. It is this perception of human nature generated from disjunctures between the demands of public and private life that lies at the center of the Baroque mind.

Finally, it is clear that in the case of seventeenth-century Spain, the Foucauldian paradigm of modern society, whereby spectacle is replaced by surveillance, does not obtain. They are both operative simultaneously, and what makes Zayas's writing so fascinating is her deft manipulation of both forms of social control.

2
Baroque Subjects: Changing Perspectives in Zayas's *Novelas*

When the Novel becomes the dominant genre, epistemology becomes the dominant discipline.

— Mikhail Bakhtin, *"Epic and Novel"*

Baroque and Postmodern

The cultural function of the literary text, currently the focus of much theorizing, is as central to the formulations of postmodern theorists as it is to cultural historians of the early modern period. As noted in the first chapter, in a number of its primary concerns postmodern thought bears a striking congruence to the Baroque, the cultural climate in which Zayas produced her text. Self-reflexivity and paradox are two fundamental features shared by both cultural movements. Instability, introspection, and change — "change expressed both through acknowledgement and resistance," in Edward Friedman's words — are essential features of the Baroque. He writes powerfully of the paradoxical nature of the Baroque — its status as "both a rewriting — a transformation and, ultimately, an undoing of the Renaissance, whose trace is always present." [1]

This deconstruction of the Renaissance in the forging of modern thought and expression is identified by John Beverly as consumately modern: "The Baroque is, as Spengler argued, already partly Modern. The contemporary 'man [sic] of letters' and contemporary literatures are, in effect, carryovers from the Baroque into bourgeois-liberal culture."[2]

The modernity of the Baroque and its conscious and problematic self-contradiction conforms strikingly to the paradoxical nature of the post-modern mentality. As Linda Hutcheon explains, "Postmodernism's distinctive character lies in this kind of wholesale 'nudging' commitment to doubleness or duplicity. In many ways it is an even-handed process because postmodernism ultimately manages to install and reinforce as much as undermine and subvert the conventions and presuppositions it appears to challenge."[3]

The simultaneous subversion and reconfirmation of hegemonic discourses of thought and practice lead some to interpret a postmodern text as subversive, others to view it as a constructive force that acknowledges structures from the past, reappropriating them selectively in order to address contemporary history.[4]

Zayas' *Novelas* exhibit all the aforementioned features attributed by theoretical consensus to postmodern fiction. Her contradictions are designed to be foregrounded and insoluble. The close readings of Zayas from the perspectives of feminist thought and narratology reveal both the irreducible historical specificity of her literary enterprise and its resistance to easy systematization with regard to strategies of literary or ideological analysis.

It is instructive to suggest—in general terms and with a purposefully polemical slant—the usefulness of viewing the contrast between periods of literary or cultural history in terms of a contrast between privileged or dominant rhetorical figures. The cultural authority exerted by a given rhetorical figure varies markedly from one age to the next; witness, for instance, the twentieth-century fascination with metaphor. The bibliography devoted to this subject is voluminous. By contrast, interest in the exemplum, has largely been relegated to the periphery by modern criticism.[5]

More precisely, both the high Renaissance and high modernist culture privilege metaphor, while both Baroque and postmodern culture privilege metonymy—specifically, example. Roman Jakobson has argued persuasively for the "alternative predominance of one or the other of these two processes."[6] In the case of Baroque Spain, however, his distinction must be qualified, for a simultaneity is operative whereby metaphor is privileged in the realm of poetry and metonymy in the sphere of prose. Nonetheless, both figures are exploited in order to undermine logocentrism.

It is not simply a matter of aesthetic taste which accounts for such de-privileging of a particular rhetorical figure. Rather it is a phenomenological issue—namely, a given culture's perception of *the cognitive process itself*—that is at stake. As a result, it is not difficult to understand why example poses a threat to certain movements in intellectual history, as John D. Lyons observes:

For a positivist or a realist, the basis of all assertion is shaken when examples of laws and rules are revealed as discursive constructions like any other rhetorical figure. A more sophisticated approach of the deconstructionist type, however, might well be embarrassed by its need to use examples (if only in the form of textual reference) for the kind of appeal for support it requires from an "outside." Every example can be deconstructed, and, in an approach that moves forward by selecting and deconstructing exemplary texts, the whole critical movement could be derailed by an excessive attention to its initial gestures. (4)

Indeed, despite efforts to the contrary, we as literary critics cannot escape example. For when we write a critical essay that attempts to situate a literary text within a broader context (be it ideological, tropological, stylistic, etc.) we necessarily exploit this literature as example. In spite of such reluctance to consider example as an object of literary-critical study, recent interest in discourse analysis has led to a renewed interest in critical attention devoted to it. Among the results obtained by this methodological perspective is a realization that example often presents itself in a deceptively simple light. Although unlike metaphor it explicitly proclaims a particular pedagogical function, let the reader beware. Writers of exempla, during the Renaissance and particularly during the Baroque, exploited the exemplum as a metacritical tool to comment on the deceptive nature of language itself. We are coming to realize, as several early modern writers did, that exempla can be effectively exploited for their powerful "ability to . . . suspend the apparent speech acts that constitute their situation of enunciation" (Lyons, p. 25).

That the Baroque is a period consumed with epistemology, with the individual subject's self-reflective interrogation of his or her relationship to society, is borne out as much by social history as it is by literary history. Seventeenth-century Spain's obsession with the novel, with the novelistic form of the picaresque, with the novella, and with the first European novel, *Don Quijote*, attest to its fascination with epistemology per se. Alban Forcione crystallizes this idea when he describes Don Quixote's famous debate with the Canon of Toledo: "Don Quijote (here uncharacteristically speaking with the voice of a "modern") defiantly responds to the Canon's neo-classical celebration of rationality, traditionality, and exemplarity in literary characterization with a compelling account of the intensities and pleasures of the private reading experience and the riches of the subjective order wherein literature reaches the sources of its greatest powers."[7] Or in broader terms, as Mikhail Bakhtin explains, "when the novel becomes the dominant genre, epistemology becomes the dominant discipline."

The staging of problems of cognition, the subjective order of reality, is foremost in the literature of the era. And it is so because subjectivity (the definition and parameters of the individual, his or her place in society) was a prime concern of Baroque culture. The fascination with the picaresque in Spain during the seventeenth-century—as opposed to the sixteenth-century's fascination with romance—offers revealing testimony to literature's function as a forum for society, for a particular era and its unique obsessions.[8]

The numerous and popular fictional autobiographies of picaros relentlessly detail and dramatize the crisis of subjectivity. These are narratives of solitude, of the radical isolation felt by the protagonist, male or female. That subjectivity, even when the subject is a destitute, uneducated "nobody," became a topic of passionate interest is aptly expressed by Marcos de Obregón, a picaro himself, when he remarks that "no hay vida de hombre ninguno de cuantos andan por el mundo de quien no se pueda escrebir una gran historia" [there is no life story of any man on earth that does not have the makings of a great story].[9]

The alienated individuals whose lives are chronicled in picaresque novels are an expression of the disaffection and dislocation experienced in Baroque society as a result of several interrelated factors that had been evolving over time. The imperial exploits of the late fifteenth and six-teenth centuries led to expansion, both spatial and economic, which, in turn, resulted in an unprecedented degree of social mobility; and even-tually the rigidly defined privileged classes no longer functioned as such. A logical and inevitable by-product of this unprecedented social mobility was the growth of individualism. As José Antonio Maravall puts it, "ex-pansion [technological, geographic, and economic], mobility, a loosening of bonds, and individualism constitute a chain of phenomena at the end of which appears the link of freedom."[10] Inevitably, however, as the trend toward expansion was replaced by economic downsizing and chaos, Spanish society experienced a crisis of massive proportions. Indeed, the second half of the sixteenth century saw a series of disastrous develop-ments (political and natural phenomena) that led to an atrophying of the economy and a decay in social order. More precisely, as J. H. Elliott puts it, "if any one year marks the division between the triumphant Spain of the first two Hapsburgs and the defeatist, disillusioned Spain of their suc-cessors, that year is 1588."[11] The material defeat of the Spanish Armada by England was small in comparison with its psychological effects, dra-matizing, as it were, the end of Spain's imperial grandeur. What ensued in the following decade made matters even worse. Another armada against the English, this time at Cádiz, was lost.

Yet of far greater implications was the fact that the economy had lost its momentum. Philip II's reign had been based on a Spanish-Atlantic revenue source that ceased to be a monopoly by the 1590s. Along with this setback, the New World itself suffered economically and otherwise: "The century that followed the great Indian epidemic of 1576–79 has been called 'New Spain's century of depression'—a century of economic con-traction, during the course of which the New World closed in on itself" (288). While Dutch and English aggression eroded Spain's domination of the New World, further disasters were generated closer to home. Plague and famine led to a depopulation in rural areas and a subsequent over-population of urban ones, with all its attendant problems, economic and social. As a result, the milieu of the picaro became a fact of life for a large segment of the population.

This state of general decline continued into the next century, although a new turn was taken by the arrival in 1621 of Philip IV and his influential royal favorite, the Count-Duke of Olivares. Charged with the restructuring of Spain's economy, Olivares implemented his task by centralizing bureaucratic power while reorganizing the social hierarchy (and mobility) operative during the previous century. New powers were granted to the upper classes, which, of course, led to inevitable tensions with those elements of society that suddenly saw themselves as dispossessed.

Repression based on race, religion, class, and gender was in evidence, and the goal was the security of the influential, the loss of strength of the bourgeoisie and the strengthening of the nobility. As Henry Kamen observes, "what seems to have concerned people the most was the *mobility* of the poor, the rising tide of beggary and vagrancy, which threatened to make poverty spill out of its old restricted channels and flood over so as to threaten the security of the upper classes." [12]

Antonio Maravall offers one of the most ambitious accounts not only of the historical events that precipitated and characterized seventeenth-century Spanish history, but of Baroque culture as a whole. He is perceptive in discerning the "control mechanisms" that Clifford Geertz sees as the defining features of culture. Yet, while he articulates with great insight various social, economic, and historical factors and documents that went into the formation of Baroque culture, he misconstrues the function of artistic texts, viewing them somewhat reductively as political propaganda. Expanding upon an idea of Karl Vossler, he writes, for example:

Lope's most agreeable and familiar dramatic subject is showing us how humankind's natural instincts behave in the realm of providential and social bonds and dependencies, barriers and echelons. The description also applies to everyone else; all of Baroque art, from Lope's comedy to the novel of Mateo Alemán, to Zurbarán's paintings of saints, becomes a drama of the estates, the gesticulating submission of the individual to the confines of the social order. The same thematics underlie arguments that on the surface seem indifferent to the question, and in works of a very different nature—by Villemediana, Quevedo, Gracián, and others. (35)

To give another example of Maravall's ideological, somewhat essentialist, appreciation of literature, he writes of Calderón as follows: "Calderón, coinciding with the general sense of Baroque *comedia*, gives us a clear example: according to him, 'to offer obedience' is one of the principal virtues—socially the most worthy of esteem—and, therefore, his virtuous character, representing the man who reaches a state of grace and salvation, is one who, although he agrees to make use of thought, has to be 'bridling it, rein and bit,/with obedience.' " (32).

This equestrian imagery, however, brings to mind the opening moments of Calderón's *Vida es sueño*, a text which exposes the oversimplification Maravall tries to impose on the Calderonian corpus. Indeed, as his quotation above indicates, Maravall would extend this view to all literary and artistic production in the Baroque. Yet Calderón's play focuses with great intensity on human subjectivity—the degree to which an individual is able to determine his own destiny, and the relationship of his subjective desires to the body politic. By no means does Calderón wish to stage simple "gesticulating submission" to the State.

Speaking of subjectivity in a critique of Maravall, Anthony J. Cascardi writes convincingly of the unresolved tension (rather than ideological predictability) of this text's protagonist, Segismundo, and of Tirso de Molina's Don Juan as follows: "In Don Juan's case, as in Segismundo's, the psyche is better seen as internally split rather than underdeveloped: as divided historically between the seignorial values of nobility and prestige on the one hand and a newly mobile individualism on the other; as cleaved metaphysically between the attractions of the finite *siglo* and the moral threats of the everlasting world." [13]

Maravall's interpretation of the literary text, like the artistic object, as an overdetermined function of ideology (both of which figure the individual as incapable of agency) reflects the basic premise of such theorists as Althusser and, to a large extent, also Foucault.[14] Of late, however, this rather monolithic rendering of the human subject has been called into question because it constitutes a glaring oversimplification. As we know, and as Paul Smith lucidly explains, "a person is not simply determined and dominated by the ideological pressures of any overarching discourse or ideology but is also the agent of a certain *discernment*. A person is not simply the *actor* who follows ideological scripts, but is also an *agent* who reads them in order to insert him/herself into them—or not." [15]

Smith elaorates the paramount importance of agency, defining the human *agent* as "the place from which resistance to the ideological is produced or played out, and thus *not* equivalent to either the 'subject' or the 'individual.'" The *individual*, by contrast, is "the illusion of whole and coherent personal organization, or as the misleading description of the imaginary ground on which different subject-positions are colligated" (xxxv). Finally, *subject* in Smith's nomenclature is understood as "the term used to describe what is actually the series or the conglomeration of positions, subject-positions, provisional and not necessarily indefeasible, into which a person is called momentarily by the discourses and the world that he/she inhabits" (ibid.). In other words, any given individual inhabits multiple subject-positions. Smith stresses the fact that these multiple subject-positions never "cohere to form a complete and non-contradictory 'individual'—let alone an 'individual' who determines the character or constitution of his/her own subjectivity" (xxxiv).

It is this unstable, dialectical notion of subjectivity—as an unpredictable, unresolved, and changing conglomeration of subject-positions—which is at the center of the most influential writers of the seventeenth century—Góngora, Quevedo, Cervantes, among others. And it is an equally complex appreciation of human subjectivity that reveals the full richness and subtlety of Zayas's text.

Since the pioneering work of Saussure, and more recently Lacan, subjectivity has come to be understood as an ever evolving and contradictory phenomenon. Rather than being a stable, coherent totality, the individual, for Lacan, is constituted by an unavoidable division and contradiction between the subject of an utterance (the "I" of the discourse) and the "I" who produces the utterance (the self which speaks, and which is only represented there in a fragmented way). Subjectivity is located in the gap created by this division, and it is constituted by a matrix of subject-positions which may be in conflict with one another, indeed, even radically contradictory of one another.[16]

The individual naturally tries to reconcile these inevitable contradictions in positions by seeking noncontradictory ones that will make for a more harmonious, less pressure-laden existence. Catherine Belsey identifies two primary responses of women coping with their contradictory subject-positions in present-day society:

The attempt to locate a single and coherent subject-position within these contradictory discourses, and in consequence to find a non-contradictory pattern of behavior, can create intolerable pressures. One way of responding to this situation is to retreat from the contradictions and from discourse itself, to become 'sick'—more women than men are treated for mental illness. Another is to seek a resolution of the contradictions in the discourses of feminism.[17]

Of course, feminism in the twentieth century differs radically from the possibilities for alternative discourses envisioned in the seventeenth. Patriarchy was a foregone conclusion, as was the fact that the man in the family wielded the political, economic, and social power. We should also bear in mind, as Thomas Laqueur has documented in the social and scientific registers, that in the seventeenth century, "*sex*, or the body, must be understood as the epiphenomenon, while gender, what we would take to be a cultural category, was primary or 'real.' . . . Sex before the seventeenth century, in other words, was still a sociological category and not an ontological category." [18]

Zayas was living in a turbulent but liminal period that was beginning to perceive sex, for the first time, as an ontological category—a potentially explosive one. Yet what still prevailed, as Constance Jordan points out, is a conception of the sex/gender dichotomy that differs substantially from our own modern appreciation. Renaissance humanists "understood that sexuality was a fact of life but they thought it related only to procreation. Gender was a far more comprehensive and significant category than was sex. For a man to be fully human meant that he had accepted his own obligations to cultivate the feminine virtues and recognized masculine virtues in women." [19] The conception of human nature was thus "androgynous": "A person was biologically male or female, but behavioristically both masculine and feminine if virtuous; brutal and effeminate or cruel and vain if vicious. . . . Sexual difference and its effects on the human person was not normally a topic that Renaissance feminists addressed directly. (Discussions of wife beating and rape are exceptions)" (8).

In her writing Zayas explores these two philosophies of the sex/gender distinction which were coming into conflict for the first time in Western history. She reveals a new understanding of sex, gender, and their implications for subjectivity in a wealth of responses to the patriarchy and to its traditional prescriptions for acceptable female behavior. This chapter details some of the many subject-positions figured by her female protagonists (and male ones as well), revealing that it is not by any means an either/or proposition—either feminism or silence—in the case of the *Novelas*.

El prevenido engañado (Forewarned but Not Forearmed)

El prevenido engañado (I, 4) offers a stunning case in point, a display of surprising subject-positions in conflict with one another that are articulated by Zayas—here in an uncharacteristically humorous vein—which is, at the same time, infused by grotesque detail. The story is a miniature bildungsroman, in which an admirably idealistic youth named Fadrique undergoes a sentimental apprenticeship, based primarily on his successive infatuation first with a young woman named Serafina, thereafter with a widow named Beatriz, finally with the beautiful and urbane Violante. Beginning from the perspective of a starry-eyed youth, Fadrique learns that the choice of partner is not between women who represent respectively, sexual ignorance, beauty, and brains. As he will realize, such masculinist stereotyping of female identity is reductive, wholly inadequate to the representation of female gender and agency. He comes to appreciate the fact that diversity, not exclusion, is the issue.

In so doing, Zayas mirrors the trajectory that modern feminism has undergone in recent times—moving from a series of univocal assertions in the name of "woman" to a recognition that such totalizing views underrepresent the wide ranging fact of female desire and response. To a considerable degree, the essentialism exhibited by feminist scholarship at its incipient stages can be attributed to two factors. The first is an issue of rhetorical impetus. As a political ideal, feminism, like any other ideological movement, finds itself compelled to articulate a universalizing model whose global implications can be readily apprehended. In addition, feminism was first conceived of along the lines of the Enlightenment subject

"Man," which was assumed to represent all men and women. Yet as Laura Brown observes: "How can we use a feminism that comes out of imperialism?" [20] Like current feminist thought, Zayas seeks to demythologize impoverishing depictions of women according to the limited categories operative in fairy tales—as either exclusively good or bad, as virtuous or depraved.

Introduced as a paragon of discretion and good judgment, the young Fadrique begins his sentimental journey by falling in love with an angelic beauty, "un serafín en belleza" (167) named, not by accident, Serafina. She reciprocates interest in him as well, although she is already being courted by another suitor named Vicente. Yet to Fadrique's surprise and delight, Vicente suddenly stops visiting Serafina, a change which he mistakenly interprets as her rejection of this suitor in favor of himself. She agrees to marry Fadrique, but no sooner has she done so than she falls ill for a period of several months, the result of an unspecified affliction that necessitates her seclusion. While keeping nightly vigil outside Serafina's house, Fadrique notices her hasty departure from it in the middle of one night. Puzzled by this suspicious behavior, he secretly follows her from her house to an abandoned building where she gives birth to a baby girl whom she immediately abandons, fleeing into the night.

These events overwhelm Fadrique, and all at once he comprehends that Vicente's disappearance resulted from Serafina's pregnancy, as obviously, did her sudden willingness to marry him instead. For his part Fadrique arranges for one of his relatives to care for the child (whom he names Gracia) until the age of three, at which time he stipulates that she will be raised in a convent—away from the corruptions of the world. In a pointedly worded sonnet Fadrique registers his bitter disillusionment toward the deceitful and desperate Serafina.[21] We suddenly find her in a state of panic because she has just lost two suitors—the second an honorable one who had wanted to marry her—because her status as an unwed mother has been detected, and because she has been unable to learn any news about the newborn whom she abandoned on an empty lot. Thus we see her wanting and not wanting to be a mother, wanting and not wanting to be a respectably married woman. Wondering whether the baby has died of neglect or perhaps been "eaten by dogs," Serafina tells her parents she wishes to become a nun, and so she enters a convent where, henceforth, she lives so devoutly that she is considered by the inhabitants of Granada to be a "saint." In this way Zayas recalls for her reader the consummately Baroque topos of the deceptive nature of appearances—of epistemological ambiguity—rather than the ideological function Maravall posits.

Incredulous at the callousness and duplicity that this seeming "angel" could perpetrate, Fadrique decides to leave Granada for Seville, where he adopts the stance of a seasoned misogynist. Chastened by the example of Serafina, he denounces all women—a view which the narrator strenuously opposes: "Por ella ultrajaba a todas las demás mujeres, no haciendo excepción de ninguna, cosa contraria a su entendimiento, pues para una mala hay ciento buenas, y no todas lo son, ni es justo mezclando unas con otras, culparlas a todas" (173) [Because of her he railed against all women without exception. His generalizations go entirely contrary to the real nature of women because there are a hundred good women for each bad one; not all women are bad, and it isn't right to confuse the good with the bad and blame them all (120)].

This defense of womankind is voiced by Alonso, the narrator of the *novela*, not by a female narrator. Thus just as we detect a number of unanticipated and conflicting subject positions in Serafina (the abusive mother who is capable of maternal concern, and even putative saintliness), we witness the idealist turned misogynist who is admonished by another male—who happens to be an outspoken female apologist. Zayas thus resists gender typecasting—in this case on the level of her assembled narrators. A sustained reading of her *Novelas* reveals, moreover, that this important feature remains constant on both the diegetic and extradiegetic levels throughout her text.

Soon after arriving in Seville, Fadrique is smitten by a widow named Beatriz. And although he holds firm in his misogyny, he manages to fall in love with this lady, idealizing her as he did with Serafina. Here too, then, we see Zayas's interest in representing the impoverishing nature of traditional male typecasting, which can be as inadequate as the reductionist representation of women as chaste or fallen, beautiful or stupid. He wants to marry her, and goes about soliciting her consent, but Beatriz explains that she must wait an obligatory year before remarrying, in deference to the memory of her dead husband. This standard grieving practice and the delay it poses are construed as honorable by Fadrique so he spends more than six months waiting patiently, courting his lady as ardently as she permits. One night, however, he is horrified to discover that Beatriz has all the while been involved with another lover, a black slave, whose impending death she has brought about by her rapacious sexual demands.

Like Serafina, Beatriz is also described as having the appearance of an "angel" (although her behavior is perhaps even more reprehensible than that of her predecessor): "Pareciéndole a [Fadrique] en la hermosura, ella un ángel y él un fiero demonio" (183) [Her great beauty made her look like an angel ministering to a fierce devil (127)]. Yet in reality she is the diabolically abusive member of the pair. In etymological terms her name means "the blessed one"; thus here too Zayas is interested in dramatizing the distance separating word from deed, etymological association from its referent, and appearance from reality. Clearly, by the repeated "angelic" characterization we are also meant to compare this putative "angel" to Serafina in order to underscore the diversity of the female psyche, as well as the circumspection with which we should regard the narrator's evaluative judgments. At the same time, Zayas accomplishes an additional task—namely, that of reminding her readers of the fact that any narrator is bound by his or her subjective constraints. In this case it is a question of a racially prejudiced storyteller—Alonso.

The slave, Antonio, complains of her "vicious appetites" that have brought him to his untimely end:

—¿Qué me quieres señora? ¡Déxame ya, por Dios! ¿Qué es esto, que aun estando yo acabando la vida me persigues? No basta que tu viciosa condición me tiene como estoy, sino que quieres que cuando ya estoy en el fin de mi vida, acuda a cumplir tus viciosos apetitos. Cásate, señora, cásate, y déxame ya a mí, que ni te quiero ver, ni comer lo que me das; morir quiero, pues ya no estoy para otra cosa. (184)

[What do you want of me, madam? Leave me alone, for the love of God! How can you pursue me even as I lay dying? Isn't it enough that your lasciviousness has brought me to this end? Even now you want me to satisfy your vicious appetites when I am breathing my last? Get yourself a husband, madam, marry, and leave

me in peace. I never want to see you again! I won't touch the food you bring me;
I want only to die, that's all I'm good for now.] (127–28)

Sexual coercion such as Beatriz exerts is distasteful, to say the least. The
fact that it comes as a result of class power—she is the master, he the slave
(and a black)—compounds the transgression, and Fadrique is understandably repulsed by this disclosure of her behavior. What is important
extradiegetically is Zayas's ability to represent the diversity of female response; a widow who is not simply having an illicit affair, but one where
she derives the kind of pleasure resulting from the power that men frequently exert over the maids who work in their households. It is an example of female sexual excess, and it is an interracial one. By this disclosure Zayas indicates that the desire for sexual domination over another
individual based on economic superiority, of lasciviousness even over a
sick partner, and of interracial liaisons is potentially as compelling for a
woman as it is for a man. In this episode, as in others across the hundreds
of pages of the *Novelas*, the situation posited by Belsey (either silenced
woman or feminist) is inadequate to Zayas's rich portrayal of the female
subject. Female fantasy—and even facilitation—of transgressive desire is
potentially as diverse for women as it is for men. There is not one exclusively gendered response for either sex in her writings.

Understandably alienated by Beatriz's activity, Fadrique leaves for Madrid, more convinced than ever of female duplicity. He stays with one of
his uncles and his son, named Don Juan who is, like all young men, it
seems, in love. Don Juan describes his beloved Ana and her cousin Violante who are as beautiful as they are witty, talented also in poetry and
music: "Son las Sibilas de España, entrambas bellas, entrambas discretas,
músicas, poetas. En fin, en las dos se halla lo que en razón de belleza y
discreción está repartido en todas las mujeres del mundo" (187) [They
are the sibyls of Spain: both are beautiful, witty, both are musicians and
poets. In conclusion, these two women possess the sum of all the beauty
and intelligence scattered among all other women in the world (130)].[22]

Discussing the accomplishments of these two cousins, Fadrique insists
that he seeks instead to find an *ignorant* woman: "Ya son todas tan agudas, que no hay quien las alcance, todas saben amar y engañar; y así me
tienen tan escarmentado las discretas, que deseo tener batalla con una

boba" (191–92) [Nowadays women are all so sharp you can hardly keep up with them. They all know how to love and how to deceive, but clever women have taught me such a lesson that I want to win only an ignorant one (133)].

It is incongruous and ironic, given his name (and its legendary association with lasciviousness), that Don Juan takes issue with Fadrique here, arguing for the necessity of intelligence in a woman for her to be truly alluring: "No sé qué hombre apetece una mujer necia, no sólo para aficionarse, mas para comunicarla un cuarto de hora" (192) [I can't imagine any man wanting a foolish woman to talk with for fifteen minutes let alone to love!" (133)]. By this single stroke of her pen Zayas deftly undermines Spain's national myth of masculinity. Her characters and narrators, as well as the anonymous authorial voice that periodically intervenes in the text, provide this type of cultural commentary that has profound implications for Spanish society, its official myths, and its objective realities.

Once more in keeping with his previous contradictory behavior, Fadrique falls totally in love for a third time—now with Violante, wanting to marry her, although she finds the prospect of marriage to be abhorrent, a definitive loss of her freedom. Meanwhile, the relationship of Juan and Ana becomes complicated by the fact that she marries a jealous older man. Undaunted by this impediment, however, she cleverly plots a way to enjoy Juan's company, having some fun at the expense of the misogynistic Fadrique in the process. Juan convinces him that his depression is so extreme that he will kill himself unless Fadrique impersonates Ana in bed with her soundly sleeping husband. With great reluctance he accepts this challenge, becoming mortified as the "husband" (in reality the disguised Violante) fondles him, acting as though he were preparing to make love. Fadrique is understandably terrified at the implications for his life and honor, should the "husband" wake up, and equally repulsed by what he is convinced is a provocative homoerotic gesture.

Once the trick is revealed, Fadrique enjoys Violante's company for several months, yet, when he seems most confident of her fidelity, she suddenly becomes aloof. He discovers her with a young lover who picks up an incongruous weapon—a shoe—and pointing it directly at Fadrique, says he will shoot if he doesn't leave immediately, which he does. This evocation of shoes—a known figure for sexual activity exploited in such texts as the *Lazarillo* and *El patrañuelo*—is utilized creatively here as Zayas transforms the power of sexuality represented metaphorically by the shoe into a putatively literal gun.[23] Violante and her new lover laugh uproriously, prompting Fadrique to strike her on the face, beating her until she screams, at which point he is forced to escape.

After this traumatic resolution the liaison he experiences more unexpected affairs, including one in which a woman, "for his sake," murders her husband, stuffing the corpse into a sack, lugging it on her back down to the river, where she deposits it. The jarring contrast of levity and grotesque behavior—one which is rapidly executed and lacking commentary—is clearly meant to arouse readers' *admiratio*, to keep them on the edge of their seats.

Sixteen years of travel and adventures leave Fadrique convinced of the wisdom of his desire to find a wife who is totally ignorant of the world. As a result, he goes to the convent where Gracia, the infant girl he had rescued, has grown up, taking her for his wife after verifying that she is both beautiful and stupid. Having married her, Fadrique convinces Gracia that wifely duty consists of donning armor and keeping watch over the sleeping husband all night, after which the wife sleeps during daylight hours. Not knowing any better, Gracia complies with these instructions, although she understandably finds this nightly vigil to be tiresome. And as we might expect, her artificial environment of sexual deprivation is shattered when Fadrique goes away on a business trip and a suitor named Alonso confronts her.

Upon his return Fadrique understands that Gracia has become erotically enlightened and that he has been the architect of his own dishonor—a fool to presume that he could deny his wife her sexuality. Finally he learns the hard way that discreet women who are also virtuous are beyond all price. If they are not virtuous, the narrator adds, they should at least know how to dissemble: "que las mujeres discretas saben guardar las leyes del honor, y si alguna vez las rompen, callan su yerro" (215–16) [discreet women know how to keep the laws of honor and, if ever they break them, they know how to keep their error secret (152)].

In terms of subjectivity and its representation, *El prevenido engañado* is quite revealing of Zayas's technique. She turns the age-old debate about beautiful women with brains—whether these two attributes are attractive to men and whether such women are capable of fidelity—into a sexual and emotional odyssey for Fadrique. By the end of his adventures, he comes to realize that, in fact, intelligence and beauty are the most desirable combination of features a woman can possess. Beyond his personal enlightenment, of course, this belief lies at the core of Zayas's literary and intellectual project—to convince men that women should be allowed to cultivate their minds, and that it is an obvious asset rather than a threat to their masculinity.

We see, in addition, Zayas's capacity for constructing complex, unpredictable characters, both male and female, who are fraught with competing subject-positions. Fadrique, who is convinced that he must avoid intelligent beauties, time and again, is drawn to them. He is capable of brutality, as when he beats his paramour Violante, but not (surprisingly) when his familial honor has been stained by his own wife, Gracia, who suffers no punishment whatsoever. This outcome is especially striking given the gory consequences of adultery in seventeenth-century Spanish theater.[24] Beatriz, who wants to project the role of the grieving widow wishing to marry an honorable suitor within a respectable time frame while concealing a black slave whom she sexually abuses, is the other most stunning example. This *novela* dramatically articulates the supremely unpredictable nature of the human subject.

Mal presagio casar lejos (Marriage Abroad: Portent of Doom)

The conciliatory tone of *El prevenido engañado*, as well as its occasional levity, makes it a tale of wife-testing that is uncharacteristic of the *Novelas* as a whole, particularly the second part, which reveals a fascination with violence overwhelmingly directed at women. *Mal presagio casar lejos* (II, 7) provides an equally original and unexpected exploration of subjectivity reflected in male-female relations (as well as an extreme example of the excessive violence that Zayas is capable of staging). Its view of female agency is quite alien to the creative expediency registered by all the women, without exception, of *El prevenido engañado*. It is diametrically opposed, in fact, since here the women are all victims of sadistic men. Angela Carter speaks of such predation in general terms, but her comments are relevant to the depiction of woman in this narrative. Carter writes of a world of male brutality in which women are transformed "from human beings into wounded creatures who were born to bleed."[25] Indeed, such intense victimization of women corresponds to the second part of Zayas's collection, the *Desengaños*, by contrast with the less macabre *Maravillas* of the first ten novellas, written a decade earlier.

Mal presagio casar lejos is a story of grotesque cruelty in which five children, one son and four daughters, lose their parents and all suffer great personal tragedies. In spite of their innocence, beauty, intellect, and nobility, however, each of the women is brutally murdered. The first, named Mayor, accompanied by her youngest sister, María, goes to Portugal when Mayor takes a Portuguese husband. In a totally feigned and unwarranted testing of his wife, this man writes her a love letter, pretending to be not her husband but a suitor. As she reads the letter, he rushes in, killing both her and the page who delivered his letter. Seeing this, the younger sister jumps out the window in an attempt to escape, breaking both legs as a consequence of her fall, an accident which leaves her an invalid for life. We are told in no uncertain terms that the Portuguese do not like Castilians, and that this is why Mayor lost her life in the unprovoked attack. We are also informed that María was rescued by some Castilians, who returned her in a permanently crippled state to the safety of her homeland.

In this way the topic of nationalism—especially the abuse of Spanish women abroad—is firmly established from the opening moments of the unfolding narrative, reinforced with each new casualty. The second sister of this unfortunate family, Leonor, marries an Italian by whom she has a son. When one day and without any ulterior motive she praises a Spanish captain within her husband's hearing, he strangles her with her hair, murdering their now four-year-old son as well. The third sister, Blanca, meanwhile marries a prince from Flanders who seems to her brother to be a suitable match. Yet as the narrator explains, if she had known the tragic fates of her three sisters, she would surely have chosen the convent instead of agreeing to any marriage.[26]

Still unaware of her sisters' deaths, Blanca agrees to this marriage of convenience on the condition that the prince come to Spain and court her for one year, a logical proviso intended to give her time to determine whether his love for her is genuine. They marry at the end of the year, and almost immediately thereafter Blanca learns of the violent ends which her sisters suffered. But now it is too late since she has officially become a commodity—her husband's property.

The issue of nationalism surfaces even more intensely since almost as soon as they leave Spain Blanca's husband begins to mistreat her, we are told, because Spanish women always suffer at the hands of foreign husbands. Of this lamentable custom the narrator pointedly asserts: "No sé qué desdicha tienen las españolas con los extranjeros, que jamás las estiman, antes se cansan a dos días y las tratan con desprecio" (273) [I don't understand the misfortune Spanish women have with foreign husbands, who never esteem them but instead tire of them in two days and treat them with contempt (286)]. Yet the misogyny extends beyond national boundaries. For even Marieta, the prince's sister, is hated by her husband, although he is not a foreigner.

By this discrepancy between the narrator's observation and the contradiction afforded by the text itself, Zayas underscores in yet a different way the need for her readers' active participation in analyzing the discourse and actions she presents. This need for skeptical analysis on the microtextual level becomes equally crucial for the macrotextual level as we are systematically confronted by a wealth of contradictory perspectives on gender, race, and class by characters and narrators alike.

As *Mal presagio* unfolds we learn that the prince's mistreatment of Blanca is nothing by comparison with that of her relentlessly cruel father-in-law. The day that the newlyweds arrive in Flanders, the prince's father, impatient at the one-year delay in the marriage, meets his daughter-in-law for the first time with the following words of abuse: "—¿Cuándo había de ser esta venida? Basta, que las españolas sois locas. No sé qué extranjero os apetece, si no es que esté desesperado" (273–74) [It's about time you got here. I can't understand why any foreigner would want you; he'd have to be desperate (287)]. This remark is indicative of his discourse with her, never treating her with anything other than rage and ridicule.

Why, then, does the prince marry Blanca in the first place, given the prejudice against Spaniards that he and especially his father feel? It would appear from the violent deaths of Blanca's three sisters, and from the equally vicious fate that Blanca will soon have, that Zayas constructs an exemplum of the perils involved for the woman who marries a foreigner. Yet other causes are suggested as well. Her sister-in-law Marieta, who is not married to a foreigner, is garrotted by her husband, either because she defended Blanca in an altercation she had with her husband, or because the husband was jealous of a servant, "un gentilhombre de la señora Marieta, que le daba la mano cuando salía fuera, mozo de mucha gala y nobleza" (281) [a young, elegant nobleman, the one who took her arm when she went out (295)]. It is never made clear whether this jealousy was justified—whether this gesture is based on courtesy or passion. Though this ambiguity is not resolved, Zayas communicates with devastating clarity the overwhelmingly misogynistic environment in the household of the prince and his father.

This tale progressively discloses that the brutal attitude toward women results less from nationalistic prejudice than from a homoerotic complication, a fact that Blanca herself realizes when she walks in on the prince as he is making love to his favorite page, Arnesto. Whereas Blanca had assumed that the prince's radical change in attitude toward her once he reached his home in Flanders was the consequence of a liaison with another woman, she is shocked to discover him in bed with another man instead:

Vió acostados en la cama a su esposo y a Arnesto, en deleites tan torpes y abominables, que es baxeza, no sólo decirlo, mas pensarlo. Que doña Blanca, a la vista de tan horrendo y sucio espectáculo, más difunta que cuando vió el cadáver de la señora Marieta, mas con más valor, pues apenas lo vió, cuando más apriesa que había ido, se volvió a salir, quedando ellos, no vergonzosos ni pesarosos de que los hubiese visto, sino más descompuestos de alegría, pues con gran risa dijeron: —Mosca lleva la española. (286)

[In the bed she saw her husband and Arnesto engaged in such gross and abominable pleasures that it's obscene to think it, let alone say it. At the sight of such a horrendous and dirty spectacle, Doña Blanca was more stunned than when she beheld lady Marieta's corpse, but she was braver. The moment she set eyes upon them, she left more quickly than she had come. They weren't ashamed or embarrassed by her having seen them, instead they were amused and roared with laughter. One of them said: "That sure spooked the Spanish woman!"] (300–301)

Finally, it would appear, we discover a motive for all the seemingly unwarranted and excessive barbarity against women that fills the pages of this narrative, namely, the fact that the prince, his father, and Arnesto form a fiercely loyal homosexual community. That Zayas would represent this possibility in an extended fashion in seventeenth-century Spain seems daring indeed. Even today many view this kind of topic as highly transgressive and controversial.

Yet this departure from the canon of "appropriate" themes corresponds to the new reading practices that Roger Chartier identifies with the privatization of reading. Silent reading created an air of intimacy that shut out the outside world, permitting the reader to indulge in all types of fantasies, including the voyeurism that Blanca—and later her sister—experience. And, while it is a wholly negative experience for her, the transgressive nature of its representation is titillating for the reader, representing as it does a forbidden activity in the context of early modern mainstream society. While it is not described in great detail, it borders on the pornographic, which private reading made possible in respectable circles for the first time. In effect, in the privacy of his or her own room, the reader is now offered the exciting prospect of becoming a voyeur.[27]

Even more remarkable than the treatment of a transgressive theme, Zayas offers a surprisingly complex, nuanced vision of homosexuality. For if we trace carefully the speech and actions of the prince, we see that he too reveals inconsistent and contradictory subject positions to a very dramatic degree. Paul Julian Smith writes insightfully of the male-female relations at issue in *Mal presagio casar lejos*, speaking of the "negative female exchange" as opposed to the "productive economy of men" embodied by the homosexual community of the prince, his father, and Arnesto. In so doing he affirms that "(according to Zayas and Irigaray) 'hom(m)osexualité' (sexual commerce between men) is the logical result of a system which persists in excluding women. In this 'circulation of the same' women can figure only as objects of exchange and can never transcend a state of permanent exile."[28]

It is true that these women are forever silenced as a result of cruel and unwarranted male brutality, but the "productivity" of the male group is debatable. In addition, such a coherent presentation of the male community is called into question given that at several important junctures in the text the prince reveals himself to be conflicted about his sexuality and affective affiliations. Why did he seek a wife at all if he formed part of a productive and stable male community? Contradictions in his behavior surface from the inception of the one-year courtship stipulated by Blanca. When Blanca's trial period is criticized by many of her associates, among them her maid since childhood, she responds quite logically, saying:

—¿Y quienes son los necios, doña María—preguntó doña Blanca—que llaman locura a una razón fundada en buen discurso, de manera que sienten mejor de casarse una mujer con un hombre que jamás vió ni habló, y que suceda ser feo, o necio, o desabrido, o mal compuesto, y se halle después aborrecida y desesperada de haberse empleado mal, que no avisarse del caudal que lleva en su esposo? *Todas cuantas cosas se compran se procuran ver*, y que, vistas, agraden al gusto, como es un vestido, una joya. ¿Y un marido, que no se puede deshacer de él, como de la joya, y del vestido, ha de ser por el gusto ajeno? (263; emphasis added)

["Doña María, who is so unwise as to call foolishness something based on solid reason?" doña Blanca asked. "Is it better for a woman to marry a man she's never seen, never spoken to, who might be ugly, stupid, harsh, deformed, so that too late she may find herself despised and despairing because of her misjudgment in not ascertaining what kind of a man her husband was? Before you buy merchandise like a dress or a jewel, you always examine it first to determine in the examination whether it pleases your taste. A husband, who can't be gotten rid of like a dress or a jewel, should be selected by others?"] (275)

Through Blanca, Zayas registers the historical fact of unfortunate betrothal practices, whereby women were promised in marriage with little or no consideration given to anything but the financial and social implications of the union. This socioeconomic perspective on marriage, of course, extended beyond the boundaries of Spain and was the standard view largely until the nineteenth century, when considerations of personal attraction began to enter into the picture. Nonetheless, Zayas has Spain in mind when she speaks through the voice of Blanca in order to decry this financial approach to courtship and marriage.

Zayas is even more pointed in her criticism of her homeland a few pages later, when she condemns the social pretentiousness inherent in the abusive appropriation of the term "Don." In a lengthy excursus (only part of which is reproduced here) the narrator laments:

En aquellos países [Flandes], ni el Italia, ninguno se llama Don, sino los clérigos, porque nadie hace ostentación de los Dones como en España, y más el día de hoy, que han dado en una vanidad tan grande, que hasta los cocheros, lacayos y mozas de cocina le tienen. (274)

[In those lands, as in Italy, they don't use the title "don," except sometimes for priests, because nobody flaunts titles like "don" as much as in Spain. This is particularly true nowadays when vanity has reached such an extreme that even coachmen, lackeys, and kitchen maids use the title.] (287)

Is this meditation on the vanity and abuse of the term "Don" inserted here in a somewhat disruptive way to indict (nonaristocratic) abusers of the title, or is it intended to signal the aristocracy's uneasiness in terms of its somewhat shaky existence vis-à-vis the lower classes? Perhaps both—it is ultimately left for the reader to decide, forging an interpretation that is no doubt heavily weighted according to his or her socioeconomic affiliations.

Returning to the thread of the narrative, we learn that the prince's father is furious at this obligatory year of courtship, yet his son seems not to be since, as the narrator points out, he wanted to "see Spain." The extent of his affective commitment is thus uncertain from his response to the delay in marrying. We also learn from Blanca's faith in pure reason that she is unaware of the complexities of human subjectivity, that her testing of her future husband may well not disclose his true nature. In part Zayas underscores Blanca's blind faith in reason as a way of pointing to the unpredictable, labyrinthine possibilities of multiple subject-positions. At the same time, she is rejecting the reductive time-worn dualism that depicts the female psyche as sentiment and the male as reason.

Further ambiguous signals concerning the prince's sexual and affective identity are given by the narrator, and by Blanca's response to the prince as well. We learn from the narrator that the prince "se enamoró tanto de la hermosa doña Blanca, o lo fingió, que el corazón del hombre para todo tiene astucias" (266) [was so enamored of doña Blanca, or so he feigned to be, for a man's heart is fundamentally cunning (278)]. Blanca liked the prince, and he was undeniably in love with her; she liked him but did not want to become his wife; she regretted bitterly that the marriage must wait a whole year, and yet at the same time wished that the delay were longer(!).

Blanca's desperate unhappiness stems from the contradictory impulses at the thought that she must reluctantly marry (thus forfeiting her freedom) and her simultaneous love for the prince. This contradictory reaction, "tan diferentes efectos de amor y desamor" (271) [such contradictory effects of affection and disaffection (284)], is a hotly debated topic among the members of the *sarao*. Some say that Blanca was wise in making the prince pay full price for her beauty, while others claim that it was sheer madness since she already belonged to him. For his part, we are told that the prince is so despairing at the one-year delay that he would have returned to Flanders had it not been for Blanca's brother, and that his father, the elderly prince, had in fact ordered him to return home.

In any event, it is clear that the father construes the one-year testing period as an insult, which would account in part for his negative reception of Blanca upon her arrival in Flanders. What is left unsaid but becomes obvious is that, given his detestation of all women (evident from his murderous acts), he does not want his son to marry at all. Did he permit the marriage in order to keep up appearances? Or was he perhaps yielding reluctantly to a desire on the part of his son to assert himself against his father's will as bisexual or heterosexual? We are not told explicitly; instead Zayas leaves it up to the reader to judge. Again, the kind of ideological clarity Maravall assigns to the literary text seems remote indeed.

Even more telling and unanticipated in the prince is the fact that he reveals himself to be siding not with the men, but with the women of the group, especially his sister Marieta and wife, Blanca, at two key moments in the text. The first is when he discovers Marieta dead as a result of the garrotting administered by her husband (his cousin) and his own father. We are told that had he known their intentions, the prince would surely have prevented his sister's death, and that he was greatly grieved by the servant's death as well: "Vino el príncipe de fuera, que no se halló al lastimoso caso, ni le sabía; que fuera cierto no lo consintiera, o la salvara, porque amaba mucho a su hermana y no sabía si del [*sic*] que había sentido menos la muerte del gentilhombre" (282) [The prince hadn't been a party to the dreadful scene and indeed knew nothing of it or you can be sure he would never have allowed it. He would have saved his sister because he loved her dearly. Nobody knew how he felt about the death of her gentleman (296)].

Seeing his sister's battered corpse on one side and Blanca's fainted body on the other the prince laments with great passion to his father, saying: "—¿Que crueldades son estas, señor, o qué pretendes de esta triste española, que la has llamado para que vea tan lastimoso caso?" (282) ["What kind of cruelty is this, sir? What are you doing to this unfortunate Spanishwoman that you call her in to witness such a doleful spectacle?" (297)]. By way of answering this question, his father angrily dismisses him as a coward, at which point the prince helps bring Blanca to her senses, all the while grieving for his viciously murdered sister.

The other crucial moment at which the prince tries to defend a woman, it is Blanca herself, as his father and Arnesto reveal their sadistic intention to bleed her slowly to death. María helplessly witnesses this repulsive spectacle through a keyhole, while the prince begs his father not to go through with his plan: "Volviéndose a su padre con algunas señales piadosas en los ojos, le dixo: '—¡Ay señor, por Dios, que no pase adelante esta crueldad! Satisfecha puede estar con lo padecido vuestra ira y mi enojo. Porque os doy palabra que, cuanto ha que conozco a Blanca, no me ha parecido más linda que ahora. Por esta hermosura merece perdón su atrevimiento'" (289–90) [He turned to his father with tears of compassion in his eyes and said: "Alas, my lord, for God's sake, do not permit this cruel act to proceed. Your wrath and my anger should be satisfied with what she's suffered. I swear to you that as long as I've known Blanca she's never looked lovlier than she does now. If only because of her beauty, her audacity deserves pardon" (304)]. His father's only response is "Calla, cobarde, traidor, medio mujer" (290) ["Shut up, you womanish coward, you traitor!" (304)]. Following this exchange, we are told in no uncertain terms that it was Arnesto and his father who had created the animosity that the prince felt toward Blanca, which helps explain his increasingly alienated treatment of her.

The prince's displays of grief and compassion and the narrator's commentary make clear that much of the time the prince feels conflicted about the consequences of his male bonding. The story does not create the unproblematic, positive male community that Smith suggests. Nor is its female community as passive as he suggests. He claims of Blanca, for example, that "her one positive act is to burn the bed in which her husband and his page have made love, a symbolic rejection of desire in all its forms" (237). Yet the urge of a wife to burn her marital bed once it has been defiled by another coupling is clearly not "a symbolic rejection of desire in all its forms." It is a sign of rage at the fact that she has been replaced, and by a union that writes her out of the economy of desire in absolute terms.

Beds function programmatically in this narrative. Blanca's bed-burning scene is the fourth reference to beds in this tale. The first refers to Blanca's sister María, who is crippled for life, hence bedridden, as she tries to elude the wrath of her brother-in-law; the second depicts Blanca while she is convalescing from the beating given her by the prince; the third is the scene revealing the prince making love with Arnesto. As a result, for Blanca beds are hateful reminders of physical pain inflicted by men on women or of her personal marital humiliation as a result of her husband's preference for men.

An additional and highly significant "positive act" is Blanca's disbursement of her jewels to her servants once she understands that her days are numbered as a result of her discovery of the affair between the prince and Arnesto. This type of bequest from one woman to another was a way by which the boundaries of the self could be affirmed by a woman in early modern Europe. As Natalie Zemon Davis explains, paradoxically: "A strategy for at least a thread of female autonomy may have been built precisely around [the] sense of being given away, that women sometimes turned the cultural formulation around, and gave themselves away. . . . The women's wills carefully describe the gifts—'my fur-lined gray cape,' 'my third-best petticoat'—and the items are distributed according to the status and closeness of the recipients."[29] Moreover, this ritual of the bequest held true for poor women as well as affluent ones. It was a way of communicating and affirming their individuality, thereby also demonstrating the bond of the female community. In this way, during her last moments of life, Blanca finally attains a margin of autonomy that had been denied to her within the bonds of the marriage she initially believed would respect her individuality. It is a vivid testimony to Zayas's ability to understand and represent the possibility of radically conflicting subject-positions, and to the importance and unpredictability of agency. Her representation of homosexuality is dazzling not simply because she broaches a "forbidden" theme, but because of her subtle appreciation of this non-canonical sexuality. In addition, the sensitivity of the portrayal makes us wonder whether it stems from her own possibly lesbian relationship with another noblewoman.[30]

Al fin se paga todo (*Just Desserts*)

If the possibilities for female agency are presented as painfully limited in *Mal presagio casar lejos*, with Blanca's disbursement of her jewels as her only life-affirming act, *Al fin se paga todo* (I, 7) offers a radically different set of possibilities for its protagonist, Hipólita. She is fortunate and resourceful, constructing a positive existence for herself in the wake of multiple disasters.

The narrative opens by focusing on García, a gentleman residing in Valladolid, where Felipe III has temporarily moved the capital from Madrid. As he looks out his door, García sees a body being hurled violently from a house, and goes to verify what he has just witnessed. Shocked at the realization that the body is that of a badly beaten woman, he takes her to his lodgings, offering her food, shelter, and words of consolation. The woman in question is Hipólita, a twenty-four-year-old beauty who looks more like an "angel" than a woman, a fact which tempts him: "Casi se atreviera a ser Tarquino de tan divina Lucrecia; mas favoreciendo don García más a su nobleza que a su amor, a su recato que a su deseo, y a la razón más que a su apetito, procuró con muchas caricias el reposo de aquella hermosísima señora" (295–96) [If don García hadn't reminded himself of the faith she'd placed in him, he might have dared to play Tarquin to such a divine Lucrecia. Showing his nobility instead of his burning love, his sensibility more than his desire, his reason rather than his lust, with many gentle caresses he tried to make the lovely lady comfortable (217)].[31]

This analogy recalls (as did *El prevenido engañado*) the paradigmatic rape scene of the Roman heroine who took her own life shortly after her brother-in-law had raped her, feeling that she had stained her husband's honor beyond repair, although she had resisted Tarquin with all her strength. Yet with García the analogy is somewhat strained in that he is not Hipólita's brother-in-law. The suggestion that he might be tempted to rape her is intended presumably by the narrator of this tale, Miguel, to indicate the extent of García's passion, but also his noble resolve and self-control.

Rape by a brother-in-law is, however, the issue that results ultimately in the deaths of Hipólita's brother-in-law (Luis), her husband (Pedro), her former suitor (Gaspar), and his unnamed servant. It turns out that since her marriage eight years earlier Hipólita has had to deflect Luis's designs on her virtue. To deal with his unseemly advances she sometimes pretends not to understand them, sometimes admonishing him to respect his brother's honor and hers, even offering him (in a somewhat disconcertingly transactional manner most often employed by men) the opportunity to marry her cousin, whom Hipólita claims is more beautiful and wealthy than she.

This situation continues unchanged until one day Luis finds an opportunity to blackmail his sister-in-law. In spite of her loving husband, Hipólita falls in love with a Portuguese named Gaspar who pursues her ardently. So smitten is he that he dares to declare his love for her in church, and when Pedro is out of the house on a hunting trip Hipólita determines to entertain Gaspar in lavish fashion. Given the oppressive summer heat of Valladolid, she orders two satin mattresses placed in the garden beneath a lovely arbor, thus creating an idyllic setting in which to entertain her lover. Yet before Gaspar has a chance to experience Hipólita's bower of bliss, her husband returns unexpectedly. When Gaspar arrives at the house moments after Pedro, finding all the doors locked, he completely misreads the scene, assuming that Hipólita has deceived him by deciding to entertain some other suitor instead. We are told that "en siendo una mujer fácil, hasta con los mismos que la solicitan su facilidad se hace sospechosa" (306) [once a woman is easy, even the very man who caused her to err becomes suspicious of her (224)], thereby underscoring male — rather than the cliché female — inconstancy. Seeing a male figure lying next to Hipólita, Gaspar draws his dagger and is about to plunge it into the body when, at the last moment it rolls over, and he recognizes it to be her husband, Pedro.

Undaunted, Hipólita consults the next day with her resourceful maid who chides her for not taking a few risks, given how madly in love she claims to be. The maid recommends that Gaspar come before the doors are locked in the evening, offering to hide him in her own room until Pedro is asleep, at which point the lovers will finally be able to consummate their passion. This time the tryst is thwarted by a different unforeseen occurrence, namely a fire that engulfs the house. A number of servants die in the blaze, but the family escapes injury and, in the confusion, Gaspar manages to get away undetected. A third encounter is planned whereby Gaspar is to enter through a little window on the ground level. This meeting also fails to materialize as Gaspar (rather comically) becomes wedged in the window frame, unable to move either in or out. Using daggers and other tools, the servants manage to remove the frame from the wall, eventually permitting his escape.

Recognizing the significance of this architectural detail, Amy Williamsen points to the episode not only as the evocation of a powerful symbol of the feminine in Golden Age literature, but also as an example of Zayas's sense of humor: "In the *Novelas*, Zayas explores the comic possibilities of the architectural sign, at times demonstrating that the rigid imposition of the patriarchal order also restricts men."[32] Aware of the relentless polyvalence in Zayas's writing, however, she recognizes the sinister potential of architectural evocation in the *Desengaños*, where "the house serves as an instrument of torture employed against women" (144). She offers the example of *Amar sólo por vencer* (*Love for the Sake of Conquest*) (II, 6), where the father and uncle kill the protagonist by making a wall collapse on her. Yet the gesture is double-edged, for while the patriarchal architecture succeeds in destroying the young woman, its own self-destruction results as well (144).

A fourth encounter in *Al fin se paga todo* begins in a promising manner, but has fatal consequences. The next morning, after Pedro leaves the house, Hipólita summons Gaspar and embraces him at long last, this being only the second favor granted by her in their year-long relationship (the first one being the kiss he stole the night he almost killed Pedro by mistake). When Pedro returns once again unexpectedly, Hipólita instructs Gaspar to hide in her trunk, and he willingly complies. Pedro lingers, however, more than an hour and a half, at which point Hipólita opens the trunk and discovers Gaspar totally lifeless. Beside herself with sadness and panicked at the thought of a dead man's body in her bedroom, she begs Don Luis's help. Realizing the potential for blackmail, he helps by taking Gaspar's corpse to a friend's house. In the process of transporting the body, he becomes aware that Gaspar is not in fact dead, and manages to revive him. Claiming to be an upstanding and outraged family member, Luis deceptively projects a concern for familial honor, telling Gaspar that he must never go near Hipólita again or he will kill him rather than allowing Don Pedro's honor to be called into question. Gaspar complies, after first informing her maid that he never wants to see her again, that he had never imagined that any woman could be as treacherous as she has been. For her part, Hipólita is disconsolate and falls ill as a result. Her husband is saddened to see her so depressed, while the perfidious Luis tries to extract payment from her in the form of sexual favors—pressures that lead Hipólita to contemplate suicide, despised and abandoned by the man she loves, pursued by the man she detests.

Aware that she will not submit willingly to his lust, Luis devises an audacious plan to rape Hipólita by tricking her into believing that he is her husband. Having cut a small door into the attic of his brother's adjoining house in order to facilitate his penetration, Luis enters it, releasing all the horses from the stable in order to create sufficient confusion to rouse Pedro from his marriage bed and send him out of the house. The release of the horses (traditionally, a symbol of male lust) is a device by which Zayas dehumanizes the perfidious brother-in-law still further. At this point Luis slips into bed with Hipólita, pretending to be Pedro, and disguises his voice so convincingly that he deceives her. Having satisfied his lust, Luis leaves, whereupon Pedro returns to his bed, and begins engaging in foreplay with his wife. Hipólita is taken aback at the timing of this second sexual encounter, coming so soon after the first, remarking to him: "—Válgame Dios, señor, y qué travieso que estáis esta noche, que no ha un instante que estuvistes aquí, y agora pretendéis lo mismo" (320) ["Good heavens, my dear, how mischievous you are this evening! Why you just finished and here you are again!" (235)]. Pedro tells his wife she must have been dreaming, at which point she understands that her brother-in-law has finally gotten his way.

Unlike the chaste Lucretia, who could not bear such dishonor, choosing suicide instead, the resilient and resourceful Hipólita plots her revenge in a cold-blooded, calculated manner. Passing carefully through that same attic door by which Luis had finally succeeded in causing her dishonor, she murders him in his sleep. Although the first dagger thrust kills him, Hipólita's wrath prompts her to stab him again and again. The savage nature of her repeated stabbings communicates the strength of her passionate hatred of Luis, and the indisputable fact that female agency can result in as much physical violence as male aggression.

Recalling the double references to Lucretia and Tarquin, one might be tempted to say that Hipólita is a "Lucretia made good," in that she punishes the vile rapist rather than sacrificing her own life—a life which was totally without fault in terms of agency. Yet, of course, Zayas is not simply offering her reader an active, vengeful, "corrected" Lucretia—a more brave, empowered version of the Roman heroine. For Hipólita, we recall, is a very determined would-be adulteress. Zayas wishes to figure complication, the multiple subject-positions at issue in "real life"; she wants to demythologize, as it were, the artificiality by which legendary exemplars represent only one exclusive human impulse or personality trait. Hipólita loves her husband but is madly in love with Gaspar; she hates Luis, but when he dishonors her she kills him viciously rather than killing herself. She is a survivor.

Indeed, Zayas's interest in creating characters who represent many (frequently conflicting) subject-positions is nowhere more evident than in Don Pedro himself. As Hipólita finishes avenging herself, she replaces the bloody dagger in Pedro's sheath, and when Luis's body is discovered, the police take the blameless husband into custody since he is the owner of the murder weapon and because the maids testify to the police that Luis had been pursuing his wife relentlessly. Once Hipólita confesses to the crime, from the protected space of the convent where García has placed her for safekeeping, her husband is released, and she is declared innocent of any wrongdoing. And, though her kind and long-suffering husband begs her to return home, she refuses, saying that "honor con sospecha no podía criar perfeto amor ni conformes casados" (326) [suspicious love couldn't lead to perfect love or to conjugal harmony (239)] — reasoning that lingering suspicions will inevitably remain, not because of Don Luis (whose transgression she had already punished), but because of Don Gaspar's former love for her.

Of equal importance, of course, this reasoning may largely be construed as a pretext to protect her passionate love for García rather than as a desire to protect her husband's reputation. Hipólita's resourcefulness and agency show through once more here. And the fact that this tale is narrated by a male member of the group (Miguel) is even more striking. Far from disapproving of her behavior, he appears rather to revel in her resourcefulness. All she asks of her husband is that he support her in the convent, which he does liberally. Like Fadrique of *El prevenido engañado*, he is thus not predictably vengeful, like the husband of Calderonian honor plays, but rather a very understanding man. Not only is he willing to fund Hipólita's existence in the convent, he is so shaken and depressed by her absence that he falls terminally ill, dying within one year. Never having felt any animosity toward his wife, Pedro leaves her his entire estate, visiting her as often as possible until the day he dies.

His untimely death has beneficial consequences for Hipólita, who suddenly finds herself "libre, moza, y rica" (free, young, and wealthy), and with an adoring suitor whose love she reciprocates ardently. As a result, she marries García, has wonderful children by this marriage, and thanks heaven for their collective good fortune. Some time later we learn that Gaspar, who had beaten Hipólita so brutally when she sought refuge with him and who had, in addition, stolen her jewels on that occasion, has been murdered by one of his servants, who is about to be hanged.

The narrator, Miguel, claims that he heard these events recounted by the people who were directly involved in them, indicating also that he decided to tell this true history so that people will understand that everyone gets what is coming to them. To take this narrative as an unproblematic illustration of poetic justice is, however, a mistake. Luis and Gaspar are both murdered, the first by the woman whom he had raped, but the second by a greedy servant, in a peripheral, arbitrary manner that has nothing to do with either his adulterous machinations or his beating of Hipólita. It is, rather, a chance occurrence motivated by greed rather than justice. In ethical terms, García is not entirely worthy of the reward he receives, either—marriage to the woman of his dreams and lovely children by her as well. He has, after all, led to the breakup of her marriage and the death of her adoring husband. Likewise, Hipólita herself cannot be said to deserve the bliss she experiences with García, at the expense of Pedro, who dies a broken man as a result of her infidelity and ultimate rejection.

That Zayas questions the validity of the title of her seventh narrative is clearly suggested by an ambiguity Miguel generates in passing directly before he recounts it: "El mal jamás dexa de tener castigo ni el bien premio, pues cuando el mundo no la dé, le da el cielo" (292) [Evil always has its punishment just as good has its reward, if not in this world, then certainly in the next (214)].[33] Yet Zayas cautions the reader not to expect simple equivalences and clear-cut exempla in her narratives, such as *Al fin se paga todo*. People tend not to behave as abstract virtues and vices in accord with the dictates of a literary or philosophical exemplum. Her appreciation of human nature, of subjectivity, is far too nuanced and labyrinthine for such simple solutions. And so is her understanding of the virtually infinite possibility for agency in both sexes.

From the analysis of *Al fin se paga todo*, with its built-in ambiguities in terms of female exemplarity, by contrast with the female victimization of *Mal presagio casar lejos*, we see also the danger involved in generalizing about Zayas's feminist project. While she has an enduring interest in defending the need for intellectual and affective equality of women and men, her total production cannot be reduced to a depiction of victimized females. Recent studies extrapolate from some of the more grisly stories, claiming, as Elizabeth Ordóñez does in her fine essay, that Zayas writes primarily about victimized females and victimizing patriarchies: "Women in the 'novelas' of María de Zayas are repeatedly victims of the misunderstanding of men: husbands, brothers, and women acting in collusion with men misread wives, sisters, mistresses, even friends. They are repeatedly too ready and too willing to believe false stories regarding their women, never checking the sources of the narrative, never doubting the reliability of the narrator."[34] Ordóñez accurately registers the often deadly power of gossip—that its sources and potential motivations usually go unexamined. Her suggestive insights hold true for many (though not all) of the narratives of part II, and still fewer of part I.[35] For example, in four of the five tales discussed in this chapter, *El prevenido engañado* and *Al fin se paga todo*, *La burlada Aminta y venganza del honor*, and *El juez de su causa*, we witness resourceful women who take charge of their destinies precisely by manipulating the men around them.

La burlada Aminta y venganza del honor
(*Aminta Deceived and Honor's Revenge*)

La burlada Aminta y venganza del honor (I, 2) is a case in point, a tale, as the title suggests, composed in two parts. In fact, as Patsy Boyer insightfully observes, this double focus characterizes Zayas's writing: "Because the novellas tend to be bipartite rather than unitary, with two separate parts to the plot and at least two distinct messages (e.g., *Disillusionment in Love and Virtue Rewarded*), it is difficult to characterize them in simple terms" (xxii). This is a key observation about Zayas's desire to construct epistemologically intricate narratives rather than totalizing cautionary tales about severely disempowered females.

La burlada Aminta is a striking case in point, another example of female resourcefulness that triumphs over perfidious male (and female) behavior. Aminta is the hyperbolically depicted beauty at the center of this narrative: "de todos era llamada el milagro desta edad y la otava maravilla deste tiempo" (85) [everybody called her the miracle of the age and the eighth wonder of modern times (48)]. Considered to be a basilisk, the mythical serpent that can kill with its lethal gaze, because of her tremendous allure, she has transformed the nocturnal streets of Segovia into the mountains of Arcadia and the Jungle of Love.

As she is waiting to marry her cousin who is returning from a trip abroad, she is noticed by a dishonorable man who identifies himself as "Jacinto," a man who, unbeknownst to her, has actually abandoned his wife, living instead with a concubine named Flora who is posing as his sister. Despite the delicate femininity suggested by her name, Flora is one of Zayas's most impressively despicable and dangerous women. Specifically, she is the type of female villain in Zayes's fiction whom Marcia Welles would aptly identify as pertaining to the category of the Terrible Mother. Drawing on the work of Erich Neumann, Welles explains that there exists the archetypal association of the Good Mother (associated with fecundity and birth), but also the ensnaring, destructive type of the Terrible Mother. Commenting on what she perceives to be a binary opposition operative in the *Novelas*, she explains that: "Characteristically in the tales of María de Zayas the negative Feminine is manifested in the figure of a sorceress, a seductress, or a wicked older woman; the positive Feminine is represented by a virginal figure who eventually consummates her holy matrimony, or instead, enters a convent to devote herself to the Church. This polarization corresponds to the opposition established in Christian mythology between the temptress Eve and the chaste Mary."[36]

Welles's work is insightful in registering and attempting to account for the malevolent females who appear in a number of Zayas's stories, and who serve to interrogate uncomplicated, essentialist readings of her work along rigid lines of victimized females and predatory men. Yet this binary conception of good women versus explicitly evil ones should be emended to make room for those who do not fall into either extreme of such a polar opposition. Where, for example, do we locate someone like Hipólita from *Al fin se paga todo*? She is neither an exemplary wife and daughter of Mary, nor is she a seductress who tempts unsuspecting males. She is, rather, a woman who, after eight years of marriage to a loving but unexciting husband, is pursued by an extremely persistent and appealing lover to whom she yields. The fact that in the year-long courtship her suitor manages to steal only one kiss and that she was embraced by him just one time indicates that she does not fall into the extreme of the lascivious Terrible Mother, nor, of course, of the Good Mother. The same can be said of Ana and Violante, the two cousins of *El prevenido engañado*, as well as many others. Welles envisions this binary opposition in accord with her reading of the *Novelas* according to the play of Good versus Evil that is a defining feature of the romance genre. Of the romance—rather than novelistic—affiliation that she perceives at the root of the *Novelas*, she explains: "The *novela cortesana* can be understood only if examined within the *nonrepresentational* and idealized conventions of romance, which as defined by Northrop Frye corresponds to a specific structural principle of *mythos*, its core being an adventure proceeding in a dialectical pattern from a lower to a higher world, and must be considered a form of prose fiction distinct from the novel" (301; emphasis added). Yet the profusion of ambiguous characters, competing and unresolved discourses, and axiologically inconsistent narrators that inhabit Zayas's imaginary universe pertain to the world of the novel, not to the clarity of the romance world.[37] Zayas insists very pointedly on the representational quality of her narratives, that they are, with the possible exception of I, 10 (*El jardín engañoso*), "true histories."[38] It is precisely the novelistic focus on subjectivity, on unresolved and shifting subject-positions in story after story, that defines her text and eludes ideological categorization.

Not functioning as part of the obscure "gray area" of novelistic discourse, Flora pertains to the sinister female type, a woman who admits to being less interested in jealousy than she is in idly amusing her paramour at the expense of another woman, an innocent one, namely Aminta. She willingly explains to Jacinto that she will lay out her snares (*redes*) and traps (*tramoyas*) (89) in order to capture the unsuspecting virgin for him. Once Aminta falls for Jacinto, Flora says that he will be able to pluck the flower of her virtue if he promises (deceitfully, of course) to marry her. If his passion persists beyond the moment of deflowering, he can then abduct her to a place where she is not known, and when he tires of her, he can abandon her in such a way that she will never know the author of her dishonor given that he travels under a pseudonym and false identity.

For her part, Flora views this vile deception which she proposes as nothing more than a game to amuse both Jacinto and herself. Deception and disguise, in this case cross-dressing, are central to her behavior, given also that she dresses in male attire in order to accompany Jacinto when he goes to serenade Aminta. Flora's ability to detach herself emotionally from the man with whom she cohabits is remarkable; she actually seems to be immune to jealousy, as she openly claims.

Yet Zayas suggests an even more unconventional, indeed transgressive dimension of Flora's personality in a fleeting suggestion of her bisexuality.[39] Wanting Jacinto to linger in the presence of Aminta, Flora tells him "—Aguarda, hermano, no pasemos de aquí, que ya sabes que tengo el gusto y deseos más de galán que de dama, y donde las veo y más tan bellas, como esta hermosa señora, se me van los ojos tras ellas, y se me enternece el corazón" (94) ["Wait, brother, let's sit here. You know my tastes are more those of a gallant than of a lady, and wherever I see a lady, particularly one as beautiful as this lady, I can't take my eyes from her beauty and my heart grows tender" (55)].

While she does not dwell further on this aspect of Flora's sexuality, it is clear that, once again Zayas seeks to emphasize the possibility of multiple, simultaneous, and conflictual subject-positions in woman. Although momentary, the suggestion is nonetheless definitively established in the text. It seems likely, moreover, that this is the reason for Flora's otherwise inexplicable immunity to Jacinto's jealousy, and to her desire to get closer to Aminta even though it might jeopardize to a considerable extent her relationship to him. With remarkable insightfulness and candor concerning the intimacies of human sexuality, Zayas dramatizes the fact that the lesbian urge is as possible for a member of a primarily heterosexual relationship as is the homoeroticism within heterosexual wedlock that we find in *Mal presagio casar lejos*.[40] This degree of perceptiveness and perspectivism on Zayas's part is stunning—programatically postmodern and consummately Baroque in its conflictual nature.

By means of Flora's machinations and those of a well-paid go-between named Elena, Jacinto conquers Aminta's virtue as Flora and Elena voyeuristically witness the event:

Le dió la mano de esposo, con cuya seguridad gozó de algunos regalados y honestos favores, cogiendo flores y claveles del jardín, jamás tocado de persona nacida, que estaba reservado a su ausente primo. Solenizaban la fiesta Flora y doña Elena con mil donaires, viendo a don Jacinto tan atrevido, como Aminta vergonzosa. (97–98)

[He gave her his hand in marriage. By virtue of this pledge, he enjoyed some free and delightful favors, gathering flowers and carnations in that garden untouched by human hand which had been reserved for her absent cousin. Flora and doña Elena witnessed these celebrations with a thousand jokes, watching don Jacinto act as bold as Aminta reacted with embarrassment.] (58)

The narrator of the tale, Matilda, seizes this moment of Jacinto's triumph —brought about by Flora's cold-blooded deceitfulness—to rail against the dangers of evil women, judging from her unconscionable function as procuress for her own lover, that an evil woman in fact poses a much greater threat than an evil man:

¡Oh falsa Flora, en quien el cielo quiso criar la cifra de los engaños, castigo venga sobre ti! ¿de tu amante eres tercera? ¿habrá quien dé crédito a tal maldad? Sí, porque *en siendo una mujer mala, lleva ventaja a todos los hombres*. A don Jacinto disculpa amor, a la triste Aminta el engaño, mas para Flora no hay disculpa. (98; emphasis added)

[Oh, false Flora! In you, heaven created the epitome of deceit! May punishment fall upon you, you who act as your lover's matchmaker. Can anyone imagine how evil you are? Terribly evil because *as a woman who's evil, you have the advantage over men*. Love excuses Don Jacinto, deception excuses the unfortunate Aminta, but for Flora there is no excuse.] (59; emphasis added)

Not only does this passage reveal an amazing array of subject-position possibilities in one woman; Matilda's extradiegetic exclamation about the superior wickedness of evil women over evil men shows that female narrators can, at times, be much more critical of their own gender than men can. In fact, the excessiveness of Matilde's indictment here in combination with the preponderance of predatory men in the *Novelas* makes her remark seems incongruously unconvincing. If we think back also, for example, to Alonso's staunch profeminist defense in *El prevenido engañado*, we note that this type of "same gender" critical detachment is a recurrent feature of Zayas's writing.

The situation begins to deteriorate when Jacinto's passion starts to wane as a result of capturing the prize of Aminta's virginity. This change is crystallized by an ominous moment wherein the instant the lovers clasp their hands together, the emerald ring she is wearing on her finger splits in half, as a piece of it flies up, striking Jacinto in the face. Aminta construes this incident as an ill omen whose importance Jacinto pretends to ignore. Given the fact that the flame of Jacinto's passion has now been extinguished, his thoughts turn to the reckless peril in which he has placed himself.[41] Fearing that Elena might reveal his whereabouts, he cold-bloodedly shoots her dead with a bullet to the heart. Able to think of little else than his means of escape, Jacinto deposits Aminta in the house of a distant relative named Luisa, who lives with her gallant and noble son, Martín. Here the emotionally devastated Aminta remains, under the ironically conceived pseudonym of Doña Victoria.

Aminta learns from Luisa that not only is Jacinto married, but that his real name is Francisco, that he is a notorious liar living with a woman who is actually not his sister, but his mistress, having totally abandoned his wife. By eavesdropping through the keyhole to her room, Martín learns of Jacinto's betrayal of Aminta, a deception that leads her to the point of suicide. As Aminta is about to slash her wrists with a dagger, Martín rushes into her room to stop her, at which point she faints. When she revives from her swoon, she can think of only one thing, namely the deception perpetrated by Jacinto and Flora, and vows to avenge herself. Martín, passionately but honorably in love with Aminta, offers to help her in this dangerous enterprise.

To underscore in yet another way the pervasive reality of competing subject-positions and the dark, unpredictable side of human nature, Zayas informs us that in spite of his correct behavior the narrator admits that he can appreciate Jacinto's impulse to take advantage of Aminta: "Concedió don Martín con todo, y no es mucho, pues que amaba y aventuraba el gozar tan hermosa dama, tanto que ya disculpaba a don Jacinto" (108) [Don Martín agreed to her conditions. That wasn't surprising because he was in love and would have done anything to enjoy such a beautiful woman; he could almost understand don Jacinto's deception (66)].

Carefully disguised as a male and bearing the name Jacinto, Aminta passes herself off as a servant, finding employment in the house where Jacinto and Flora reside. They do not recognize her at all. After serving as a page for one month, Aminta stabs both her perfidious seducer and Flora, not once but repeatedly, as they lie sleeping

Sacando la daga, se la metió al traidor don Jacinto por el corazón dos o tres veces, tanto que el quexarse y rendir el alma fue todo uno. Al ruido despertó Flora, y queriendo dar voces, no le dio lugar Aminta, que la hirió por la garganta, diciendo: — 'Traidora, Aminta te castiga y venga su deshonra.'" (117)

[Aminta drew her dagger. Two or three times she plunged it into the treacher-ous Don Jacinto's heart, so sharply that his cry and his giving up the ghost were simultaneous. At the sound, Flora awoke and was about to scream but Aminta didn't give her time. She stabbed her in the throat uttering these words: "Traitor! Aminta punishes you and avenges her dishonor!"] (73)

When servants discover the bloody corpses, the authorities look for a muleteer and a page (the disguises used by Martín and Aminta), but find-ing no one fitting that description, the case is closed. The secret of the murders never becomes known, in fact, except to the narrator, Matilda, who discloses it in order to show Aminta's great courage in avenging her dishonor. Aminta keeps the name Doña Victoria, which is now (finally) a meaningful appellation, marries her beloved Martín, and, we learn, lives happily with him and her mother-in-law in Madrid. The only thing that could have improved upon this situation, according to the narrator, would be the birth of children to this devoted couple.

Zayas may choose not to represent them as a nuclear family perhaps because it is the predictable cliché form of romance resolution or perhaps to underscore Aminta's "masculine" resolve rather than her childbearing potential, the other traditionally prized female quality along with chas-tity—which the raped Aminta did not possess when the informed Martín very willingly proposed marriage to her.[42] Here too, then, we see some very unexpected resources of agency, with Flora's utterly perverse affect and Aminta's formidable courage in avenging her dishonor—a tradition-ally male activity, as the compellingly popular honor plays of the time attest. We also see atypical responses in the male register, with Martín's unexpected level of compassionate understanding regarding Aminta's de-filed honor, his reluctant willingness to assume the more passive role by allowing her to execute the murders rather than doing so himself, and his exemplary love of her as his wife. These two characters, among many others who inhabit the pages of Zayas's *Novelas*, underscore the crucial importance of agency—its unpredictability whereby women can and do assume the role of male agents and men of women. Predictable gender typecasting runs contrary to Zayas's epistemological project.

El juez de su causa (Judge Thyself)

While Zayas's experiment with temporary female cross-dressing permitted both Flora and Aminta to masquerade as Jacinto's pages in *La burlada Aminta*, her exploration of its possibilities yields extended and truly astounding effects in *El juez de su causa* (I, 9), straining the reader's credulity in the process with her tongue-in-cheek narrative.[43] For in this tale the cross-dressed heroine's resourcefulness and daring seems to know no bounds as her admirable valor gets her appointed to the exalted position of viceroy by Charles V. Everyone is deceived about her sexual identity, believing her to be a man; and the misperception continues until the very moment when she decides to reveal her true identity.

This narrative is notable in the Zayesque repertoire, among other reasons, because it pertains to the tradition of the Moorish tale, the *novela morisca*, initiated in Spain with the *Historia del Abencerraje y la hermosa Jarifa* in the sixteenth century, a form that enjoyed tremendous popularity during that century and beyond, especially as a result of Cervantes' numerous exploitations of it.[44]

As a result of her choice of the *novela morisca* for her ninth tale of part I, Zayas uncharacteristically expands her narrative beyond the boundaries of Spain, across the Mediterranean to Morocco's inland city of Fez, and ultimately back to Spain. In so doing she produces an intriguing meditation not just on gender (especially female gender and the parameters of agency), but on race, religion, and class as well. It is axiomatic with all of the true lovers we encounter in the *Novelas* that the hero and heroine are beset by seemingly insurmountable obstacles, and we soon learn that the paradigmatic couple of *El juez de su causa* is no exception. Estela, an inhabitant of Valencia, is beautiful, wealthy, and, indeed, a paragon of womanly virtues. She is the only child of loving parents, and she is courted by many suitors. Of all her admirers she favors one named Carlos, who possesses in the male register all the desirable qualities one could ever hope to encounter. The complication to their marriage comes first in the form of another woman named Claudia, who consults a crafty old former servant of Carlos, Claudio, who arranges for Claudia to enter the service of Carlos by posing as a page named "Claudio." By this choice of pseudonym, and very close to the surface of the text, we see Zayas's interest in conflating female motivations and identities (in this case with the Claudia/Claudio correspondence) similar to the Jacinta/Jacinto association in *La burlada Aminta*. Claudia's reason for this cross-dressing is to win Carlos away from Estela by serving as the messenger of their courtship, which she hopes to end by her personal intervention. A further impediment arises when a wealthy Italian count falls in love with Estela as well. Both he and Carlos petition Estela's parents on the same day to marry her, as the parents opt for the count, given his social pedigree and financial means, informing Estela of this choice only after the papers have been signed.

Desperate at this news, the couple decides on the extreme plan of eloping to Barcelona where they can marry without the complications that exist in Valencia. Yet Claudia, inspired by a clever Moorish nobleman named Amete, manages to derail their plan. He himself is as in love with Estela as Claudia is with Carlos, proposing, therefore, a mutually advantageous plan whereby he will abduct Estela and take her to Fez, where his father is a wealthy and influential pasha. Presumably time and geographical distance will make Estela accept Amete, who reasons that if she converts, becoming a Muslim, he will marry her. By a similar line of reasoning, Amete convinces Claudia that Estela's definitive absence from Spain will permit her to win the heart of Carlos.

The perfidious Moor, however, abducts not only Estela but Claudia as well, thus foiling her plan entirely by reasoning to her that "por conseguir tu amor quitas a tu amante la vida, quitándole la presencia de su dama; pues a quien tal traición hace como dármela a mí por un vano antojo; ¿cómo quieres que me asegure de que luego no avisarás a la ciudad y saldrán tras mí, y me darán la muerte?" (380) [to gain your love, you have deprived your beloved of his very life by removing her from his presence. Well, what does the kind of person who'll do such a deed as to betray her beloved for a whim deserve? How can you expect me to be sure you wouldn't turn around and tell the whole city what happened to Estela; then they'd be after me and sentence me to death?" (279–80)].

In this same speech Amete hypocritically declares that "no es razón que ninguno se fíe del que no es leal a su misma nación y patria" (380) ["one should never trust a person who's not loyal and true to his own land and nation" (279)]. Ironically, while in the abstract these words ring true,

Amete will lose his own life for not following this advice as he attempts to kill the prince of his own country. By making this remark, Zayas registers the potential chasm separating word from deed, appearance from reality. This capacity for verbal deception is insightfully acknowledged by Patsy Boyer as a general tendency of Zayesque narrative: "Words belie and lead astray within the stories just as the characters and the narrators use words to their own misleading ends."[45]

His machinating cruelty persists and, when he sees that Estela will not yield to his lust as a result of his verbal pressure, he determines to use force instead, treating her as nothing but a slave: "Como Amete viese que por ruegos ni caricias podía vencerla, empezó a usar de la fuerza, procurando por malos tratamientos obligarla a querer por no padecer, tratándola como a una miserable esclava, mal comida y peor vestida, sirviéndole la casa, en la cual había su padre de Amete, cuatro mujeres con quien estaba casado, y otros dos hijos menores" (382) [When Amete realized that his kindness and cajoling wouldn't win Estela, he began to use force. He thought to obtain her favors by punishing her, so she could put a stop to her suffering only by being nice to him. He treated her like a wretched slave; he dressed her in rags; he gave her leftovers to eat and made her serve the entire household, which consisted of Amete's father, his four wives, and two other younger sons (281)].

The motif of Christian woman as slave (rather than a male slave) is unusual in the *novela morisca* tradition. By this gender reversal Zayas expands the possibilities for female experience still further here—as she will in the first tale of part II, *La esclava de su amante (Her Lover's Slave)*, where a white Christian woman turns herself from a figurative "slave of passion" into a literal slave masquerading as a Moor.

While Carlos languishes in prison, where he has been consigned as a result of an incriminating love letter in which Estela confessed to her parents her intention to marry him, Estela suffers ever increasing grief and danger. After she has survived for over a year in the ignominious role of slave, Amete's patience runs out and he determines to rape her, aided in his evil plan by Claudia, who lies to Estela by telling her that she has planned their escape back to Spain. As Amete ties up and beats Estela mercilessly, she courageously fends him off until, utterly exhausted, she has no other defense left but to scream.

As luck would have it (and according to the impossibly felicitous co-incidence that pervades such romance narratives), her screams are over-heard by a noble Moor named Xacimín, the prince of Fez. Estela's good fortune is compounded by the fact that this prince is not only unwill-ing to permit any man to brutalize a woman, as Amete was doing, but he feels, in addition, a genuine affinity for Christians in spite of his own faith.[46] By juxtaposing him both implicitly (and explicitly) with Amete—two Moorish noblemen who behave in totally opposed ways in terms of morals, social conventions, and religious tolerance, we see Zayas once again breaking down the possibility of constructing ironclad categories of race, gender, or class.[47] Clearly, she effects a similar complication if we consider the noble, Christian, and female categories as they function in the diametrically opposed figures of Estela and the wicked Claudia.

Not only has Amete transgressed against Estela by his beating and at-tempted rape of her, he commits treason by attacking and attempting to kill Xacimín, his prince. For these crimes he and his accomplice Claudia are sentenced to death and shortly thereafter impaled. In retrospect, the considerable amount of money offered by Amete's father was obviously to no avail.

Here too, Zayas wants to offer a nuanced presentation of the Infidel and his system of justice. Whereas she often remarks on the power and pro-tection exerted by money for Spanish nobles and aristocrats, of its abu-sive power in the judicial system, here she inverts the racial stereotype—offering an admirable portrayal of the Infidel, who is usually portrayed as lawless. In one and the same text, as with its prototype El abencerraje, we find the Moor presented both as the demonic Other and the idealized Other. Thus we see that even her position as a member of the aristocracy, and that of her storytellers as well, is compromised here as elsewhere.

Xacimín grants Estela's request that she be allowed to return to her own land, giving her, in addition, money, jewels, and a Christian slave to ac-company her. Meanwhile, all of Estela's adventures have been unfolding at the time that Charles V, the Holy Roman Emperor, has been waging his famous offensive against Fredrick Barbarossa in Tunis. Aware of the pres-ence of Spanish troops in North Africa, Estela decides to join the cause, cutting her hair and dressing as a man in order to enlist in the army. So consistently valiant is she in the operations in France and Italy that (using the name Fernando) she distinguishes herself especially one day when Charles's horse is killed, thus obliging him to fight on foot. Without hesitating Estela offers him her horse, thereafter fighting at his side until the king is safe. As a reward for this exemplary act of heroism the king bestows upon "Don Fernando" the prestigious Order of Santiago and the title of duke.

By one of those impossible coincidences that seem to motivate romance, Estela notices that her long-lost Carlos is among the soldiers in the army, and without disclosing her true identity, she takes on Carlos as her personal secretary, asking him about his background in order to determine whether he has remained faithful to her. He discloses that he spent two years in prison, accused of abducting, raping, and killing Estela, who seems to have disappeared from the face of the earth. He explains further that he spent the entire year after his release from prison looking for her, but in vain.

Assured now of his fidelity, Estela vows to help Carlos, indicating that after the campaign is over she will convene a court that will definitively exonerate him of all the charges. And, in a stroke of unbelievable good fortune (another incredible coincidence), she is named viceroy of Valencia, where she is obliged to judge her own case as the very first order of business. After lengthy testimony is given, the viceroy concludes that the only way Carlos can be cleared of the death penalty is if Estela herself appears before the assembled citizens. The viceroy reveals that "he" is the woman in question, and everyone is astonished that the valorous soldier is, in fact, a woman. King Charles, we are told, is even more amazed, since he had witnessed the extraordinary valor repeatedly exhibited by "Don Fernando" on the field of battle.

In this way Zayas dramatizes the fact that in the last analysis, few things other than anatomical detail, distinguish the capacities of men and women. The king sends congratulations and jewels to mark the restoration of the deserving couple, reconfirming the estates he had previously awarded Estela, bestowing upon her the additional title of Princess of Buñol. Estela's habit of the Order of Santiago is officially transferred by the king to Carlos, who also assumes her former title as viceroy of Valencia. The final achievement recorded by the narrator occurs with the birth of the couple's beautiful and worthy heirs.

One final observation deserves mention regarding distinctions of gender and agency in this narrative; namely, the fact that this story is narrated by Juan, the most frivolous of the frame characters—and one whose name conjures up the relentless seducer of women (Don Juan) who has no interest or belief in their potential for valor—makes the outcome of *El juez de su causa* even more striking. It underscores once again that the subjective states of human nature are ultimately inscrutable, often shockingly so. In this context, Marcia Welles is right when she notes that each of the narrators is "indistinguishable from the other . . . functioning as a 'second self' of María de Zayas."[48] It must be added, however, that by the variety of positions these narrators represent, that Zayas's "second self" can only be characterized as an encyclopedia of possibilities for gender and agency.

The five stories considered within this discussion of subjectivity offer a representative sampling of the diversity at issue in the *Novelas*. Woman as wife, mother, daughter, sister, and mistress in a wide range of successful and unsuccessful familial relationships is fully articulated. Woman as helpless victim, as acquiescent partner, as playful adulteress, as sinister agent or as triumphant avenger are all portrayed here. And the possibilities for male agency are equally varied. To be sure, part II of the *Novelas* offers more victimized females, but there too we should not minimize the complex presentation of the female psyche that is constructed. After all, some of the most heinous deeds depicted in the second ten *novelas* are masterminded by women.

Zayas—as so many of her narratives attest—is not attempting to bring down the patriarchy but to endow it with a greater measure of gender equality. While some narrators are outspoken critics of men, finding no value in them, others (including a number of the women who narrate the *desengaños* of part II) do. Some of the male partygoers criticize other men for their injustices toward women, praising the women instead, and, as we have seen, women from the group are often critical of the actions of other women. The stories considered thus far reveal the infinitely more complex set of possibilities Zayas envisions. The remaining *novelas* further confirm her nuanced presentation.

At times (particularly in the second part) she is totally outspoken, advocating escape to the convent as the only logical solution for woman, yet it must be remembered that Zayas, as Paul Julian Smith notes, is unable (or unwilling) "to create an integrated female subject and a coherent female narrative."[49] Although he does not elaborate the idea of unintegrated female subjectivity (one lacking in coherent ideological views), Smith expresses the possibility of a choice on Zayas's part. Clearly there is value in refusing to figure woman according to one exclusive psychological or sociopolitical posture. Addressing this issue in the broader context of Europe as a whole, Traub, Kaplan, and Callaghan affirm that "the absence of investment in a fully articulated, coherent subject may have allowed for the establishment of subcommunities, pockets of resistance, and alliances between subordinated groups." They make the additional—crucially important—point that "resistance" is a relative thing: "it is important look for resistance in relative terms, rather than to hold early modern women's words and actions up to post-Enlightenment standards of subjective self-consciousness."[50]

Zayas is able but unwilling to construct a coherent female subject and female narrative. Her attainment of bestseller status was not the result of a monologic feminist discourse relentlessly aimed at exposing the evils of the patriarchy. She is aware of and accepts in principle (albeit reluctantly) the fact that the father has total control over his offspring, and the Zayesque heroines who avenge their honor do so within the dictates of that code. As so many of the *novelas* attest, she does not condemn the so-called honor code itself, but rather its illegitimate, hypocritical practitioners.[51]

The whole notion of the "gendered subject" is a problematic one for early modern literature, and for much later literature as well. As Carol Neely remarks a propos of feminist Shakespeare criticism, but with implications for feminist approaches to literature in general: "If feminist criticism abandons the notion of the subject, replacing it with the much more slippery concept of subject positions, and by so doing calls into question the notion of gendered subjects, gendered authors, gendered texts, the ground for its critique is eliminated."[52] Neely is clearly being polemical in this remark. In the final analysis, she is calling not for a rejection of feminist criticism but for a valorization of subject-positionality as a way of combatting the dangerous urge to be "monolithic, monological, monogendered, monomaniacal" (16).

Female perspectives are represented by Zayas in her characters and narrators, and they invite, indeed demand, analysis, especially since the prologues and extradiegetic interventions (particularly in part II of the *Novelas*) are so explicit. Yet, to view subjectivity as a necessarily gendered phenomenon is a recent development originating in large measure with historical changes in the domestic sphere, especially the intensified division of labor that resulted in the nineteenth century.

More important than distinctions based on gender in seventeenth-century Spain, it was instead the aristocracy's obsession with issues of lineage (blood purity) and the honor code that defined the subject's perception of him or herself. And, as George Mariscal writes, here too it is a question of contradictory subject-positions: "the aristocratic subject itself was the intersection of a variety of contradictory positions and . . . in concrete practice any single subject was simultaneously situated in a variety of ways. . . . The subject of Castilian legal discourse, for example, which invoked blood as the source of its authority, was distinctly opposed to the subject figured by religious writing, which cited virtue."[53]

Mariscal's study of subjectivity does not attempt to deal with female writers. But his words of caution regarding class-based readings hold true as much for the female authors of the early modern period, as for the male. The idea of the bourgeois individual and the bourgeois family are concepts unfamiliar to the seventeenth century, although they are—anachronistically—of crucial importance in most twentieth-century psychoanalytical readings of early modern literature. As a result, we must strive to recognize other forms of subjectivity and social behavior that result from cultural formations which may be quite alien to our own. We should refrain from misrepresenting the Baroque period's epistemological concern with multiple subject-positions by reducing it to the status of predictable ideology. While exploring the female psyche represented by Zayas, we should resist the ever present temptation to turn early modern Spanish culture into a reflection of our own cultural preoccupations. Paradoxically, as Amy Katz Kaminsky notes, the same jewels which are used by Zayas's women to gain a measure of autonomy from men are also designed to attract them.[54] The ambiguities and contradictions figured by Zayas's characters and the imaginary universe they populate are paradigmatically Baroque subjects.

3
Reading Magic: Mass Printing, Mass Audience

Neither political, constitutional, ecclesiastical events, nor sociological, philosophical, and literary movements can be fully understood without taking into account the influence which the printing press has exerted upon them.

— S. H. Steinberg, Five Hundred Years of Printing

The Magic of the Book

The plural readings and contradictions of the Baroque subject that Zayas stages so intriguingly in her writing reflect developments in the publication industry. Her art and that of other contemporary authors was not determined exclusively by their literary self-expression, but to an equal if not greater degree in some cases, by a new reading market and the reading practices from it. One of the most fascinating aspects of seventeenth-century Spanish culture and society has to do with the implications of mechanical book printing. Because books came to be mass produced at little expense, they could reach for the first time an unprecedented number of consumers.

Cervantes inscribes this phenomenon and its importance in the *Quijote* with a visit to a book-publishing factory in part II, chapter 62, wherein are depicted "toda aquella máquina que en las emprentas grandes se muestra" (997) [all the processes of a large printing house (876)]. The materiality of the text and its mass production, as well as the implications of copyrights and royalties, are all elaborately depicted by Cervantes. Yet, of equal, indeed greater, importance to the material and mass-produced nature of books for him is their impact on the individual reader. That is why he figures readers of all types in his text—the young and the old, readers of all reading abilities, literacy levels, social classes (from peasant to royalty), and degrees of sophistication. That is also why Cervantes inscribes many of the strikingly varied interpretations elicited by part I at the beginning of part II, chapter 3.

Indeed, as Roger Chartier explains, "in the course of the sixteenth and seventeenth centuries in Western Europe, reading, for the literate élite, became the act *par excellence* of intimate, private, and secret leisure."[1] The pleasurable retreat from the cares of the world made possible by one's personal library is thematized in a variety of texts from this period. Although we do not hear Don Quijote speaking explicitly of his library as a secret refuge, Cervantes makes very clear at numerous junctures in his text the meaningfulness of the library for him in these terms. The scrutiny of his library undertaken by the priest and barber in I, 6, further emphasizes the impact exerted by libraries on the human imagination, offering an extended meditation on the existentially compelling nature of books.

Commenting on the uniqueness of Don Quijote's library, Edward Baker makes the important observation that: "There is no precedent in Early Modern Castile for the kind of library that Don Quijote has assembled, no library composed chiefly, much less exclusively, of recreational books."[2] Devotional books tended to be the mainstay of private Spanish libraries in the seventeenth century. The book-burning scene which concludes the examination of the library—referred to alternately as an *auto da fé* and its opposite, a "massacre of innocents"—dramatizes even more vividly the perceived allure and perceived threat of books.

It is, on the most basic level, Don Quijote's desire to emulate the chivalric heroes of his carefully chosen tomes that provides a model of behavior for his life. His is an extreme case of "the pleasure of the text," as Roland Barthes describes it. Speaking of one of the many pleasurable aspects of reading (which seems particularly appropriate to Don Quijote), Barthes writes: "A certain pleasure is derived from a way of imagining oneself as individual, of inventing a final, rarest fiction: the fictive identity. This fiction is no longer the illusion of a unity; on the contrary, it is the theater of society in which we stage our plural."[3] And, while most readers do not fall into the deluded category to which Don Quijote pertains, we find many of the most notable figures of the period attesting to the power of reading, the sanctuary represented by their private libraries. Montaigne describes his own: "J'essaie à m'en rendre la domination pure, et à soustraire ce seul coin à la communauté et conjugale, et filiale, et civile" [I try to make my authority over it absolute, and to withdraw this one corner from all society, conjugal, filial, and civic.][4] In similar fashion, Shakespeare depicts Prospero as preferring the seclusion of his study to the ego gratification of government in the often cited remark: "Me, poor man, my library/Was dukedom large enough."[5]

Books are represented not only as necessary tools for magicians, which is a long-standing association, but books can, it seems, turn ordinary readers into magicians of a sort. No longer is it a question of the humanistic belief in books as instructional aids or, at the other extreme, of the humanistic admonition concerning the vanity of books (that book learning in and of itself can be a sterile pursuit if not accompanied by good judgment). Now the activity of reading is perceived as offering, in addition, a wealth of unprecedented pleasure to the reader.

This new perception of the reading process and its effects is also closely tied to the issue of Baroque subjectivity that is reflected in a variety of ways in Zayas's *Novelas*. Principal among the features of this new, intimate individual reader is the belief that knowledge is constituted by the subject *per ipse*. No longer is the collective, universal view of timeless exemplary truth to be sought. Speaking in general terms of this phenomenon, Jean Marie Goulemot notes that "all literature of the late seventeenth and early eighteenth centuries is influenced by [an] affirmation of private life. . . . The private became an essential element in fiction, the foundation of its truth as well as the truth of historical causality."[6] Zayas makes explicit in each of her stories at the beginning and end of the narration, that they are not fiction, but *true* and historically verifiable. Indeed, more often than not we are told that the names of the real protagonists have been changed so as to protect the reputations of the innocent. For the same reason, her narrators are presented either as having participated in

the narratives themselves or as having had the material meticulously recounted by participants in or witnesses to the events.

In thematic terms, the focus on intimacy is also at the core of the new
reading practice and of Zayas's text. We read about the bedroom and
marital relations and their transgressions in tale after tale, and the divulg-
ing of such details has a double effect. On the one hand, it endows the
narrative with the appearance of truth, on the other it constitutes a viola-
tion. The private affair warrants belief because it has been made a public
matter.

By extension, the transgressive effect of this disclosure of secret information turns the reader into a voyeur. As Goulemot observes of such literature and its consequences for the reader, "Reading places [the reader]
in the position of the voyeur who glimpses the most intimate of secrets.
The reader, who violates the sanctity of private space, always knows more
than the protagonists who reveal themselves. . . . The paradox is that the
secrecy of private space produces its effects only by ceasing to be secret"
(387). In the *Novelas* we find such incidents as a wife walking in on a
homosexual affair involving her husband, two women who watch a third
lose her virginity, keyhole surveillance, and other things of this sort, all
calculated to shock and titillate the reader.

We see the physical attraction of one woman for another, the male concubine who is exhausted to the point of death by his mistress's rapacious
sexual appetites, and another who treats her chosen partner—blindfolded and in the dark for the duration of their month-long affair—like
a whore who is paid for his services each time: How are we to account
for such details in Zayas? They are pornographic in that they reduce the
individuals to their most basic sexual functions.[7] How, we may ask, can
such interests on the part of Zayas be reconciled with her stance as female
apologist? They can, given that Zayas is much more than an advocate
of women who suffer injustices at the hands of an unconscionably cruel
male order. Her twenty tales show an interest in exploring not only subjectivity—especially female subjectivity in all its dazzling complexity,
sexual and otherwise—in a way that had never been attempted, but she
is equally committed to exploring the new mass market of private readers
with a taste for the sensational, the erotic, and the forbidden. As Giovanna
Formichi observes, "la preminenza dell'interesse economico-sociale porta

ad una soluzione edonistica della narrativa postcervantina" [the preeminence of socioeconomic considerations leads to a marked hedonism in the post-Cervantine narrative].[8]

This was the age of mass-produced tabloid pamphlet literature as well. These *relatos de sucesos*—allegedly "news stories" recounting true occurrences, actually pamphlets detailing all kinds of grisly sex, violence and other crimes, as well as bizarre supernatural events—were, as Henry Ettinghausen notes, "no doubt the most widely consumed form of reading in sixteenth- and seventeenth-century Spain."[9] Thousands of these proto-newspapers survive, and they indicate that, unlike the honor plays which were tremendously popular at the time, the *relatos* lack the social or ethical dimension, offering narratives of unredeemed lawlessness and debauchery instead.[10]

The ways of understanding the world changed appreciably with the advent of print in the early modern period. Print is linked, as Benedict Anderson observes, to the emergence of the novel and the newspaper in Europe—it being "the first modern-style mass-produced industrial commodity."[11] Sold in great quantities yet ephemeral in their one-day life span as bestsellers, Hegel notes that for many modern citizens, newspapers serve as substitutes for morning prayers; they are, in other words, a new, secular ritual, a medium that, as Elizabeth Eisenstein observes, "encouraged silent adherence to causes whose advocates could not be located in any one parish and who addressed an invisible public from afar."[12]

Print has also had a surprising impact on the production of literature, as S. H. Steinberg observes: "Neither political, constitutional, ecclesiastical events, nor sociological, philosophical and literary movements can be fully understood withou taking into account the influence which the printing press has exerted on them."[13] Zayas is an interesting case in point—a writer of seventeenth-century short stories whose violent, often lurid tales capitalize on the emergence of the craze for tabloid literature that gripped the Spain of her day. She is often cited for her gendered perspective, whereby each of her twenty stories addresses male-female relations, obsessively detailing abuses of the patriarchal structure of Spanish society with gory detail. One wonders, however, who was buying and reading her? Given the overwhelmingly male literacy in Spain, if she was bent on exposing the state-sanctioned cruelty male heads of household would surely not purchase her texts or let them circulate among the women of their domestic sphere. Not to mention—as several critics have—that the sheer mass of violence done to women as represented in Golden Age literature does not conform to fact: it is grossly exaggerated. Representation of this violence points to transference or sublimation of some kind—it represents something *other* than what it appears to.

It figures the fear—both the politically sanctioned variety (the *auto da fé* mentality) and its subversive opposite—of society's crisis on the individual level, that is, the emergence of the fragmented subject that interrogates its role *amid and against* the discourses of the state. The very notion of "Spanishness" (in terms of race and class—as well as gender) is, as George Mariscal reminds us, hotly contested during this period. And, as Joan Kelly-Gadol observes, gender must be considered not only as "a constitutive element of social relationships based on perceived differences between the sexes," but also as "a primary way of signifying relationships of power—at its highest levels"—as Zayas is keenly aware.[14]

Zayas, like the tabloid press—which was, in fact, read more widely in her day than any other kind of reading material—plays on the fear and fascination at issue as the modern subject struggles to define itself in relation to the official, totalizing discourses of the state. Tabloid journalism during the period tends to be viewed by twentieth-century critics largely as government propaganda. Two basic categories of Spanish tabloid circulated: those detailing political events—pageants, military triumphs, and the like—or natural phenomena: volcanic eruptions and earthquakes (including human disasters such as heinous crimes and monstrous births). The passion for this journalism emerges as a result of the "increased interest in historical immediacy rather than the historically non-immediate."[15] Indeed, many of the houses publishing this material were located next to the local post office of a given city. Yet much of the material presented as historically accurate—replete with names, dates, and even eye-witnesses—is patently false given its sensationalist, "media porn" nature. (Eyewitness accounts of a 380-year-old Bengali, the Turkish boy born with three eyes and three horns, and the gypsies who murder and then eat a priest are indicative of these accounts.) Even more odd is the fact that a great number of these tabloids were written not in hard-hitting expository prose, but rather in the form of poetry—thereby belieing their status as spontaneous, unmediated, unadorned, faithful reporting. Why, then, was it so compelling for its consumers? What were the motives of its producers? Several possible motivations for the production of these often grotesque and/or terrifying accounts suggest themselves.

The first is that they are instruments of social control, cautionary tales that illustrate the grisly fate of citizens who do not obey the law: one woman (Ana de Flores), for example, whose mother gives birth to twin sons, asking Ana—their sister—to suckle one of them. No sooner has she cursed this suggestion (saying she would rather suckle a Devil), than a terrifying snake appears and attaches itself to her left breast. The vicar-general orders her breast cut off, at which point the serpent attaches itself to her remaining breast. Given that it is impossible to rid the town of the beast, she keeps it permanently in a basket beside her. In this case, the event is clearly a bit of propaganda, fostering social control by reinforcing the importance of responsible civil speech. This is also in keeping with the mentality resulting from the Council of Trent. The same mindset accounts for the proliferation of miraculous occurrences documented by the tabloid press. An atmosphere of censorship was clearly at issue given also the prohibition of the publicatin of plays and novels that existed in Castile between 1625 and 1634.

An additional impetus stems from the wondrous discoveries of the New World transmitted back to the Old World. The *Ripley's Believe It or Not* appeal of countless natural wonders can not be overstated. The iguana, for example, is first identified for a European audience by Gonzalo Fernández de Oviedo in his *Crónica general y natural de las Indias* (1478–1557), wherein he debates its classification as either an animal or a fish [sic], indicating also its mysterious form of nourishment—since it appears to eat nothing at all even when observed for days on end. Yet the seemingly fantastic *relatos* of this sort respond to new impulses of scientific inquiry and exploration in Europe in general. Moreover, they are by no means confined to sightings in the New World. Indeed, the most famous natural wonder of all—a fabulous monster—is probably the shell-covered boy alleged to have been born in Lisbon in 1628.

As with most depictions of monsters, this event is construed as an omen—but it is important to note that *no* consensus exists as to its message. And the indeterminacy generated by this alleged occurrence poses a real problem for modern interpretation of such ephemera—whose critics tend to assume a decidedly exemplary thrust. Even if a tabloid gives an explicitly moralizing message, it may serve, as in so many of the novellas of the period, as a smoke screen to endow the narrative with a veneer, at least, of decorum.

The central emotion generated by these texts is *fear*—fear of monsters and earthquakes, lawlessness and debauchery. It is a form of sublimation of the historically real, empirically experienced societal chaos of seventeenth-century Spanish life onto people and events found in print —which offers a measure of solace or contentment to the reader who considers himself fortunate not to have suffered similar catastrophes. Yet it also offers pleasurable escape—voyeurism of forbidden, potentially alluring situations—a dimension of which Zayas was acutely aware.

A few examples suffice to illustrate the compelling nature of this material. Race relations between whites and blacks are addressed by Zayas in the expository, sensationalist manner of these tabloid sheets. Indeed, one well known narrative published in Cuenca in 1603 relates in a "relación verísima" how a (white) lady of Seville gave birth to a black boy as a result of making love to her equally white husband while her black maid's baby happened to be lying in the bed with them. This is the initial event in a narrative that records the husband throwing the baby in the river, two kindly friars rescuing and raising it in Utrera, whereupon the biological mother is reunited with her son after making a vow to the Virgin of Victoria. The now grown-up son searches North Africa for his father, who has been captured by the Moors, renounced Christianity for Islam, married a Moorish woman, and had a son by her. The adventure ends with the four of them attempting a daring escape to Ceuta, failing and being executed: "Murieron como christianos / invocando al buen Jesus."

The narrative illustrates, first of all, the whites' fear of racial impurity— a topic associated with the codes of blood purity designed to isolate the Jews converted to Christianity, the so-called *cristianos nuevos*, from the *cristianos viejos* who claimed to be untainted by any Jewish lineage, an analogue to the Muslims in Spain, who were definitively expelled in the early seventeenth century. But at the same time this news item celebrates the exemplary, redemptive potential of Christianity. The message is thus a double one—a paranoid fear revealing cultural anxiety about race (a message of cultural exclusion), but at the same time, a conversionary tale revealing the universal appeal of the Faith (a message of cultural inclusion), which conforms to Spain's—avowedly crumbling—imperial identity.

Zayas is similarly polysemous in her representations of gender, class, and magic. The issue of black-white relations offers a dramatic testimony to her use of social, political, racial, sex, and gender categories to figure the newly emerging appreciation of human subjectivity and its manifold complexities.

Slavery, as we have already seen in Chapter 2, is a case in point, an interrogation of black-white relations that Zayas addresses provocatively. Amid the existence of white as well as black slaves owned by various masters, we find depicted in (*El prevenido engañado [Forearmed but Not Forewarned]*), a widow who fends off a suitor, invoking as the reason for her behavior the obligatory year of celibacy to which she must adhere in deference to her dead husband's memory. Yet what we learn from her suitor's surveillance is that she is sexually involved with her slave—who is a black man. Far from being the bereaved widow, she is actually the cause of the slave's death, which occurs as a result of her monstrously insatiable sex drives.

This scene is striking in its implications in terms of both gender and class. Namely, it figures woman as being potentially as libidinous and predatory as men are. Yet, given the relentlessness of her excess, the widow seems even more sinister. The fact that her partner is sick adds to the repugnance of this impression. That the tables are turned—that it is a woman sexually abusing a man rather than the normatively male predator—offers a comment on the abuse of women, as well as a meditation on class difference; usually it is the male head of household who takes advantage of a female servant.

The shock value of this black-white liaison clearly reflects the fascination and fear of the Other—the obsession with blood purity which had been, since the mid-1400s in Spain, official policy with respect to Jewish converts to Christianity, soon thereafter extending to Muslim converts. Here the white woman seems demonic by comparision with her God-fearing black partner—whose dying words are that his mistress should marry legitimately. He is, shockingly, presented as morally superior to her. And the implications for the colonizer and colonized in the New World enterprise are as clear as the implications for Spain's racial intolerance at home. Zayas's social critique is hard to miss.

A different instance of racial anxiety surfaces in her tale entitled *Tarde llega el desengaño* (*Too Late Undeceived*), a narrative modeled on Marguerite de Navarre's thirty-second and forty-third *Heptameron* tales. In the French model text, a wife commits adultery, for which she is chastised by her husband—who shaves her head and hangs her lover's skeleton up in her bedroom (where she is confined until the husband forgives her)—in compliance with a suggestion made by a visitor to their house. The couple are reconciled, produce heirs, and live harmoniously.

For her part, Zayas offers a lurid remake of this scenario. The husband recounts how he fell in love with a woman whose identity was a mystery to him, and who accepted him as a lover only on condition that he would be taken to her blindfolded, keeping his eyesight obscured each night for the duration of their sexual intercourse, until he is guided back to his own house. This bizarre arrangement, whereby he is paid for his services like the typical female whore, continues for a month, at which time he tries to ascertain this lustful woman's identity. We learn that her name is Lucrecia (an obvious inversion of her famous Roman namesake). By contrast, this latter-day Lucrecia orders her lover (Don Jaime) killed because he has ascertained her identity against her will. He escapes to the Canary Islands, where he establishes a household and marries a Lucrecia look-alike name Elena. Yet unlike her ancient namesake, Helen of Troy, this Elena is passively (yet brutally) victimized.

The Spanish text depicts a black female slave who abuses the exemplary wife by convincing the lady's husband that she has dishonored him in a liaison with her cousin. In order to punish the unjustly maligned wife, the husband substitutes the mendacious slave for her mistress in every way—giving her the jewels, clothes, even, we assume from the lavish affections he showers upon her at table in the presence of guests, the sexual prerogatives of the lady—who must witness the substitution in public and on a daily basis, while she competes with the dogs in scavanging for bones under the dining-room table, living in a painfully small cupboard. The slave, finding herself about to die of undisclosed but seemingly natural causes, confesses to Don Jaime that she had unjustly maligned Elena because she herself was in love with Elena's cousin, who refused to reciprocate her passion. At this, he stabs the slave to death and rushes to forgive Elena, who has expired with her hands positioned in the form of a cross. Horrified by the injustice in which he has played such a decisive role, he goes mad, ultimately dying in a deranged state.

In the case of this narrative, the effect of the mixed couple on the inscribed audience (like the effect on the extradiegetic reader), is one of fear and loathing—given the totally predatory nature of the black slave who destroys the life of her exemplary white mistress in a "dilatado martirio" (protracted martyrdom; 208). Yet in this story it is not a neatly drawn essentialist treatment that confronts us. A stern indictment of the husband is also registered given his—like other husbands'—lamentable haste in condemning their wives before attempting to determine their guilt or innocence. The overwhelming number of chaste wives in Zayas's stories are similarly condemned, a pattern by which she indicts the ease with which the so-called "honor code" can be misinterpreted, leading to such injustice.

At the heart of Zayas's presentation is a cultural commentary that exploits the tabloid ethos very visibly. As well as being a powerful writer of fiction and social critic, she is a shrewd marketing strategist who "cashes in" on the sensationalist ethos of the day—becoming the best-selling author of the Spanish literary scene after Cervantes, Quevedo, and Alemán. By means of her grisly portrayal of bleeding and broken bodies, Zayas offers an early instance of Elizabeth Grosz's notion that "bodies have all the explanator power of minds." [16]

The association of books with magical, extraordinary powers has a very long history, indeed. Every institutionalized religion, for example, makes reference to a unique text that documents the superhuman accomplishments of its particular deity or deities. In literature, as well, witches, sorcerers, and magicians always have recourse to a special book that endows them with their particular abilities. [17] If the book is lost or stolen these practitioners invariably become powerless.

It is no exaggeration to say that the Renaissance was a period obsessed by magic—its origins, its possibilities, and its implications. The attraction of this subject derives in large measure from the age's determination to understand science as a rational discipline disassociated from the theocentric framework within which it had been understood for so many centuries. Related to this inquiry into natural science as an independent branch of learning is of course, the Renaissance focus on the self, the period's attempt to define in precise terms the parameters—the potential and the limits—of human power. As such, magic is endowed with a serious epistemological valence.

María de Zayas reveals her own keen fascination with magic by offering her readers numerous magicians, male and female, who control either white or black magic—successful ones as well as imposters.[18] These figures are of prime concern to the imaginary universe she constructs for a number of reasons, offering yet another level of complication within her intricate work. And in terms of agency, these versions of the magus are virtually as varied as the other human types who populate her text. No possibility exists for construing these characters as monolithic in either their conception or their efficacy. They are not cast uniformly as charlatans whose imposture is designed to be dramatically exposed so as to comply with the inquisitorial criteria of the censors. Here, as at virtually every turn in her text, Zayas creates a kind of Baroque tension and unresolved polysemy, managing at the same time, however, to evade the disapproval of the nationally sanctioned expurgators.

In the century during which she wrote, the perception of books as being endowed with magical properties was an especially timely topic, one that far exceeded the time-worn association of books with magic. This topos came to be a real obsession not only for its epistemological value, but for a commercial reason—namely, as a result of the facility with which books could be purchased by large segments of the population. The book as mass medium resulted in an unprecedented moment in the cultural history of Europe in general, and of Spain in particular. From the mid-sixteenth century onward, mechanical printing created the possibility of a private library for an individual reader of even modest means. And, as Suárez de Figueroa observed at the time, obviously in awe of this new technological advance: "It is not unknown that in this way one can put out more work in a single day than many learned writers in a year." [19]

This new-found resource for the private reader was received with awe, but also with disapproval. Reading as an activity that could now be practiced in private came to be regarded as a potentially dangerous commodity. Chartier, investigating the impact of this intimate reading practice in early modern Europe, explains that the activity was viewed as immensely influential in both positive and negative ways. As is the case of Prospero, who refers repeatedly to his books and their power, and Caliban, who decides to burn them in order to destroy Prospero's power, "there emerges a strange alliance between reading, the most private and hidden practice, and true, effective power, power far more effective than that of public office."[20] The mystique of private reading and the sense of tremendous energy endowed by it becomes so intense during this time that, as Chartier explains, "the reading of books of magic (such as the *Books of Experiments* in sixteenth-century England or the nameless book of magic widely read in rural Aragón and Languedoc in the nineteenth century) became the paradigm for all reading, which had to be done in secret and which conferred upon the reader a dangerous power" (ibid.).

Documenting some of the more outspoken negative assessments of this new intellectual resource in Spain, Fernando Bouza Alvarez recalls the existence of *bibliotafios* (book gravesites), places to which books considered by the *enterradores de libros* (buriers of books) to be a menace to society were relegated. In this context he offers a fragment from Juan de Zabaleta's *El día de fiesta por la tarde* (1660), a strikingly callous description of worm-eaten "book corpses" that would repulse any latter-day bibliophile:

[él] se encierra por de dentro en la librería y empieza a entresacar de los estantes los que tenían las encuadernaciones maltratadas, para hacerlos encuadernar de nuevo. Esto es lo mismo que si se anduviera uno por los sepulcros a sólo renovarles las mortajas a los muertos. Cuerpos muertos son los cuerpios de los libros que hay en estos estantes pues a nadie son de provecho, ¿qué importa que tengan las mortajas carcomidas?[21]

[He (the book burier) shuts himself up in the bookstore and begins to take off the shelves those books with worn bindings in order to have them rebound. This activity is analogous to going through the graves in order to put new shrouds on the dead. The bodies of the books on the shelves are dead bodies. Since they are of no beneficial use to anyone, what does it matter that their shrouds are worm-eaten?] (my translation)

Perhaps the most virulent attack on books Bouza chronicles is contained in a book entitled *Memorial por la agricultura*, published in 1633, a text that goes so far as to blame the destruction of the nation itself on books:

Y la lengua de la pluma es la mayor que hoy se conoce para obrar este efecto, cuando la ocasión de la comunicación, por su medio, alienta a desterrar a tantos de sus propias tierras, con sólo las alas de la pluma y libros, pesándoles de la perseverancia y virtud del trabajo en sus oficios en que están dependientes unos de otros. (58)

[The tongue of the pen is the most powerful medium that exists today. Communication by books urges so many citizens to abandon their own homelands, dissuading them from the perseverence and virtue of work and the collective enterprise.] (my translation)

Beyond the book's perceived power in the seventeenth century as a form of white or black "magic" (in its positively perceived attractiveness for the individual reader or its negatively condemned perversion of ethics and civic responsibility), the cultural impact of its mass production has still further implications. As S. H. Steinberg observes, "Neither political, constitutional, ecclesiastical events, nor sociological, philosophical, and literary movements can be fully understood without taking into account the influence which the printing press has exerted upon them."[22] While one is accustomed to considering the impact of printing as state propaganda, it should be noted that it has exerted an equally significant influence on literary movements as well. This double effect of the book as mass medium has been explored in the Spanish seventeenth century by D. W. Cruickshank and, specifically in the case of María de Zayas, by Maravall and Salvador Montesa Peydro in interesting ways.

Reflecting the dramatically negative appraisal of many critics against print, and especially against the ephemera that were circulating at the time, Lope de Vega inscribes this controversy in his play *La octava maravilla*, in a dialogue that takes place between a master and his servant concerning the value of these proto-newspapers. When the latter reveals that he has read in a pamphlet about a man who has given birth in Granada, the master responds with an indictment of the mendacious medium and of the gullible public that falls prey to its absurd and irresponsible journalism. The servant is taken aback at the master's incredulity, responding with the question "¿Está de molde, y te burlas?" [It's in print and you doubt it?]. Of course, Lope himself is probably the most notorious exploiter of the masses of any Golden Age author, as he happily acknowledges in his flippantly conceived poetic tract, the *Arte nuevo de hacer comedias*, when he affirms that the public must be entertained: "aunque se ahorque el arte" [though art be hanged].[23] In this connection, Cruickshank also recalls Don Quixote's innkeeper in I, 32, who claims that the romances of chivalry are obviously true, given that they all were all properly licensed by the royal council, which is clearly incapable of permitting the printing of lies. It is this pandering to the *vulgo* that prompted Pedro de Tapia to proclaim in 1649 that Lope "había hecho más daño con sus comedias en España que Martín Lutero en Alemania" [had done more damage with his plays than Martin Luther had done in Germany].[24]

While ephemera, akin to our tabloid journalism, is not really literature, both it and the literature of the day were, at the time they were composed, consciously written with the new, largely undiscriminating urban reader of little education (referred to collectively as the *vulgo*) in mind. This reader is consistently juxtaposed in countless literary prologues and texts of the time to the discerning, educated *culto* reader.[25]

From the creation of the common (overwhelmingly urban) reader that resulted, beginning in the sixteenth century, with the publication of romances of chivalry, to the seventeenth, with its keen interest in novelistic forms, Maravall makes a leap of logic, concluding that the literature of the time is primarily "kitsch": Everything that belongs to the Baroque emerges from the necessities of manipulating opinions and feelings on a broad scale."[26] From Bernini's *Santa Teresa* to Calderón's *La vida es sueño*, all Baroque art is construed by Maravall as kitsch. Yet kitsch, according to Webster's *New Twentieth-Century Dictionary*, derives from the German *kitschen*, "to smear. Art, writing, etc. of a pretentious, but shallow kind, calculated to have popular appeal." Thus, to reduce all of Baroque literature (and art), including the profoundly philosophical *La vida es sueño*, the epistemologically revolutionary *Quijote*, Lope's existentially dazzling *El castigo sin venganza*, and other texts of this caliber to kitsch is unconvincing. To construe and reduce a text that can appeal to a wide audience that includes less educated members as necessarily kitsch constitutes inaccurate usage. To his credit, Montesa Peydro modifies Maravall's reductive equation, allowing for an additional possibility, namely, that bestsellers can result either from legitimate literature of quality that by nature appeals to many social and educational levels (*un arte genuinamente popular*) or kitsch literature (*arte populista*).[27] Yet he, like Maravall, relegates Zayas to the second category (295–334). There is merit to his observation that kitsch literature can be a form of escapism for the urban masses, "muchas [obras] contribuyen, sin duda, a restablecer el equilibrio interior en el lector (por compensaciones, excitaciones . . .) roto o descompuesto en su vida diaria" (299) [many works no doubt help the reader regain perspective (compensating in some way or providing escapism) which is so often disturbed by daily life]. Certainly the intimate details of the private lives of Zayas's characters, the love intrigues, and even the grisly details of murder, dismemberment, rape, and so on do provide a kind of sensationalism that rivals the popular appeal of the soap operas and similar melodramas of today. The *Novelas* clearly were designed to have this type of mass appeal, but that is only one aspect of Zayas's literary project. To reduce her twenty tales to "pretentious and shallow" writing bereft of artistic quality is to distort the polysemy they project.

Zayas is immensely literate, relying on the novelistic tradition of the canonical Italian *novellieri* such as Boccaccio, Bandello, Sercambi, as well as Marguerite de Navarre, Lope, and Cervantes. Moreover, the literary self-consciousness she displays from the opening lines of her prologue to part I as well as the all-pervasive perspectivism that she generates (both implicitly for her readers as well as explicitly in the conflicting gender, social, political, and religious interpretations her storytellers derive), clearly prevent our classifying her writing as *arte populista*. She was a shrewd businesswoman who succeeded in producing a profound text that would also be a financial success. But financial success should not necessarily be equated with kitsch, as Montesa Peydro and Maravall assume. If we follow this line of thinking, we would have to relegate *Lazarillo de Tormes* and *Don Quijote*, two all-time bestsellers, to the status of "pretentious but shallow" kitsch, which is clearly not the case.

Another reason for which Maravall's kitsch framework must be rethought has to do with his interpretation of this cultural phenomenon as stemming from its function within a "guided culture." He says that literary censorship during the Baroque was a tightly controlled twofold phenomenon. First, the nationally administered boards of censors ensured that no printing of objectionable books would be permitted, and that those texts granted publishing licenses would be determined as a function of their propagandistic value, for their unproblematically positive support of the issues and concerns of the State—"kitsch in the Baroque correlated to what there was of the technique of manipulation: the same thing, therefore, that made it a 'guided culture' " (88). Here too, however, what do we make of Zayas's calculatedly polysemous, conflicting interpretations? How could the State use her text (or the *Quijote*, for example) as propaganda? The multiple subject-positions that proliferate within her text seem to defy any clear-cut function that would promote official institutional values. Ignoring the indeterminacy she generates, Maravall offers an additional meditation on Zayas and her text as propaganda by linking the preponderance of violence and cruelty in her text to what he terms the "aesthetics of cruelty" fostered by the State. Referring to a letter written by a Jesuit priest in 1634 that speaks of the laughter provoked by a public hanging, Maravall concludes, "There is no doubt that the spectacle of violence, pain, blood and death—a spectacle that was popularly supported and displayed before the masses—was used by rulers and their collaborators to terrify people and in this way to succeed more efficiently in subjecting them to their place within the order" (162–63).

Here too, however, we must distinguish between the spectacle of a public execution of a criminal and the private violence we find in Zayas. Maravall writes that "for (her) cruelty was little less than an obsessive aspect of her confrontation with the other sex: 'En cuanto a la crueldad, no hay duda de que está asentada en el corazón del hombre, y esto nace de la dureza dél' " (II, p. 199) [As for cruelty, there is no doubt that it is located in the heart of man and is born of his harshness (162)].

Here too, however, Maravall fails to make an important distinction. As with his interpretation of the *Novelas* (and all other Baroque literature as well) thought to convey a monolithic, officially sanctioned discourse, he errs by not distinguishing between the ritual violence of the public execution and the private violence of domestic crimes of passion. Perhaps one could interpret the murder of an adulterous wife by her husband or other family member as a valorization of the honor code, but what do we make of the preponderance of virtuous wives who are wrongly and cruelly sacrificed? Is this group of novellas not detrimental to the official belief in the integrity of the so-called honor code which provided a cornerstone of social ethics? Beyond the considerable problem posed by these cases of unjust behavior (whose perpetrators go unpunished, as a rule), what do we make of all the other indeterminacies of her polyvalent text? Maravall's view ignores the tension of unresolved axiologies that are so visible in the pages of Zayas's novelistic enterprise.[28]

It is precisely the unresolved nature of multiple tensions that keeps Zayas's readers on the edge of their seats, not a monolithically conceived, predictable formula. The magic of the book stems from the *Novelas*'s thorny and unpredictable situations and signals about the characters' private lives. While the melodramatic nature of her writing no doubt contributed to its enormous popularity at the time when it first appeared and long thereafter in Spain and abroad, its literary, experiential, and ideological nuances and tensions very likely did not—designed, as they are, to be savored by the discriminating, educated reader—to say nothing of her often convoluted, hence difficult, style and syntax, in the prose as well as the poetry.[29] Rather than offering a tool of mass psychology whereby the government can invade the minds of its readers and impose its policies, Zayas's texts achieve the opposite effect, granting the private reader free rein to exercise his or her imagination with an appeal to the two Aristotelian emotions of fear and pity and a kind of voyeuristic satisfaction.

The sensationalism exploited by Zayas was not exclusively an appropriation of the shock value of the ephemera merely calculated to pander to the masses; it was simultaneously predicated on the venerable compositional quality of *admiratio*, the author's ability to engross the reader in a text that elicited admiration in the etymological sense of "wonder," a marveling at the strangeness of the event recounted, but also at the aesthetically pleasing, artistic manner by which it is recounted.

The fact that part I of her *Novelas* is referred to by the author herself not as *novelas* but as *maravillas*, (marvels), and part II as *desengaños* (disenchantments), underscores her desire to elicit wonder, surprise, and/or shock in her readers. An additional motivation for her atypical nomenclature may well be related to the censors, who were stymied by a work bearing an unaccustomed or hybrid generic marker—hence uncharacteristically tolerant of features that would be construed as unacceptable in the more canonical genres. Cruickshank illustrates this authorial strategy by explaining that "an author could produce a hybrid which defied classification, or a novel disguised as history: Lope's *Dorotea* (Madrid, 1632), which he called an 'acción en prosa,' is an example of the former, and Pérez de Montalbán's *Vida y purgatorio de San Patricio* (Madrid, 1627), called a *novela a lo divino* in the preface, is an example of the latter."[30] This change from the accustomed generic marker of *novelas* also reflects the fact that Zayas's emphasis is on the work as it affects the reader rather than the inherent nature of the work per se. Marcia Welles insightfully formulates this shift as "mirroring the change in aesthetic criterion at the theoretical level from the 'mimetic' to the 'pragmatic.'"[31]

Indeed, the focus on the consumer and consumerism is crystallized in the choice of words (especially *engolosinar* and *apetecidos*) Zayas uses to insist, implicitly but firmly, on the readers' pleasure as her prime concern: "Como he dicho, ya los nobles, reducidos a no seguir en esto la vulgaridad [el decir mal de las mujeres], se habían engolosinado con los *Desengaños*, que aunque trágicos, por verdaderos apetecidos" (II, 334) [As I have already said, these, once persuaded not to go along with the public opinion like that, have become addicted to our disenchantments which, although tragic, are appealing because they're true (II, 305–6)]. Of this quotation Welles remarks that it "reveals the pleasure of the readers as being the prime consideration for the insistence on credibility" (303). Yet, while it is important to foreground Zayas's obsessive concern with the reaction her writing has on its audience, there is an additional reason for the insistence on credibility, namely the belief that if a work was not believable (although it might in fact be a total fabrication) it would not be pleasurable to the reader. As Lugo y Dávila expressed in the "Prohemio al lector" of his *Teatro popular: Novelas morales* of 1622 (a text regarded as a kind of poetics of the Golden Age novella):

La mayor valentía y primor en la fábula que compone la novela, es mover a la admiración con suceso dependiente del caso y de la fortuna; mas esto tan próximo a lo verosímil, cuya es toda esta doctrina, al poeta no le toca narrar las cosas como fueron, sino verosímiles a lo que debieron ser.[32]

[The greatest virtue to be found in the plot of the novella is to elicit wonder based on a particular incident and on the vicissitudes of fortune; one that is believable, without any unbelievable details; because according to the philosopher (Aristotle), whose theory this is, the poet should not narrate things as they were, but as they should have been]. (my translation)

Of course, Zayas departs from this well-known precept of poetic believability rather than historical veracity, of moral rather than historical verisimilitude, for while she invokes the need for credibility she goes to great lengths to insist that all of her *novelas* (except perhaps I, 10, *El jardín engañoso*) are, in addition, historically real occurrences. Here too, however, she reveals her subtle contradictoriness. While insisting repeatedly that her narratives actually occurred, that they are *relaciones de sucesos*, she also indicates in an insolubly slippery manner that her plots are founded on gossip.

Gossip is always compelling, she admits, once more having recourse to literary (and gastronomic) consumption: "eso tienen las novedades, que aunque no sean muy sabrosas, todos gustan de comerlas" (II, p. 102) [this is the nature of gossip, that although it may be unappetizing, everyone loves to consume it (my translation)]. Indeed, with tongue in cheek she attributes her stories at one point to court gossip rather than fact: "Habían de ser las damas las que novelasen (y en esto acertó con la opinión de los hombres, pues siempre tienen a las mujeres por noveleras)" (II, p. 10) [The women should be the ones designated to tell the stories (and the men all agreed since they always consider women to be inveterate gossips (my translation)].

Speaking of the evident contradiction in the authority with which she endows her tales (true history, poetic truth, or gossip), Kenneth Stackhouse accurately notes that Zayas "associates the noun *novela* with the adjective *novelero* in its pejorative connotation of 'fond of gossip'": "El vulgo es novelero y no todos bien entendidos" (II, p. 167) ["People love a good story (gossip) and not everybody is well-intentioned (132)].[33] The awareness of the power of gossip for her readership is yet another indication of Zayas's clever marketing strategies. And her ability to create and purposely leave unresolved the tension between the antithetical sources of gossip and/or history as authority attests to her deft ability in the literary marketplace.

While Zayas cagily exploits the perennial lure of gossip to sell books, she also capitalizes on a carefully chosen period-specific consideration, namely, the seventeenth century's relentless fascination with epistemology of the supernatural, ranging all the way from apparitions of the Virgin and her miraculous powers, to false ghosts. The heavily used topos of appearance versus reality that we find throughout the literature of the period is generated from a profound philosophical and existential unease about the truth-status of what we perceive; that our fallible perception will almost necessarily result in misperception, hence misinterpretation and, ultimately, wrongful action. From Lope's *El castigo sin venganza*, to the perspectivism so elaborately detailed in the *Quijote*, to Calderón's *La vida es sueño*, the issue of reality and man's ability to influence it were of prime concern.

So too were the attempts to define the natural world and its relation to the supernatural; this involved a notable increase in the exploration of allegedly magic phenomena—both "natural magic" and "superstitious magic." Suárez de Figueroa represents the common belief held at that time regarding these two forms of magic when he explains that: "Natural magic . . . views celestial and terrestrial things and considers their advantages and drawbacks, discovering the faculties hidden in nature, and consequently mixes the ones with the others in a necessary proportion and in a certain constellation"; this magic, then, combining the beings' occult properties whose knowledge has been attained, "produces what appears to be unheard-of miracles." The other is "superstitious magic": "It is done by invoking evil spirits and is manifest idolatry, always prohibited by well-ordered republics."[34]

Throughout all of Europe, in fact, the final years of the sixteenth century and the successive century brought with them not just this interest in magic, but an obsessive concern with witchcraft and its pernicious possibilities. This holds true equally for Italy, France, Spain, and England, about which the historian Hugh Trevor-Roper writes of the "witchcraft epidemic."[35] In her *Novelas* Zayas capitalizes on these related interests in magic, the supernatural and witchcraft, by including numerous instances of each phenomenon, thus exploiting not only new reading practices but these popular issues of timely concern in the writing of her text. In this way, the "magic of the book" is twofold in her literary enterprise, a reference both to one of her predominant themes, and to her far-sighted ability to "cash in," becoming a best-selling author because she dares to take on subjects that figured among the most hotly debated cultural controversies of her day, thereby captivating her readers. She is quite pointed in discussing the type of books that sell: those that are "llenos de sutilezas se venden, pero no se compran, porque la materia no es importante o es desabrida" (I, 23) [many works filled with subtlety are offered for sale but never bought because the subject is unimportant or not pleasing (2)]. It is no accident that Zayas represents herself in the prologue to part I as something of a witch figure when she writes of her text, and of print in general, as a "crucible of letters" ("crisol donde se averigua la pureza de los ingenios" [I, 21]).

El jardín engañoso (The Deceitful Garden)

The fascination with magic along with its original, unanticipated possibilities is dazzlingly revealed in *El jardín engañoso* (I, 10), by its original solution to the very familiar literary situation of a man who decides to sign a pact with the Devil. This tale reveals Zayas's wide reading and clever exploitation of a Boccaccian tale (*Decameron* X, 5), as well as her creativity in exploiting magic for the purposes of generating further indeterminacy, further polysemy in her enterprise as a whole. And, like other aspects of her text, we will see that Zayas's deployment of magic and related phenomena virtually defies categorization.

In a study that makes important observations concerning magic and the supernatural in the *Novelas*, Kenneth Stackhouse posits a useful four-part typology of these issues, namely that 1—"Magic is real and efficacious; 2—those who employ magic pay an extreme penalty; 3—magic occurs more abroad than in Spain due to the influence of the Church and the Inquisition; 4—when magic occurs, it does so only temporarily, seemingly only by divine dispensation" (68). As a framework that tries to make sense of the complex poetics of magic confronting the reader it is a useful conceptualization, yet, as the texts reveal, it oversimplifies somewhat the Zayesque perspective.

Decameron X, 5, is—like all of Day Ten—devoted to the theme of magnanimity. More precisely, this tale offers a dramatization of the power of language. In order to protect her virtue, the married woman makes an impossible request of her suitor—that he create a splendid garden in the dead of winter. When, with the help of a magician, he actually accomplishes the request, she must yield to him. The distressed wife explains this problem to her husband, at which point he amazes both her and the reader by indicating that she must *keep her word* and comply with her suitor, who, in turn, is so impressed by the husband's commitment to *linguistic integrity* that he annuls their verbal contract. Indeed, he and the husband further illustrate their reverence for the word by their mutual admiration, becoming the best of friends.

Variations on this theme can be found in Boccaccio's *Filocolo*, Chaucer's *Franklin's Tale*, in Boiardo's *Orlando innamorato*, and a variety of ancient sources. Despite the particular test involved, in each text what is being tested is the power of language. In every case the tale concludes with a celebration of referentiality. Keeping one's word leads to reward—an unproblematic, prelapsarian view of language is imposed. Like Boccaccio, Zayas is interested in the power of language; unlike him, she focuses on the darker, labyrinthine possibilities of the garden.

The *Jardín engañoso* tends to be interpreted as a lighthearted conclusion to Zayas's first collection. E. B. Place, for instance, sees it as "rival[ling] some of the most brilliant passages in the French burlesquing *nouvelles*."[36] This is due, in part, to the fact that Zayas replaces the magician with the Devil himself; the suitor makes a pact with the Evil One in order to furnish the required garden. And, like Boccaccio's magician, the Devil ultimately grants the suitor freedom from his contractual perdition, which is uncharacteristic demonic behavior, to say the least. In fact, according to Place, Zayas is credited with having written the only known example of such diabolical magnanimity (37).

Yet we may rightly ask, why does she emphasize this atypical behavior? In addition, does she not run the risk of incurring the wrath of the nationally sanctioned literary censors? Here as elsewhere in her strategically written pages, she shows herself capable of transgressions that she always couches in an acceptable manner so as to appeal to as wide a readership as possible. Her subtly worded ambiguities and often irreconcilable disagreements of interpretation by the *sarao* participants themselves allows the discerning, careful reader to savor the Baroque openendedness of the text, while the more conventional reader can extract a single, unproblematic interpretation.

In attempting to ascertain who has been the most magnanimous—the husband, the lover, or the Devil—Zayas writes: "Principiaron a disputar [y] cada uno daba su razón: unos alegaban que el marido, y otros que el amante, y todos juntos, que el demonio, por ser en el cosa nunca vista el hacer bien" (422) [Each person defended an opinion: some favored the husband, others the lover, and everyone agreed that the Devil had outdone himself because it's unheard of for the Devil to do a good deed (312)]. Is it magnanimity, the sin of pride or—more likely—weakness verbally disguised as its opposite that motivates this extraordinary behavior? The Devil exclaims: "Toma don Jorge: ves ahí tu cédula; yo te suelto la obligación, que no quiero alma de quien tan bien se sabe vencer" (420) [Take back your pact! I don't want the soul of a man who's learned to conquer himself (311)]. If one has learned to conquer himself, then he cannot be conquered by the Devil.

Zayas understands the paradigmatic function of the Boccaccian narrative in terms of pre- and postlapsarian language. That is why she makes the linguistic dimension explicit by transforming Boccaccio's magician into the Devil himself. That is also why she entitles her story *El jardín engañoso, The Deceitful [or Deceptive] Garden*. Boyer mistranslates it, in my opinion, as *The Magic Garden* (296), presumably because part I of the *Novelas* is traditionally—and, to my mind, somewhat erroneously—viewed as largely unproblematic stories of connubial coexistence, in comparison with the violently predatory domestic scenes of the *desengaños* in part II. As analysis makes clear, the first ten stories unmask scenes of hypocrisy, deceptive seduction, violence, and disillusionment that are intensified in the second ten. At issue is a quantitative not a qualitative difference.

Textual specificity belies an unproblematic reading of the model text. Zayas renames Boccaccio's wife-figure (Dianora) Constanza, at the same time inventing for her a sister (Teodosia), who will, in fact, eclipse Constanza's role as female protagonist. And in a move that is characteristic of the exemplary narrator, both women are presented as being paradigmatically perfect in every way. Their names are carefully chosen as well — "constancy" and "a divine offering" lead us to expect an illustration of the semantic value indicated for each woman. (Yet as with the overdetermined nature of the names Lucrecia and Helen, whose traditional association Zayas inverts, here too we find an interest in etymological transgression, for Constanza and Teodosia will show themselves to be very alien in their comportment from what their names signify in etymological terms.)

Zayas is decidedly uninterested in following the path of predictable exemplarity. Instead her intent is to expose the potentially mendacious power of words to deceive — and deceivers who triumph. And in so doing, she offers a compelling example of the appearance-versus-reality topos, of the difficulty of ascertaining the truth. She constructs a superficially exemplary narrative that uncovers a sinister truth. Briefly stated, Zayas complicates Boccaccio's basic plot by giving the wife a sister and the suitor a brother. Teodosia falls in love with her married sister's suitor (Jorge) and tries to turn his attention away from Constanza to herself. As a result of her lies, the suitor secretly kills his brother, thereafter fleeing the country. For over two years Constanza remains faithful to the inexplicably absent Jorge, at which time a new suitor (Carlos) tricks her into marrying him. He pretends to be on his deathbed and to have chosen Constanza to be the executrix of his substantial estate; this is his dying wish. She is so moved by it that she marries him, at which point he recovers rapidly from what was obviously a feigned illness. And, although he discloses to Constanza his double deception (in terms of his health and his estate), they live happily thereafter. The narrator fills in the reasoning that prompts Constanza to accept this husband who has lied to her in such extreme form on two occasions, indicating that "era Constanza tan discreta, que en lugar de desconsolarse, juzgándose dichosa en tener tal marido, le dió por el engaño gracias" (420) [instead of resenting the deception (she) considered herself fortunate (303)].

Meanwhile, four years after his disappearance, Jorge returns and attempts to woo Constanza once again. She refuses and, in order to rid herself of him, indicates that she will favor him only if he produces a splendid garden over night:

Hagamos, señor don Jorge, un concierto; y sea que como vos me hagáis en esta placeta que está delante de mi casa, de aquí a la mañana, un jardín tan adornado de cuadros y olorosas flores, árboles y fuentes, que ni en su frescura ni belleza, ni en la diversidad de páxaros quien él haya, desdiga de los nombrados pensiles de Babilonia, que Semíramis hizo sobre sus muros, yo me pondré en vuestro poder y haré por vos cuanto deseáis." (414)

[If, between now and tomorrow morning, you will make for me in the square in front of my house a garden with flowerbeds full of perfumed flowers, trees, and fountains that, in all its beauty, freshness, and diversity of birds, surpasses the famous gardens that Semiramis had built on the walls of Babylon, then I shall place myself in your hands for you to do with as you please.] (306)

With the Devil's help he produces the fabulous artifact and, struck by the husband's magnanimity when he insists that Constanza keep her word, Jorge frees her from her promise and marries Teodosia in accord with her sister's wishes. The narrator (Laura) ends by relating that: "Vivieron muchos años con hermosos hijos, sin que jamás se supiese que don Jorge hubiese sido el matador de Federico, hasta que después de muerto don Jorge, Teodosia contó el caso como quien tan bien lo sabía. A la cual, cuando murió, le hallaron escrita de su mano esta maravilla" (422) [They all lived for many years and had lovely children. No one ever found out that Jorge had murdered his brother Federico until after his death, when Teodosia told the story she alone knew. When she died this (narrative) was found written in her own hand (312)]. As a result, Teodosia, Carlos, and Jorge (each one guilty of unconscionable verbal deception) go unpunished (indeed, they are rewarded with great happiness).

Needless to say, from the perspective of ethical exemplarity this resolution is shocking indeed. Carlos (a fraud) and Jorge (a fratricide) are literally hailed as "exemplars" of nobility and virtue by the assembled listeners. Even more shocking is the fact that the storyteller's motivation in telling the tale is entirely forgotten. We will recall that Laura had introduced her tale by observing that

matar un hermano a otro, ni ser una hermana traidora con su hermana, forzándolos al uno celos y al otro amor y envidia, no es caso nuevo; pues desde el principio del mundo ha habido hermanos traidores y envidiosos, como nos dicen dos mil ejemplos que hay escritos. Pues que la pobreza enseña ardides, y más si se acompaña con ciega afición, tampoco es cosa nueva. Ni lo es que un amante aventure la perdición de su alma por alcanzar lo que desea. Ni menos lo será que una mujer, si quiere guardar su honor, busque ni haga imposibles. . . . Pues el decir [mi maravilla] yo no es más que para dar ejemplo y prevenir que se guarden de las ocasiones." (400)

[it's nothing new for a brother to kill a brother or for a sister to betray a sister if they're driven by jealousy, love, and envy. From the very beginning of the world there have been invidious and treacherous brothers and sisters, as we see in a thousand stories that have been written down. Neither is it new for poverty to produce ingenious trickery, particularly when inspired by blind passion. Nor is it novel for a lover to risk his soul to get what he wants, or for a woman trying to protect her honor to ask a lover to do the impossible. . . . I'm telling (this story) only to make a point and to warn people to be careful.] (295)

The inscribed audience interprets this last tale of the collection in precisely the *opposite way*—as an exemplum of magnanimity—having totally forgotten Laura's motive. Although none of the listeners reveal it as a possible motive, Stackhouse indicates that the Devil was doing nothing more than revealing once more his original vice, pride, as the motive for his extraordinary act of generosity: " 'No me habéis de vencer, aunque más hagáis' " (69). Pondering the possible motivation for the Devil's magnanimity, the narrator affirms that "para eso puede haber otras secretas causas que nosotros ignoramos" (400) [there may be other, secret reasons of which we are ignorant (my translation)]. We see Zayas's determination not to close down interpretation, and, indeed, this indeterminacy is an enduring feature as much of her tales as it is of the remarks and discussions of her inscribed narrators.

Thus the "intricate labyrinths" (*tan intricados laberintos*) of the Devil's garden may well be construed as the *verbal labyrinths* that stem from the original garden, Eden. Etymologically, *exemplum* meant a "clearing in the woods." However, Zayas—while ostensibly clearing the woods—points to their unredeemed darkness, and to the magical quality of the book in its capacity to seduce its readers in markedly different ways.[37]

El desengaño amando y premio de la virtud (*Disillusionment in Love and Virtue Rewarded*)

The obvious humor generated within *El jardín engañoso* as a result of the benevolent Satan illustrates one extreme of the Zayesque exploitation of magic, namely, her interest in amusing her readers by presenting the Evil One oxymoronically in this tale as being essentially good. An entirely different, sinister appreciation of the subject is afforded by *El desengaño amando y premio de la virtud* (I, 6), a tale told by Filis in order to "probar cúanta es la fuerza de la virtud, dando premio a una dama a quien el desengaño de otra dió méritos para merecerle" (249) [tell about the power of virtue . . . about how a woman is disenchanted by the experiences of another woman and ultimately is rewarded (181)].

Like *La burlada Aminta y venganza del honor*, already discussed in terms of gender and agency, and as both titles reflect, this one narrative is also constructed by means of a story in two parts. In the imperial city of Toledo there lived a young man of noble lineage referred to in this story by the pseudonym of Fernando. In spite of the nobility of his blood and natural gifts, however, he preferred a life of vice instead of virtue. We are called upon to muse over the controversy, current even today, of nature and/or nurture, whereby an attempt is made to understand how a person develops into maturity. The narrator informs us that he came from a good home in which "desde su tierna niñez procuraron sus padres criarle e instruirle en las costumbres que requieren los ilustres nacimientos para que lleven adelante la nobleza que heredaron sus pasados" (252) [his parents tried to rear him and teach him the manners required by his noble birth so that he would carry on the family tradition inherited from his ancestors (182)].

The ignoble behavior of this titular noble is reiterated for the reader with a clear double focus—to discredit this individual offender, but also to underscore the problematic perception of nobility in the seventeenth century, the often tremendous gap separating the nobility of inherent worth as opposed to the often considerable ignobility, even infamy, of the titular nobles.[38] Again, this is a very timely topic, one which engrossed all strata of society in the period during which the *Novelas* were produced and that surfaces as the focus of many literary texts—Lope's *Fuenteovejuna*, to name one of the most popular examples—and it is a topic that has a direct bearing on the aristocratic author and the partygoers who narrate and listen to these stories.

The reader learns that Fernando's vices are, as we might expect, the offenses of reckless dueling, gambling, and womanizing. So negligent is he, in fact, so disruptive, that he is cast in hyperbolic terms as the incarnation of debauchery. Upon the death of his parents, his outrageous behavior takes on such extremes that he becomes the "aborrecimiento de los hombres. No parecía que era criado para otra cosa que para acabar y destruir la hacienda y opinión de sus antecesores, porque como no había quistión en que no se hallase, ni bellaquería que no favoreciese" (252) [abomination of men. He seemed to have been brought up purposefully to ruin and destroy the good name as well as the inheritance of his ancestors. There was no trouble from which he was absent, no disturbance of which he was not a part (183)].

We also find out that in the midst of all his indiscreet and excessive behavior, he falls in love with a young lady who is identified simply as Juana, whose beauty, grace, and discretion leave him totally smitten. The narrator is quick to point out, however, that, as with Fernando, there is more to this woman than initially meets the eye. As we observe in other tales, here too the tension of appearance and reality serves as a fundamental structuring principal in this narrative. In spite of her "hermosura, donaire, y discreción" [beauty, charms, and wit] (253), we learn that she is not, in fact, as given to *discreción* as we might first expect. Again, we see Zayas's characters evolving, not conforming to the predictable categories of good or evil, chaste or fallen.[39] While reprehensible ones can have laudable qualities and primarily positive ones can have serious flaws, as we have seen already in the case of Hipólita, for example—the adulteress who causes her husband to die of grief while she marries her lover. The

Zayesque corollary to this axiological complexity, and breech of traditional character decorum, is that evildoers may go unpunished (as in *El jardín engañoso*), and virtuous citizens may unjustly suffer unspeakable torture and death (as in *Mal presagio*).

In the case of Juana, she suffers from what is perceived as the disadvantage (rather than advantage) of her age. She is twenty years old and, instead of dwelling on her beauty or innocence, the narrator informs us that she is given to vanity and lasciviousness: "Era doña Juana de veinte años, edad peligrosa para la perdición de una mujer, por estar entonces la belleza vanidad y locura aconsejadas con la voluntad, causa para que no escuchando a la razón ni al entendimiento se dexen cautivar de deseos livianos" (252–53) [Doña Juana was twenty, a dangerous age for a woman's virtue because at this time, beauty, vanity, and folly are governed by the will, and a woman tends not to heed reason or judgment and, instead, lets herself be carried away by lascivious desires (183)].

It is interesting in terms of gender that a female narrator makes this remark. Is she prompted to do so from the perspective of a moralizer who believes that women should be closely guarded so as not to tarnish their virtue? Or is it her desire to underscore that the transgressive desires of the female psyche are every bit as real and powerful as those of a man? Or is it, perhaps, yet another motivation? The information that she was an orphan and without any surviving relatives may be supplied to explain, or at least temper somewhat, Juana's indiscreet comportment. The multiple possibilities and the debates and controversies generated within the group of partygoers and, no doubt, for the readers of the 1630s and 1640s attest to the enticing (and universally appealing) nature of this book—to its magical quality for the reader.

While intent on amorous intrigue, Juana is naive with respect to masculine verbal deception. For his part, however, being astute and knowing that she would only yield to him under the promise of marriage, Fernando proposes, courting his lady with passionate words both spoken and sung. Among the arsenal of images he employs is the description of his plight as akin to that suffered by the mythological figures of Tantalus who can never reach the crystal vessel (Juana) that would quench his thirst, and by Sisyphus laboring against virtually insurmountable odds. Juana finally capitulates, yielding her virtue as a result of the deceitful promise Fernando swears to marry her. This particular lie, we are told, is the "oro con que los hombres disimulan la píldora amarga de sus engaños" (258) [the prize men offer in order to sugarcoat the bitter pill of their deception (187)].

Their affair continues for six months and has the effect of increasing her passionate desire for Fernando, just as his diminishes, having sated himself with the pleasures of her body. As such, Fernando embodies the axiom that one can only desire that which he does not possess, a perspective that Zayas frequently evokes in her male protagonists. Yet, as if to question this proverbial male cynicism, Filis, in her capacity as narrator, adds that love is an uncontrollable force, and that we are incapable of willing ourselves in or out of love (258). Once more we see Zayas's refusal to prescribe interpretation.

As it turns out, Juana has a good friend from Rome, forty-eight-year-old Lucrecia, who is very attractive in spite of her age and a woman famous for her prowess as a witch. The narrator's comment concerning the nationality of this woman is significant, a way of signaling the perennial rivalry of Spaniards and Italians, but it is also an ambiguous one since it refers to Lucrecia as a "buena señora": "éste era el nombre desta buena señora, porque era natural de Roma, mas tan ladina y españolada, como si fuera nacida y criada en Castilla" (259) [this was the good woman's name. Lucrecia was a native of Rome but as clever and Spanish as if she'd been born and brought up in Old Castile (188)].

Beyond the nationalistic caricature, this remark is significant in that it conforms to Stackhouse's important observation that Zayas carefully chooses the nationality of her witches and sorcerers, that "magic occurs more abroad than in Spain due to the influence of the Church and the Inquisition."[40]

As a consequence of Juana's descriptions of Fernando, Lucrecia falls madly in love with him. (Here we see, once again, Zayas toying with the traditional association of this female name by offering her reader a lascivious witch instead.)[41] Juana becomes aware of the betrayal perpetrated by Lucrecia (who is described as being in league with the Devil when she resorts to her magic). She too enlists the aid of magic by means of a student from Alcalá who gives her two magic rings which her maid borrows without permission when she is doing the laundry and scrubbing floors. The rings not only reveal themselves to be animate but, taking great offense at their misuse, abuse the student who gave Juana the rings in the first place. The rings (that are in reality devils) beat him mercilessly, leaving him for dead. We are never told why this student from Alcalá had these powerful rings in his possession—an incongruous detail, to say the least.

The fact that he does not know how to control the rings, that he is nothing more than a student, in addition to the fact that his initial acquisition of the rings is not explained, makes this whole episode mysterious indeed. Stackhouse's reading here is debatable since it is not because Juana and the student "fail to make the necessary pact with Satan" that the rings rebel. It is, rather, the unforeseen appropriation of them by the maid that makes the plan backfire.

While Juana had been in the initial stages of courtship with Fernando, another gentleman named Octavio sought her hand and, seeing that she would not marry him, left Spain to serve the king in Naples. Realizing her remorse once Fernando has abandoned her, the student convinces her that he would ensure the return of Octavio if Juana would be willing to resort to magic once more. Faithfully following the student's directions, Juana utters on a nightly basis incantations containing words so scandalous that the narrator refuses to reproduce them for her readers—a ploy which allows each individual reader to construct his or her own set of abominable possibilities, in keeping with Zayas's commitment to stimulating her audience, leaving the possibilities open for each reader to determine.

The words take effect after three nights or, more likely, we are told, the will of God manifested itself by bringing Juana back to the true faith, using the Devil's magical artifice as a means to effect it. During her conjuring on the third night Juana is suddenly terrified as she beholds the ghost of Octavio, who warns her to give consideration to her soul before it is too late: "si no miras por ti, ¡ay de tu alma! (267) [if you don't take care of your soul, woe be unto you! (195)]. After repeated fainting spells, Juana tells Fernando that she is disenchanted with the world and has, therefore, decided to end her days as a nun in the convent. She asks Fernando for financial support so that she can take the veil, which he grants very readily, delighted to have gotten rid of the obligation to marry her.

Meanwhile, true to his ways, Fernando squanders not only his own inheritance, but Lucrecia's assets as well, the result being that all he can look forward to is the sum he would inherit from his aged mother. In the meantime, his mother, wanting to do the best for her son, arranges for him to marry a beautiful and chaste young woman named Clara. To Fernando this seems to be a golden opportunity since his future wife has, he believes, a very wealthy father who had made a fortune in Spain, Italy, and the Indies. What the father does not want people to know is that he subsequently lost this fortune, retaining only a modest sum. In order to keep his business failure a secret, the father gives his daughter six thousand ducats, stipulating that the rest is tied up in business deals, but that she will eventually inherit his entire estate, given that she is an only child. Fernando immediately spends this sum and leaves Spain for the Indies, abandoning Clara with no means of support for herself and their two daughters.

Lucrecia, in the interim, decides to punish him for marrying Clara, and so she resorts to her diabolical arts, impairing him with a grave illness for a period of six months. Once this period has passed, Lucrecia revokes her spell, reasoning that by this infirmity she is punishing herself more than she is him. His health is restored, thereby permitting him to return to his wanton existence in the company of Lucrecia. Given that the relationship of Lucrecia and Fernando has become common knowledge, the police determine to arrest the infamous couple. They have anticipated this legal action, however, fleeing to Seville to feign an existence within the lawful bonds of matrimony.

Clara lives for more than a year and a half without so much as a word from her husband, at which point she must dismiss the maid and work delivering embroidery for a nearby shop in order to provide, albeit meagerly, for herself and her two small daughters. As she sings one night she is overheard by a suitor of long standing, Sancho, who has loved her since the early stages of her courtship with Fernando. His love is so steadfast that he offers her a donation of one thousand *escudos*, with no obligation on her part, simply to alleviate her suffering and that of her children. In response to this gesture of magnanimity, Clara thanks Sancho, but says that she is honor-bound to her husband, to whom she must remain faithful.

As her name indicates, Clara is "clarity" itself with respect to her unobscured integrity, the exemplary behavior she exhibits in spite of all the cruelty she has undergone at the hands of her reprehensible husband. She waits for him patiently until she learns that he is living in Seville with Lucrecia, obviously without any intention of returning to his family. Juana, now a nun with a comfortable existence, generously offers to be the guardian of Clara's daughters, thus enabling their mother to search for the father who has abandoned them. The offer is accepted immediately, and not only does Clara find the debauched·couple; she works in their service as a maid for more than a year. Fernando does not recognize her even though he sees her throughout the day, and in spite of the fact that she has not disguised her name. This notable lack of recognition is attributed to the magic spell that Lucrecia has cast over him by means of a blindfolded and shackled cock she keeps in a trunk in an attic room that only the witch can enter. Given the conventions of witchcraft, and given the efficacy of this particular spell (repeatedly verified later on by the authorities), we can understand why Fernando would not recognize his wife. (Why the artful and ruthless Lucrecia does not recognize her, however, is never made clear.)

One day Lucrecia becomes mortally ill and, confiding in Clara, speaks to her affectionately, saying that she has treated her more like a daughter than a maid. This affection takes the reader aback, given that Lucrecia has been responsible for destroying Clara's marriage. Lucrecia's words are prompted either by a real attachment she may feel to Clara (of whose true identity she is inexplicably unaware), or because she has no other person to whom she can entrust the task of feeding the cock and keeping it blindfolded. Finally seeing her chance, Clara removes the blindfold, at which point Fernando regains his natural perception and is shocked to see his lawful wife whom he admits to having left penniless, reviling himself because of it, terming his treatment of Clara as "desordenado y mal cristiano" (285) [dastardly and un-Christian]. Realizing that the spell is definitively broken, Lucrecia takes her own life by stabbing herself, but not before taking her revenge. Racing to her desk, she grabs the wax figure of a man, piercing it violently with a very large pin, after which she hurls it into the fireplace where it is consumed by flames.

Clara tells her story to the authorities, who verify repeatedly the power of the blindfolded cock by alternately covering and removing the blindfold, which has the effect of either bewitching Fernando or returning him to his senses. Unlocking Lucrecia's desk the police find a thousand articles of her trade which she repeatedly used to empower herself. Everything of this sort is burned in the public plaza, as is the body of the dead witch, in a scene that is reminiscent of an *auto da fé*.

It is important to note, however, that unlike the teleology of the *auto*, where the republic is meant to be definitively freed of a pernicious influence by the ritual burning of the offender's body, here we learn that Lucrecia's magic lives on even after her death. The minute the authorities burn the charms, amulets, and other props used by the witch to practice her black magic, Fernando becomes terminally ill. Examining him, the doctors determine that his body suffered no physical illness, thus concluding that his death must be the result of the witchcraft. During his last days, Fernando treats Clara with such devotion, that she nearly accompanies him to the grave, so great is the love that she feels for him.

In the meantime, Sancho arranges for his funeral to be as sumptuous as possible, escorting the body to the cemetery with great dignity and in the company, we are told, of "all the gentlemen of Toledo." Having interred the body with the utmost decorum, Sancho asks for Clara's hand in the presence of the assembled nobles, praising her unwaveringly virtuous behavior, offering in addition a dramatic speech in praise of women: "Justo es que pagues este amor y deuda en que estás a mi firmeza con un solo sí que te pido, y yo a ti, y no sólo yo, sino todos los hombres del mundo deben a las mujeres, que a fuerza de virtudes granjean las voluntades de los que las desean" (289) [All men in the world are indebted to women like you, who, by their great virtue, earn the love of those who had simply desired them (211)]. Clara immediately grants his request, thereby turning the condolences into congratulations. Sancho offers dowries to Clara's two daughters, who choose the convent as their lifelong vocation. Meanwhile she and Sancho have "beautiful children," experiencing a life of great happiness together. We learn also that Juana's wise choice inspired the first part of the title, "el desengaño amando," and that because of her steadfast love, Clara found happiness since "desta suerte premia el cielo la virtud" (290) [this is how heaven "rewards virtue" (212)].

What follows the narrative proper is the accustomed discussion of the auditors, which highlights, like the tales themselves, the "magic of the book" in terms of human subjectivity and the diversity of interests and interpretations to which it gives rise. In the case of *El desengaño amando y premio de la virtud*, the group members comment on seven different aspects of the story: Juana's prudent "awakening," the diabolical rings, Octavio's ghost, Clara's fidelity, Fernando's blindness, Lucrecia's obstinacy (*obstinación*), and especially about "el gracioso suceso del gallo con antojos" (290) [the funny detail about the rooster with his little blinders (212)].

Some of the topics chosen, and even more so the way in which they are phrased in terms of the theme of magic and the supernatural, are striking. The explicit linking of the two-part title to Juana and Clara offers a clear religious exemplum concerning the wisdom of chaste love, be it of a divine or human husband. This reading obviously appeals to the reader looking for edification of an ethical sort. Octavio's supernatural apparition, as well as Fernando's metaphorical blindness stemming from his lascivious nature and poor judgment and his literal blindness that occurs while he is under the spell of Lucrecia's witchcraft, also fit nicely into this moral category. What is harder to explain is the rather casual way in which the auditors refer to the episodes involving magic and the supernatural.

Yet the issue of the diabolical rings, the incongruity of their human agent (a student), their frightening capabilities, and their ultimate teleology surprisingly do not elicit much curiosity or comment. It is not the usual Christian conception of the singular Devil; rather, multiple devils wreak havoc on the student not because of some transgression committed by the student or even Juana, but because a maid wears them while she does the housework, which the devils consider to be a breech of decorum. They are, moreover, arbitrary devils because they beat the student as a result not of his but of the maid's misappropriation, giving the impression in their harangue that had she not surreptitiously borrowed the rings from her mistress they would have performed their magic as promised. On the other hand they also appear to be aware of Christian cosmology, since they mention that Fernando and Lucrecia are destined for eternal torment in hell. Are they emissaries of the Devil, of God, or, as we are led to believe most strongly, of black magic unrelated to Christian axiology? From this inconsistent presentation of them we must conclude that they are calculatedly fashioned by Zayas to be ultimately ambiguous devils.

Even more curious and unexpected than the offhand treatment by the auditors of the rings is their choice of "obstinacy" as the most salient feature associated with Lucrecia. This is a rather insignificant aspect of her characterization, compared to the demonic powers she has, it seems, even from beyond the grave. Given the foregrounding of the Christian reading given to Juana and Clara by the *sarao* audience, we would expect something even more extended and dramatic in the case of Lucrecia and her function as an incarnation of the Devil. The only association between her and the Devil is a brief, passing reference made at an early moment in the tale, when Filis remarks that "al fin podía más Lucrecia, o por mejor decir el demonio, a quien ella tenía muy de su parte" (261) [in the end Lucrecia—or more precisely, the Devil, who was very much on her side—would win out (190)].

The stranglehold exerted by Lucrecia's power after her death virtually requires an ethical gloss in terms of Christian demonology so as not to give the heretical impression that witches exert power from beyond the grave. This ending seems to contradict Stackhouse's fourth precept, that "when magic occurs, it does so only temporarily, seeming only by divine dispensation." He makes no mention of the fact that Lucrecia's magic is not temporary, that it in fact continues even after her death.

By this omission Zayas clearly seeks to generate ambiguity and to highlight the fascination her public feels for magic—a dangerous topic in the atmosphere of inquisitorial Spain. Equally surprising and revealing is the deflationary manner in which the cock's blindfold is alluded to as a "funny detail," it being the direct source of Fernando's absolutely debilitating spellbound condition. Is the choice of adjective meant to diminish the potentially threatening power of witchcraft (that a believing Christian cannot logically fear)? Is it intended, rather, as a safety device for the board of censors? Or is it designed perhaps to underscore the fact that Zayas is acknowledging the fact that her heterogeneous readership will be interested in and either pleased or disturbed by different facets of the text. The acknowledgment of these multiple possibilities, and still others yet to be explicitly articulated, reveals her remarkable narratological abilities and her will to open-endedness, to refrain from indicating a restricted set of interpretational possibilities.

It appears then that this tale, besides offering us a glimpse at the forbidden world of the occult, treats magic not as something exploited overtly to be rejected in favor of official Church views, but as a titillating world to be savored by the individual reader, in this way adding yet another dimension to Zayas's irreducible axiological complexity.

La inocencia castigada (Innocence Punished)

Possibilities contained in a voodoolike image of a lover are explored even more fully than in *El desengaño amando y premio de la virtud* in *La inocencia castigada* (II, 5). And while we may anticipate from a comparison of the two titles that the latter tale will be more straightforward in its use of magic and its interpretive valence, such is not the case. For while the exploitation of an effigy itself by, in this case, a Moorish necromancer, is presented in clearly negative terms, the reaction to its power uncovers some very convoluted human motives and unanticipated perspectives.

As with her other narratives, this story has an urban setting. Zayas no doubt chooses the famous urban centers of her homeland for at least three reasons: first, because her readers (and readers of the time in general) were city dwellers; second, since she includes all the major cities around Spain, and some less significant ones as well, she achieves a kind of geographic universality that will have a wide appeal to her audience.[42] Finally, then as now, the city was perceived as the locus of transgression, where anonymity and/or its opposite—fame—made vices of all kinds more accessible than in less populated areas.

The city in question this time is located close to Seville; no more precision is offered, so as to protect the parties involved in the intrigue. Francisco is a prominent citizen, a "caballero principal" who is married to a woman of equal standing. He also has a sister named Inés, an eighteen-year-old beauty who is actively looking to get married not as an end in itself, but rather as a means of escaping the stifling domestic environment of her brother's house, which is described in such undesirable terms as a *cautiverio* (captivity) and *martirio* (martyrdom): "aceptó el casamiento, quizá no tanto por [su hermano], cuanto por salir de la rigurosa condición de su cuñada, que era de lo cruel que imaginarse puede" (110) [perhaps not so much for his sake as to escape the harsh temper of her sister-in-law, who was more cruel than you can imagine (175)].

The narrator (Laura) takes this opportunity to revile husbands, saying that they are infinitely affectionate at first, but that after a year of marriage they invariably come to hate their wives. Expanding on this idea, she produces a lengthy exclamation to her audience concerning the seemingly universal mistreatment of women by men:

¿Qué espera un marido, ni un padre, ni un hermano, y hablando más común-mente, un galán, de una dama, si se ve aborrecida, y falta de lo que ha menester, y tras eso, poco agasajada y estimada, sino una desdicha? ¡O, válgame Dios, y qué confiados son hoy los hombres, pues no temen que lo que una mujer desespe-rada hará, no lo hará el demonio! Piensan que por verlas y celarlas se libran y las apartan de travesuras, y se engañan. (110–11)

[What does a husband, a brother, a father, or even a suitor expect of a woman who finds herself neglected and lacking the affection she requires, no longer fondled or even esteemed? What else but misfortune? Heaven help me! How over-confident men are these days since it never occurs to them that a desperate woman might do things even the Devil wouldn't do. They think that by keeping women clois-tered and by guarding them closely they keep them from mischief and they are free of any other responsibility, but they're wrong.] (175–76)

Since Inés was described before this passage as cloistered and marry-ing by default (not motivated by love), the reader is led to assume that she suffers such neglect and the resultant desperation that so often occurs. Yet, in a maneuver reminiscent of Cervantes, the narrator pulls the rug out from under us, as it were. Far from being neglected, her husband es-teems her as befits her worth and beauty. Once more we see Zayas toying with her reader, leading us to predict an inevitable outcome, which, in this case, turns out to be the opposite of the anticipated marital situation.

Nonetheless, continuing with the topic of female vulnerability, the nar-rator tells us how the faithful and affectively fulfilled Inés becomes a vic-tim of male lust. A wealthy young man named Diego is smitten by Inés, and begins to pursue her indiscreetly, being so bold as to sing to her out-side her door. Seeing that Inés will not respond to his audacious advances, Diego enlists the aid of a go-between reminiscent of Celestina, to whom he gives a gold chain. The crafty bawd promises to deliver Inés to him, at which point she puts her deceitful plan into action. By obtaining one of Inés's dresses and instructing a woman of ill repute she knows to wear it, the bawd manages to convince Diego in the dark that he was in fact enjoying Inés herself. As a result, Diego confronts Inés, claiming that he has enjoyed sexual intimacy with her while she, of course, is disgusted at this allegation. She insists that the chief magistrate investigate the matter and, when the go-between confesses her deception, she is given as punishment two hundred lashes and exile from the city for six years.

Blinded by his passion and unwilling to give up, Diego now enlists the services of a Moorish necromancer who produces an effigy of Inés, telling his client that if he places this image on the desk next to a lighted candle, she will come to his house at night and lie with him. The power of the necromancer is attributed to his dealings with the Devil—activities that are identified by the narrator as running counter to the Catholic faith. For more than one month Inés (in a trancelike state) gets out of her bed, goes to his house, and spends the night with him, until one night while en route from her house to his, she is spotted by the magistrate in the company of her brother (Francisco), both of whom follow her to Diego's house. The unprincipled lover is imprisoned for his offense and the Moor is sought, but never found. (Here, too, one must nuance Stackhouse's rules of magic in Zayas's text, "if the practitioners of magic do not repent, they suffer a severe penalty" (70): the offending Moor pays no such penalty. Diego goes before the inquisitorial tribunal and is executed.)

While the magistrate has cleared the innocent Inés of any guilt, the reaction of her family—her brother, sister-in-law, and husband—is quite a different matter. The husband, Alonso, is summoned from Seville and after hearing the sequence of events he, Inés's brother, and her sister-in-law determine to punish her in spite of the fact that she had been found innocent of any wrongdoing. In hatching their plan for revenge on the innocent woman, the sister-in-law, we are told, is the most vicious of the three. More precisely, the narrator registers surprise at this fact, remarking: "De quien más pondero la crueldad es de la traidora cuñada, que siquiera por mujer, pudiera tener piedad de ella" (131) [What surprises me most is the cruelty of the treacherous sister-in-law who, being a woman, should have taken pity on her (192)]. In voicing this sentiment, Zayas reveals, yet again, her commitment to the representation of human complexity, and the rejection of gender type-casting.[43]

The three decide that a fitting punishment would be to seal her up in a room that is painfully small. So narrow is this space that she cannot even sit down, reduced to either standing or crouching slightly. The only open space is a tiny opening the size of a folded sheet of paper through which she can breathe and also receive the miserable rations she is given in order to make her death a protracted one. The sister-in-law is in charge of the key and of the food and water by which the innocent Inés somehow manages to live for a period of six years. At the end of this period, a kindly neighbor discovers her, which leads to Inés's release and her relatives' incarceration. She is by now thirty years old, her formerly beautiful hair infested by animals, her flesh worm-eaten, and she is totally blind.

Each of the three treacherous relatives is condemned to death, in spite of the sister-in-law's claim that she was simply following the husband's orders. Meanwhile Inés's health is restored except for her blindness, which is incurable. We learn, moreover, that she lives in saintly fashion within a convent, enjoying the sizeable inheritance left by her husband and brother. From this allegedly true story, the narrator offers an explicit lesson to be extracted, namely that the cruelty of men knows no bounds:

Ved ahora si [esta narración] puede servir de buen desengaño a las damas, pues si a las inocentes les sucede esto, ¿qué esperan las culpadas? Pues en cuanto a la crueldad para con las desdichadas mujeres, no hay que fiar en hermanos ni maridos, que todos son hombres. Y como dijo el rey don Alfonso el Sabio, que el corazón del hombre es bosque de espesura, que nadie le puede hallar senda, donde la crueldad, bestia fiera y indomable, tiene su morada y habitación. (138)

[See now if (this story) serves as a good disenchantment for women: if this is what happens to the innocent, what can the guilty expect? Regarding cruelty to unfortunate women, one can't trust in brothers or in husbands for they are, after all, men. As King Alfonso the Wise said, man's heart is a deep and trackless jungle where cruelty, a wild and savage beast, has its home and its hearth.] (197)

At the conclusion to the tale, the members of the *sarao* discuss the aspects which have made the greatest impression on them. The brother is blamed more than the husband, given that the latter wasn't a blood relation. The extremity of the torture is condemned given that, even if she had been proven guilty of willed adultery, she would have deserved the quick execution that results from that offense. The sister-in-law is found to be the most reprehensible since the most cruel when she should have been the most merciful, given that she was a woman: "A la que más culpaban era a la cuñada, pues ella, como mujer, pudiera ser más piadosa, estando cierta, como se averiguó, que privada de sentido con el endemoniado encanto había caído en tal yerro" (139) [The one they blamed most was the sister-in-law because she, being a woman, should have been merciful, particularly when it had been proven that the diabolical spell had deprived doña Inés of all consciousness when she'd fallen into error (198)].

Although no one in the assembled party remarks about the necromancer's magic, we see how it serves in *La inocencia castigada* to provide an exotic alternative to the predictable domestic honor-revenge *comedias*, and even more to reveal the *bosque de espesura* (dense, i.e., dark forest) that is human nature itself—irrespective of gender.

El verdugo de su esposa (His Wife's Executioner)

The supernatural, in the case of *El verdugo de su esposa* (II, 3) centers on a different form of supernatural power, namely the intercession of the Virgin Mary. Yet in spite of such extraordinary intervention, we find in this tale another case of unconscionable torture committed by an unjust husband. Also related to *La inocencia castigada* is the fact that the wicked murder of the innocent wife (Roseleta) results directly, even more directly than in the previous tale, from the jealousy of a woman (Angelina), who is anything but angelic, as her name would have us believe.

We learn that in Palermo there are two men, named Juan and Pedro, who are such good friends that they are routinely referred to as "los dos amigos." The topos of the two friends has a very long history, but the best known literary exploitation of it during Zayas time is the intercalated tale of *El curioso impertinente* (*The Tale of Foolish Curiosity*), which Cervantes includes in part I of *Don Quijote* (chaps. 33–35). Nise begins her narration by telling us that Juan and Pedro are the characters' real names and that they are in fact:

Tan grandes amigos, por haberse desde niños criado juntos, mediante el [sic] amistad de los padres, que en diciendo *los dos amigos*, ya se conocía que eran don Pedro y don Juan. Juntos paseaban, de una misma forma vestían, y en no estando don Pedro en su casa, le hallaban en la de don Juan, y si faltaba éste de la suya, era seguro que estaría en la de don Pedro, porque un instante no se hallaban divididos, aunque vivían en casas diferentes, todo lo más del tiempo estaban juntos. (146)

[Because their parents were close friends and they'd been brought up together from earliest childhood, Don Juan and Don Pedro (these were their proper names) were dear friends. When anyone referred to "the two friends," everyone knew they meant Don Pedro and Don Juan. The two always went around together and even wore the same clothes; if you couldn't find Don Pedro at home, you'd find him at Don Juan's and likewise, if Don Juan wasn't home he was sure to be over at Don Pedro's because they were never apart for an instant even though they lived in different houses.] (115)

Difficulties ensue for these paradigmatic friends, however, when Pedro marries Roseleta. She is as predictably beautiful as all the other females who populate Zayas's text, and she serves as an emblem of the paradoxical curse that beauty so often represents: "[Era] esta señora como [bella] desgraciada, que por la mayor parte se apetece lo mismo que viene a ser cuchillo de nuestras vidas (146) [The beautiful lady (was) as unfortunate as she was beautiful, for as a rule we desire exactly that which will become a dagger to our lives (109)].

As in Cervantes' story, here too the unmarried friend determines that he should no longer frequent his friend's house given that he had just married and his wife is so beautiful. On repeated occasions Juan makes excuses in order to avoid frequenting his friend's house as before, but Pedro (like his Cervantine counterpart, Anselmo) insists on his company. And, as we might expect, the inevitable happens as Juan falls hopelessly in love with his best friend's wife, reproaching himself very sternly, but ultimately unable to restrain his passion.

Repeated attempts by Juan to mask his emotions fail and, recalling Cervantes' extensive use of architectural and military metaphor in his analogous tale, he lies to Pedro "por empezar a poner la primera piedra en el cimiento de su pretension" (149) [to begin laying the foundation for his campaign (118)]. In order to dissemble his love for Roseleta, he claims to be suffering for love of Angelina. After living with this lie for two months, Juan finally declares his love in a moment when Pedro is absent. Roseleta is horrified at this admission, and for days thereafter refuses to take any meals with him. The oblivious Pedro even asks Juan to sing a love song he has composed, one whose context Roseleta understands all too well, but her husband not at all.

Juan is angry at Roseleta's rejection, but undaunted in his pursuit, writes a total of six love letters to her. She, in turn, is so angry that she takes the risk of showing them to her husband, although the narrator is careful to underscore the danger involved: "sin mirar riesgos, ni temer peligros, con una crueldad de basilisco, tomando éste [papel] y los demás que tenía guardados, se fue a su marido" (157) [without considering risk or fearing danger, cruel as a basilisk, she took it and all the other letters she'd kept and went to her husband (124)].

As we would expect, words fail to express Pedro's emotional state at this double revelation, first to know that his wife is being shamelessly pursued by another man, and second, that the man in question is his best friend. After reading the letters over and over again, Pedro plots a secret revenge, telling Roseleta to write back to Juan a letter feigning reciprocal love. For his part, Juan prays to the Virgin "que no mirando la ofensa que iba a hacerle, le librase de peligro y le alcanzase perdón de su precioso Hijo (159) [that she would overlook the offense he was about to commit, that she would protect him from peril, that she would intercede on his behalf begging her precious son's pardon (126)].

Directly after offering this prayer, he hears a voice that is coming from one of three hanged men who calls him by name. We learn that a miracle has occurred, whereby God has not only revived a man from the dead, but, in addition, given him the likeness of Juan so that he can elude the assassins who shoot and stab him before throwing his corpse down a well into which they hurl many rocks to ensure that the corpse will not be discovered.

Juan repents of his sinful thoughts not only to God and the Virgin, but to Pedro (who assumes that he must be a ghost). It was, we learn, only the temporary impostor—who was already dead—whom Pedro shot and stabbed. And, although Roseleta had never offended Pedro in thought (much less in deed), he resolves to kill her. There follows a lengthy series of motives for Pedro's resolve to kill his wife. The extensive nature of these multiple interpretations is striking, once more illustrating Zayas's concern for the effect that it will have on her readers and the wealth of possibilities which can give rise to human agency.

Reflecting on this very unwarranted reaction by the husband, some readers assume that he simply tired of Roseleta's beauty, others that he could not live with the shame caused by his association with Juan since it had become known throughout the city. Zayas observes the pleasure elicited for the audience by this unfortunate turn of events: "como el vulgo es novelero, y no todos bien entendidos, cada uno daba su parecer" (167) [People love a good story and not everyone is well intentioned so everyone had a different opinion about what had happened (132)]. The effect of this comment about the universal love of gossip is to underscore the pleasure derived from this sensationalist topic of unwarranted wife-murder. Beyond pathos, Zayas knows that her readers and auditors are experiencing titillation.

Further observations regarding Pedro's plan are offered, such as the issue of whether he satisfied his honor by killing Roseleta in spite of her innocence. Some say that he acted in the right since the slightest innuendo besmirches one's reputation. Others question why she revealed Juan's courtship to Pedro. Some criticized her for telling Pedro, that she would have been able to end the attempted liaison herself. Still others averred that she could not have maintained her honor without revealing Juan's perfidy to Pedro. No consensus is reached; some condemn him while others applaud his action.

To make matters worse for the innocent Roseleta, Angeliana decides to take her own revenge on her, furious at the fact that Juan had courted and then rejected her for Roseleta. She puts her plan into action by wooing Pedro, and when Roseleta becomes aware of this affair she writes to

Angeliana with an ultimatum: either she will desist in the adultery or she will die because of it. In order to further her treacherous plan, Angeliana shows this letter to Pedro, telling him in addition that she knows for a fact that Juan has already enjoyed Roseleta's body: "le dixo: que ella sabía por muy cierto que don Juan había gozado a Roseleta" (169) [she told him that she knew for sure that don Juan had in fact enjoyed Roseleta's favors (134)]. She then convinces Pedro that he must kill Roseleta both as a cuckolded husband and for Angeliana's own sake, as revenge for her having stolen away Juan.

Pedro not only bleeds Roseleta to death, but, in addition, exhibits the grotesque ability to feign laments and tears of mourning. His exclamations of grief are accompanied by similarly false gestures—frenetically embracing her lifeless body and kissing her hands. Roseleta is laid to rest amid great mourning and that very night Angeliana brazenly stays in Pedro's house, which leads people to suspect that he killed his wife, yet nothing can be proved. Pedro marries his new lover after a scandalously brief period of mourning for Roseleta, after which he looks for Juan in order to murder him, but fails to do so because "no lo permitió Dios" (171).

Roseleta's suffering is referred to by the discussants after the story as a *martirio* (martyrdom) unwarranted by her innocence—yet, they agree that given God's inscrutability, there must be a reason for it. Pedro and Angeliana go unpunished in this life, but will presumably suffer in the next. Juan, we are told, died in peace. The miraculous transformation of the hanged man into the likeness of Juan is accepted as entirely possible, although Zayas goes to considerable lengths to register the group's awareness of the disparity between civil and divine justice. The exemplary Roseleta dies cruelly while the man who led to her domestic peril, Juan, dies peacefully. Likewise the perfidious couple of Pedro and Angeliana we are told, lived "en paz, aunque no seguro[s] del castigo de Dios, que si no se les dió en esta vida, no les reservaría dél en la otra" (171) [in peace fearing only God's punishment which, if it didn't catch them in this life, surely would in the next" (135)].

The supernatural, in this case a miracle, leads to several interpretations. It signifies, of course, God's omnipotence. Yet the recipient of this benefit is the instigator of Roseleta's suffering. He made her life impossible so that she met an untimely death while both he and her murderous husband are rewarded; Juan enjoys a peaceful death, and Pedro a long life with his monstrous new bride. The suggestion that they will burn in the hereafter somehow fails to satisfy the group, which dwells on the disparity between civil and divine justice. Again, we see Zayas's ability to weave a compelling narrative tapestry that will gain the approval of the literary censors while appealing to a diverse readership; those looking for an example of God's supernatural power, of His inscrutability, of the chasm separating human and divine law, of justice or injustice as it pertains to the honor code, of transgressive romantic intrigue, or, ultimately, of the imponderability of human existence.

La perseguida triunfante (Triumph over Persecution)

A much more elaborate intervention by the Virgin, in fact a series of appearances by her, play a crucial role in La perseguida triunfante (II, 9). Indeed, of all the tales Zayas constructs, this one reads most like hagiography, so protracted and extreme is the martyrdom of the protagonist, Beatriz, whose name means "the blessed one." In etymological fidelity to her name, this Beatriz, unlike her perfidious namesake in El prevenido engañado (Forewarned but Not Forearmed), is blessed by witnessing the repeated incarnation of the Virgin who rescues her from extraordinary danger on a number of occasions.

The scene opens in Hungary, where King Ladislao dies, being succeeded by his son who bears the same name, a man known as a "príncipe generoso, gallardo, de afable condición y bien entendido, y de todas maneras amable" (340) [a generous, handsome, good-natured prince, intelligent and pleasing in every way (311)]. Yet, as so often happens with people initially described in such totalizing ways, as paragons of virtue or embodiments of evil in its various forms, here too the paradigm breaks down. The prince, soon to become king, shows himself to be unjustifiably cruel and profoundly inconsiderate as far as his wife is concerned.

Against his will, Ladislao is pressured by his kinsmen into marrying, as a result of which he chooses Beatriz, daughter to the king of England. Even before the wedding, however, Ladislao's beloved brother Federico falls madly in love with her, pursuing her wrecklessly even after the wedding has taken place. He persists in his audacity to the point where, once Ladislao has left to wage a military campaign, Beatriz is forced to imprison Federico in a cage for a period of more than one year in order to defend herself from his lecherous advances. Unlike the torturously small space in which Inés was confined in *La inocente castigada*, however, the cage devised by Beatriz is a rather spacious and luxurious one, where the prisoner is allowed to play cards, read books, and indulge in other pastimes as well.[44] The intent of this space is not to deprive Federico of his accustomed pleasures, but simply to guarantee that he cannot rape his sister-in-law. And as Ladislao's return becomes imminent, Beatriz releases her lascivious brother-in-law.

Upon Ladislao's return, Federico falsifies the situation entirely, telling his brother that he was imprisoned by an insanely vindictive Beatriz because he would not yield to her inappropriate advances. Without pausing to hear her side of the story, Ladislao immediately instructs some of his men to take her to a remote part of the forest at which point they are to cut her eyes from their sockets since "por mirar deshonesta había causado su deshonor" (361–62) [(they) had brought about his dishonor through their immoral glance (329)]. She is to be left there in her helpless blind state to be eaten by wild beasts or to die of hunger, two punishments deemed appropriate by the monarch for the crime he believes his wife to have committed against his brother and himself.

Beatriz's overt association with hagiography, specifically with martyrdom, is alluded to by her from this point in the tale and until its ultimate conclusion.[45] More precisely, she indicates that God is testing her, thereby offering an example of literal versus metaphorical blindness, of the physical blindness that symbolizes spiritual insight.

As the blinded Beatriz invokes the Virgin Mary a miracle occurs; her eyesight is restored by a woman whom she feels certain she has seen before. Found wandering in the forest by a German hunting party, Beatriz calls herself Rosamunda and is befriended by Octavio, the duke of Germany, who offers her honorable lodging with his family. In the meantime, Ladislao ascertains his wife's innocence, at which point Federico says he wants to find her, to restore her to her rightful place in society—whereas, in fact, he wants instead to find her in order to rape and then kill her.

Magic figures prominently in this tale, entering the scene first in the form of a ring supplied to Federico by a magician who is actually the Devil in disguise. The purpose of the ring is to help the machinating Federico kill his brother so that he may inherit the kingdom of Hungary. The prodigious quality of this ring is that it allows the wearer to change identity, and Federico takes advantage of it by successfully disguising himself in a way that "en virtud de su anillo no podía ser conocido" (376) [by virtue of the ring could not be recognized (339)]. He accompanies the "doctor," who informs the duke that he will soon die at the hands of someone he loves. The duke finds forged love letters written by his enemy, Duke Fabio, to Rosamunda/Beatriz, and by her to him.

At the discovery of these letters the duchess demands that Rosamunda be killed, while Rosamunda herself just wants to die, weary of death threats resulting from the various false accusations leveled against her. Even more predictable than Rosamunda's desire to die is Federico's entrapment of her, telling her that she is about to be raped and then killed. Yet while we may anticipate that this will indeed be her grim fate (bearing in mind all the other unjustly maligned and abused females we encounter in the *Novelas*), this is not the way Rosamunda's life ends. Instead we witness a second miracle as she undergoes a startling double metamorphosis, first into a giant and then into a ferocious lion who wounds Federico severely. Having aided Rosamunda, the mysterious and kindly woman disappears leaving her safe from her perfidious brother-in-law, but once again abandoned.

A third miracle occurs when she meets the emperor of Germany, his wife, and especially their six-year-old son who—to their surprise—embraces her as if she were his closest relative. As a result of this response by their child, the emperor and empress invite her to live with them as the little prince's governess. Yet this amiable situation is also thwarted by the Devil and Federico, as they drug Rosamunda and kill the child, placing the bloody dagger in the unconscious woman's hand. When she awakens she invokes God, after which the emperor orders her head and hand to be severed, and the child buried. Described by the narrator as an "inocente y mansa corderilla cercada de carniceros lobos" (392) [the gentle and innocent lamb surrounded by ravening wolves (352)], and on the point of execution, Rosamunda is rescued a third miraculous time by her secret friend who offers her refuge now in a hidden cave containing a large crucifix, the *Horas de Nuestra Señora* (*Book of Hours of Our Lady*), various saints' lives, and hay which can serve as her bed.

Known by the name of Florinda during the time she has spent with the emperor's family, she is found to have disappeared on the point of execution. This event is judged variously to be either a *milagro* or an *encantamiento* (394), whose effect is magnified by the added discovery that the young prince has been brought back to life. He implores his father not to kill Florinda, saying "No maten a Florinda, que no me mató Florinda; antes por Florinda tengo vida. Tráiganme a Florinda. Vayan presto, no la maten, que está inocente; que no me mató sino un traidor, por hacerle mal a ella." (395) [Do not kill Florinda! Florinda didn't kill me. It's thanks to Florinda that I've come back to life. Bring Florinda to me. Go quickly, don't kill her, for she's innocent. I was killed by a traitor who wanted to do her harm (354)].

After Beatriz/Rosamunda/Florinda has spent a total of eight years in the cave, the kindly woman who had led her there returns and reveals her true identity as the Virgin Mary, "la Madre de Dios." Beatriz is dazzled by the Virgin's appearance, beholding her wearing the raiments of her traditional iconographic portrayal: the diaphanous blue mantle, surrounded by radiant light and a host of angels (397).

The narrator (Estefanía) takes this opportunity to speak disparagingly of men by citing the authority of Alfonso X, recalling once again the image of ferocious beasts invoked by Laura in narrating *La inocencia castigada*:

de lo que más me admiro es del ánimo de las mujeres de esta edad, que sin tener el amparo y favor de la Madre de Dios, se atreven a fiarse del corazón de los hombres, bosques de espesura, que así los llamó el rey don Alfonso el Sabio, en lo verdadero, y el dios Momo en lo fabuloso, donde no hay sino leones de crueldades, lobos de engaños, osos de malicias y serpientes de iras, que siempre las están despedazando el honor y las vidas, hartando su hambre y sed rabiosa en sus delicadas carnes, que bien delicada es la vida y bien débil el honor. Y con ver salir a las otras despedazadas, se entran ellas sin ningún miedo en ellas. (400)

[What most surprises me is the courage of women in this day and age who, without the favor and succor of the Mother of God, dare to trust in the hearts of men.

The great king Alfonso the Wise said man's heart was like the hypocritical god Momus with regard to falseness and like a dense wilderness as far as truthfulness is concerned, a wilderness filled with lions in cruelty, wolves in deception, bears in malice, and serpents in wrath, always tearing to shreds women's lives and honor, sating their ravenous hunger and thirst on their delicate flesh, for fragile is honor and delicate is life. But fearlessly women enter the fray, even knowing how many are torn to shreds.] (424)

In a final transformation, the Virgin instructs Beatriz to dress as a man, giving her the identity of a *médico milagroso* (miraculous physician) who can heal the victims of the plague that is decimating Hungary. Among those afflicted by the plague is Federico, who finally confesses the perfidy he committed against Beatriz, his "false magic" as opposed to her "true cure." And as a result of his confession, Beatriz cures Federico whereupon she reveals her true identity to Ladislao. The ineffectual "doctor" who is actually the Devil, vanishes—literally—in a puff of smoke, admitting his defeat, whereas: "A la parte que estaba Beatriz con su divina defensora era un resplandeciente paraíso, y a la que el falso doctor y verdadero demonio, una tiniebla y oscuridad" (407) [Where Beatriz stood with her heavenly protrectress, they beheld a perfect light and, where the false doctor and true demon had been, darkness and black shadow (363)].

After Federico has been forgiven by Beatriz, she becomes a nun, and Ladislao becomes a monk once he has given his kingdom to Federico who, in turn, marries Beatriz's sister, Isabel. After Ladislao has died, Beatriz writes down his life and also her own, at which point she too expires.

Perhaps as a result of the tale's clarity with respect to Christian ideology, the auditors do not register discussion of it. We are simply told by the narrator that they enjoyed it in spite of its great length: "Con tanto gusto escuchaban todos el desengaño que doña Estefanía refirió, que, aunque largo, no causó hastío al gusto, antes quisieran que durara más" (409) [Everybody so enjoyed the disenchantment Doña Estefanía told that even though it was very long, their interest hadn't flagged; indeed, they wished it had lasted longer (365)].

This virtual silence on the part of the group is especially striking given the auditors' routine observations and disagreements at the conclusion of the other narratives. Beyond this accustomed interpretive practice, the extreme nature of the events that transpire and Zayas's extensive use of magic in *La perseguida triunfante* invite commentary. The tale's confrontation of diabolic magic with the Christian supernatural is dramatized by the triple victimization of a woman by a man, the heroine's brother-in-law. Indeed, Patricia Grieve sees this tale as "the one in which [Zayas] develops her attitudes towards violence against women, the silence of heroines, rewarding the villain, and the question of experience and learning as forms of education."[46]

While the representation of the female condition and its implications for societal attitudes are key here, so is magic; indeed the narrative details several different types of magic. As Stackhouse has observed, the mysterious doctor (the Devil in disguise) exhibits three categories of diabolical magic: (1) magic that is not restricted either by space or time, as when he acknowledges that "pues con [la ciencia] alcanzo y sé cuanto pasa en el mundo" (371) [by means of my science I know all that happens in the world (my translation)]; (2) secret knowledge of the natural world (e.g., the marvelous properties of certain plants and stones), as when he employs a soporific herb to induce sleep in his victim, and lends Federico a stone by means of which he can metamorphose himself at will; (3) the ability to interpret symbols (verbal and otherwise), as registered by his use of the description contained in Federico's ring to convince Ladislao of Beatriz's alleged infidelity.

In effect, "at their initial meeting, the magician already knows the prince's history and his unhappy circumstances. Second is the knowledge of the special virtues or hidden powers of plants, stones, and animals. Federico's cohort uses an herb to induce sleep; he uses a stone to enable the prince to change his appearance at will. The virtues of symbols—effigies, glyphs, and words—comprise the third. The inscription on Federico's ring enables him to convince his skeptical brother, the king, of Queen Beatriz' infidelity."[47]

Addressing the first issue, that of female victimization, its presence in this tale virtually from beginning to end is indisputable. Yet we must interpret it according to the epistemology of hagiography, rather than grafting a dehistoricized, secular, modern-day reading onto it. Grieve's discussion of three *novelas* and their hagiographic paradigms is impressively insightful in many ways, yet to say that by means of *La perseguida triun-*

fante Zayas "dismantles the very foundation of hagiography," (104) "subverting the ideology of the Church-sanctioned genre," (86) seems somewhat debatable. Neither the narrative itself nor Estefanía's recounting of it dismantle the very foundation of hagiography. To be sure, it is the story of a woman who is unjustly mistreated in the extreme, and the narrator offers a number of intercalated expressions of outrage at the way in which men treat women. But this does not diminish Beatriz's function as a paragon of Christian forbearance. Likewise, it does not vilify men definitively, given that Ladislao and Federico confessed and repented their unjust treatment of her. Since the time when the writing of female saints' lives began, men have been, to an overwhelming degree, the victimizers. Indeed, the female saints themselves often reproach men as Estefanía does. Her remarks may be quantitatively greater in number and even in length, but they are not qualitatively different than those we find in hagiography.

The fact that Beatriz becomes a nun is also entirely predictable if we think of the way in which saints' lives end. If the protagonist actually survives to make a choice, he or she invariably chooses the chastity of the monastery or convent rather than the corruptibility of conjugal life. Beyond evidence from the hagiographic paradigm that confirms Zayas is not subverting Christian ideology, we also have to think of the tale's effect on its readers. Clearly the Inquisition would never have permitted a hagiographically subversive text to see the light of day.

We should bear in mind the central importance of the frame commentary here as in the other stories. For while the auditors register surprisingly little discussion at the end of *La perseguida triunfante*, the narrator, the nun Estefanía, reveals a notable degree of distance from the story before she tells it. In the sentence before her narration begins, she addresses the men in the audience in a humorous vein, saying: "Si de mi desengaño no quedaren bien castigados, lo quedarán, si me buscan en estando en mi casa, porque los entregaré a una docena de compañeras, que será como echarlos a los leones" (339) [If the gentlemen aren't properly castigated by my disenchantment, they will be when they seek me at home in my convent because I'll turn them over to a dozen of my sisters, which would be like throwing them to the lions (310)]. Not only is the equation of nuns with ferocious lions incongruously humorous, it is striking because Beatriz, we recall, was transformed—in a very serious, indeed miraculous manner—into a ferocious lion when Federico sought to rape and kill her.

The lion motif in this tale warrants particular comment, revealing the many—frequently conflicting—levels of interpretation at work throughout the collection. Estefanía's image of the nuns as vicious lions is not only humorous, it functions ultimately as black humor, given that Beatriz's metamorphosis into a lion was designed to underscore in graphic terms her somber theme, namely the terrible threat posed by men for women. To further complicate the issue, Estefanía's reference to Alfonso X's depiction of men as "cruel lions" effects an additional reversal, this time in terms of gender.

The reason for this program of leonine references is to underscore the Zayesque obsession with polysemy, symbolic and thematic, that we find at so many turns in her text. This magical aspect of interpretation is reinforced by the fact that Estefanía speaks so bitterly about men, not on the basis of personal experience, but of reading: "Me consolaré con saber que no he sido engañada, y que no hablaré por experiencia, sino por ciencia, porque me sacrifiqué desde muy niña a Esposo que jamás me ha engañado ni engañará" (339) [I do not speak from my own experience but from knowledge. At a very young age I dedicated myself to a spouse who has never deceived me and never will (310)].

That Zayas makes explicit the abuse of women by men by means of Estefanía's overt condemnations is indisputable. Yet rather than subverting Church doctrine, Zayas, I believe, evokes the blood and gore characteristic of hagiography for a number of reasons, but without devaluing it. For the devoted reader of religious literature, Zayas offers a beautifully written saint's life. For the readers who have already read eighteen of the *Novelas*, many of which are full of horrific bodily cruelty, this tale provides suggestions of further gruesomeness (removed eyes and a nearly severed head and hand), but with the unexpected restoration of these body parts.

The appeal of violence in hagiography is attested to by Marina Warner as she explains the genre's pornographic, sadomasochistic sensationalism:

In Christian hagiography, the sadomasochistic content of the paeans to male and female martyrs is startling, from the early documents like the Passion of *Saints Perpetua and Felicity* into the high Middle Ages. But the particular focus on women's torn and broken flesh reveals the psychological obsession of the religion with sexual sin, and the tortures that pile up one upon the other with pornographic repetitiousness underline the identification of the female with the perils of sexual contact.[48]

The reader is excited by the sadistic detail that is anticipated, but here is surprised as the narrator reveals the miraculous healing effected by the Virgin Mary. An additional use of hagiographic violence is made by Zayas in her nineteenth tale in that it serves to justify or authorize the displays of excessive violence found at so many points in her twenty-story text.[49] In this tale, as with the other four magical narratives, we find wide appeal generated by the polyfaceted construction of her text to be the true magic of the book.

4

In the Labyrinth:
Exemplary Excess

The world as a confused labyrinth . . . expresses the situation of a profoundly disrupted society.

— Maravall, Culture of the Baroque in Spain

Countering the Example

Exemplum denotes a dynamic process consisting of two apparently opposite terms — a *model* and also its representation or *copy*. This idea persists in the Spanish noun *ejemplar*, meaning a copy of a book. If we consider the model — the ideas Zayas explicitly articulates — by comparison with its representation within the text, we are faced with an undeniable degree of axiological contradiction or interference.

Zayas actively invites us to consider the issue of exemplarity, didacticism, in her *Novelas amorosas y ejemplares*. Both her sharply explicit exhortations to the reader (delivered through her narrators) and the implicit observations and multiple disagreements that arise in the *sarao* participants lead us inevitably to question the actual pedagogical efficacy of her text. Indeed, this exercise has resulted in a surprising diversity of responses. The stories have been construed (antithetically) either as a celebration of the status quo or a virulent rejection of it. One view, the conclusion arrived at by Marcia Welles is that, taken as a whole, "the tales depict the quest out of the chaos or evil in the actual world towards an idealized state where opposing forces are united. The final harmony is represented by the institution of the Christian marriage (or 'marriage' to God in the convent), which by uniting the individual with the community maintains the *status quo* and insures social stability."[1]

Allegory is frequently an agent of exemplarity and Welles finds the men and women whom we encounter in Zayas's tales to be participating in this discursive mode, serving as abstractions rather than individualized characters: "the specific character portrayed is clearly depersonalized of any individual sense and converted into an abstract 'Everyman,' acquiring generic significance as 'Man' and 'Woman'" (29). Allegory is also at the heart of feminist readings of Zayas, but with the opposite results; the *Novelas* are not designed to "maintain the *status quo* and insure social stability," but its antithesis, to interrogate the system, pointing out its inherent failings.[2] A third possibility, voiced by Allesandra Melloni, finds not a feminist message, but rather an acceptance of masculinist discourse.[3]

Less wedded to binary oppositions, more invested in the unresolved tensions operative in Zayas, are critics like Melveena McKendrick and Alicia Redondo. Pointing out the three basic lures of literature, with universally appealing themes of violence, eroticism, and sentimentality, Redondo observes the clearly problematic juncture of Zayas's "conservadurismo ideológico, que exige castigar a las mujeres, y su feminismo que puede llegar a ser muy agresivo"[4] [ideological conservatism which reproaches women, and her feminism, which can be very aggressive at times]. Along these lines, María del Palomo sees as a key structuring principle in Zayas the tension between a given *desengaño* and the frame discussion that surrounds it.[5] As noted above, McKendrick also perceives an ultimately problematic (unresolved) work in terms of gender issues: "Melodramatic as her stories are, her views are balanced. She does not denounce men and she offers no practical suggestions for the improvement of women's lot."[6] I would modify this statement by saying that she does denounce men, but she also denounces women. And that, by the end of the work, she is calling for a return to the (mythical) paradise of gender relations represented within the poetic economy of her text by the age of the Catholic Kings:

¿De qué pensáis que procede el poco ánimo que hoy todos tenéis, que sufrís que estén los enemigos dentro de España, y nuestro Rey en campaña, y vosotros en el Prado y en el río, llenos de galas y trajes femeniles, y los pocos que le acompañan, suspirando por las ollas de Egipto? De la poca estimación que hacéis de las mujeres, que a fe que si las estimarais y amárades como en otros tiempos se hacía, por no verlas en poder de vuestros enemigos, vosotros mismos os ofreciérades, no digo yo a la guerra y a pelear, sino a la muerte, poniendo la garganta al cuchillo, como en otros tiempos, y en particular en el del rey Fernando el Católico se hacía, donde no era menester llevar los hombres por fuerza, ni maniatados, como ahora, infelicidad y desdicha de nuestro Rey católico, sino que ellos mismos ofrecían sus haciendas y personas: el padre, por defender la hija; el hermano, por la hermana; el esposo, por la esposa, y el galán por la dama. (455)

[I swear if you did love and cherish women as was the way in former times, you'd volunteer not just to go to war and fight but to die, exposing your throat to the knife to keep them from falling into the hands of the enemy. This is the way it was in earlier days, particularly under King Ferdinand the Catholic. Then it wasn't necessary to conscript men, forcing them into service almost with their hands tied, the way it is today (causing our Catholic king unhappiness and great misfortune). Men used to offer up their possessions and their lives, the father to defend his daughter, the brother to defend his sister, the husband to defend his wife, the suitor to defend his lady.] (400)

How do we account for this notable disparity, indeed *copia* of contradictory interpretations? We should, I think, recall the insight articulated by Cesare Segre: "The codes employed by the addresser, and his motivations as well, derive from the cultural context within which he is inserted, while the addressee [or reader of the same or later eras] will have recourse to the codes at his disposition in order to interpret the text."[7] In other words, the reception by readers of any era is contingent on the cultural codes of the time. And the era in question for Zayas is the tension-laden perspective of the seventeenth century.

Exemplarity during this period was a highly developed discursive mode, one that Cervantes and all of his novelistic exponents addressed in one form or another. And here, too, the work of Zayas is especially thought-provoking. In responding to the notable lack of explicit exemplarity in Cervantes' *Novelas ejemplares* in his own novella collection, the *Novelas a Marcia Leonarda*, Lope is highly critical of his rival. Beginning with a rather lukewarm endorsement, "No le faltó gracia y estilo a Miguel de Cervantes" [Cervantes didn't lack grace and style], he moves on to a stern judgment of these short stories because of their somewhat ambiguous exemplarity, "Podrían ser ejemplares como algunas de las *Historias trágicas* del Bandelo, pero habían de escribirlos hombres científicos o por lo menos grandes cortesanos, gente que halla en los desengaños notables sentencias y aforismos"[8] [they could be exemplary like some of Bandello's *Tragic Histories*, but they should be written by moralists or at least great writers, people who find noteworthy *sententiae* and aphorisms in the disenchanting tales (my translation)]. By contrast, Peter Coccozella judges Zayas to be immune to this charge of ambiguity: "Lope's tendentious criticism of Cervantes could never apply to Zayas' *novelas* simply because Zayas went to great lengths to compensate for the pointlessness that only Lope would dare impute to the author of the *Quijote*."[9] Lope's reproach is, however, tongue-in-cheek, given the ponderous, calculatedly ludicrous academic exemplarity with which he encumbers his four tales, an attack directed at the conservative neo-Aristotelians (the so-called *hombres científicos*) who were actively condemning his work.[10]

We should bear in mind that whereas we are in the habit of thinking that the *exemplum* is a rather transparent and easily interpreted discursive form, it can also be a very slippery one, as John D. Lyons explains:

The example is a dependent statement drawing its meaning from the controlling generality. As dependent statements grow into complex narratives, however, the number of other concepts that can be illustrated by the narrative begins to threaten the control of the generality. The dependent statement may bring details that cast an entirely new light on the apparently simple generality being illustrated, or both writer and reader may be carried away by the richness of the concrete instance to the neglect of the concept being illustrated. (34)

It is precisely this *threat*, the often protean quality of words, that Zayas dramatizes in her narrative. Aware of the potential distance separating words from the things they seek to describe, Zayas seems to enjoy this threat, reveling in the ambiguity of discourse, of perception — in the ambiguity of epistemology itself. And she does so in keeping with her interest in creating a text that will appeal to a wide readership, one that will *engolosinarse* (become tempted by, addicted to) her text. Such polysemy or "excess" is what Barthes defines as the "pleasure of the text." Zayas accomplishes this semantic complexity by discrepancies in the perceptions of characters and narrators on the diegetic level, and by the group frame-discussions that surround each tale. We are never allowed to lose sight of Emile Benveniste's crucial distinction present in the narration of any objective *histoire* (third-person speech in the past without intervention of the speaker) by the inescapable subjectivity of *discours* (speech in which the speaker tries to influence his audience): "[*Histoire*] characterizes the narration of past events . . . events that . . . are presented without any intervention of the speaker in the narration. . . . [*Discours*] must be understood in its widest sense: every utterance assuming a speaker and a hearer, and in the speaker, the intention of influencing the other in some way."[11]

El castigo de la miseria (The Miser's Reward)

If we consider, for example, *El castigo de la miseria* (I, 3), we see an early instance in the collection of exemplarity turned into a proliferation of excess. Resorting once more to etymological inversion, we see that Zayas chooses for her protagonists names which signify the opposite, in fact, of their true nature. This tale involves a miser named Marcos (which is also the name of a monetary unit), and a fallen woman, Isidora (whose name means a "gift of Isis," hence fecundity, bountifulness), who falsely convinces him that she is wealthy. She pursues the miser in matrimony so that she and her lover (oxymoronically referred to as Agustín, the "little august one") can run off with the six thousand ducats the miser has managed to save over the course of many years and privations. She is forced to carry out the theft when one night Marcos sees her without any makeup, revealing her false teeth and wig. Not only is he horrified to see that she is old and shriveled, but even more so as her false teeth become grotesquely entwined in his beard.

After Isidora's deception of Marcos, it is Agustín's turn to deceive his paramour by stealing the six thousand ducats from Isidora with his real girlfriend, Inés. By the conclusion of the narrative, not only does the miser die depressed and deceived, Isidora ends her days as a beggar seeking alms. It is from this chastised and destitute perspective that Isidora recounts for Alvaro, the narrator of this tale, the sequence of events.

Recalling Cervantes' novella *El casamiento engañoso (The Deceitful Marriage)*, Zayas turns a tale of a mutually deceitful pair offering an overt and stable example of justly punished deceit into a substantially more elusive one. What complicates considerably the Cervantine portrayal of classic swindlers, male and female, in Zayas's rewriting is the perspective of the narrator. He feels torn between ridicule and compassion for Marcos, although he claims in his prefatory remarks to be recounting his story for one purpose alone, namely to illustrate, "Es la miseria la más perniciosa costumbre que se puede hallar en un hombre, pues siendo miserable, luego es necio, enfadoso y cansado, y tan aborrecible a todos, sin que haya ninguno que no guste de atropellarle, y con razón. Esto se verá claramente en mi maravilla" (123) [Avarice is the most pernicious vice a man can have. When a man is greedy then he's foolish, boring, irritating, and hateful to everyone. No one wants to cross his path, and rightfully so, as you will see in my enchantment (79)].

Rather than offering an objective account with a transparent message, Alvaro reproduces as empirical truth the unreliable gossip that Isidora has either picked up or invented herself. She never lived with Marcos long enough to know the habits he practiced as a bachelor and yet she reports them as if she had been an eyewitness herself. For example she says that "hasta en verter sus excrementos guardó la regla de la observancia" (127) [even in the matter of doing his duty he was stingy (81)], or that he never lighted any candles in his house, that before they were married he would look for a discarded candle stub which he would light, then start undressing in the street so that by the time he reached his room, he could extinguish the stub. Indeed, true to the spirit of the picaresque narrator, Isidora totally dehumanizes the picaresque protagonist, speaking of him with hyperbolic contempt: "[Con el ayuno] se vino a transformar de hombre en espárrago" (126) [(Given the delicacy of his eating habits), he turned from a youth into a stalk of asparagus (80)]. In addition to the scathing indictment of his miserliness by means of these details, Alvaro even appropriates the use of contemptuous euphemism, a hallmark of the picaresque narrator, to narrate Marcos's case. For the purposes of indicating that Marcos's father was a professional beggar, we are told that he had "un padre viejo, y tanto que sus años le servían de renta para sustentarse, pues con ellos enternecía los más empedernidos corazones" (125) [(a father) so old that his many years had been their major source of income, for he used his age to soften even the hardest of hearts (80)].

Because of his extraordinary self-control, and the fact that he is neither a womanizer nor a gambler, Marcos receives, almost on a daily basis, offers of matrimony. Isidora is one of the women who has designs on him. And, in a very laconic and uncharacteristically evaluative remark, the narrator introduces her, saying that there is often a disparity between appearance and reality, that "siempre se adelantaba el vulgo más de lo que era razón" (128) [the masses exaggerate more than is reasonable].

From Alvaro's account (filtered through Isidora's malice) we get the impression that Marcos has replaced any possible sex drive entirely with pecuniary drive: "a no . . . tenerle el poco comer tan mortificado, por solo [las dos criadas] pudiera casarse con su ama" (109) [if his meager diet hadn't diminished his energy, he might have married their mistress just to get the maids (83)].

For all of the ridiculous details conveyed to us by Alvaro, however, it is clear that he also values Marcos's lack of duplicity. Unlike Cervantes' analogous figure, Campuzano, here the man is not out to trick the woman. He makes no claims about himself that are not true. And while we can surely reproach him—if he actually did say what Isidora claims, that "no woman is ugly if she is free"—he is never duplicitous. Isidora is the one who tries to ensnare him for his money. In fact, Alvaro is programmatic in his respect for Marcos's undevious ways, his guileless simplicity. When Isidora dazzles him, lying through her teeth, he is swept away, so ingenuous is the miser. Because of his simple, trusting nature, he does not perceive that Agustín is Isidora's lover, and so touchingly vows that if their marriage does not produce any children Isidora's "nephew" Agustín will inherit everything. And to top it all off, he speaks of the unscrupulous procurer as "his good friend," although, in the same breath, Alvaro refers to him as a "procurer of sorrows."

While he considers Marcos a fool, Alvaro repeatedly presents his incapacity for deceit in positive terms. We encounter the narrator's example of Marcos's trusting nature, which leads him not to request verification when Isidora presents what he assumes is her house and twelve thousand ducats for her dowry. Embroidering upon this facet of his personality, Zayas through her narrator uses another example of Marcos's simplicity to tease the members of her own aristocratic audience: "Como era Marcos de los sanos de Castilla y sencillo como un tafetán de la China, no se le hizo largo este romance, antes quisiera que durara mucho más, porque la llaneza de su ingenio no era como los filateados de la Corte, que en pasando de seis estancias se enfadan" (144) [Since Marcos was a typical Castilian rustic and as pure as silk from China, the ballad didn't seem long to him. Indeed, he wished it had lasted longer because his simple wit wasn't like the wooly wits at court who get bored after six stanzas (95)].

Perhaps the most striking example of Marcos's gullibility comes at the moment when he tries to recover the six thousand ducats which Isidora has stolen from him by resorting to the services of a magician. The magus in question is actually a student friend of Marcela, whose magic book of spells turns out to be none other than *Amadís de Gaula*, the chivalric romance which elaborately celebrates idealistic love. The narrator informs us a propos Marcela's cruel desire to utterly deceive the victimized Marcos, that evil people prey on good ones who, in turn, tend to be credulous. And such is certainly the case with Marcos. The "magician" plans his false conjuring of demons in a way that is reminiscent of the abuse inflicted upon Don Quixote with the cat in II, 46, that scratches his face mercilessly.[12] In Zayas's story the sadistic magician sets the cat on fire and it, in turn, lands on Marcos's head, scorching his hair and face. He falls to the floor in a dead faint, and eventually recovers only to feel totally humiliated as the law officers laugh when they discover that the book of conjurations he shows them is in fact the *Amadís*. When "Doña Isidora de la Venganza" sends him a letter that condemns his frugality, inviting him to contact her when he has saved up another 6,000 ducats, this is more than he can bear. Upon reading this cruel letter, Marcos is stricken by a high fever.

At this point Zayas offers her reader two different endings to *El castigo de la miseria*, one that appeared in the first Spanish edition of part I, which was omitted from all subsequent editions. It is unclear whether the rewriting occurred as a result of Zayas's concern for possible censorship by the Inquisition (something to which she was never subject) or to the very pathetic tone that the ending achieves in the first version, a tone which she may have felt was too melodramatically heavy-handed, one which tipped the scales of reader sympathy too much in favor of Marcos.

The ending in the first edition claims that everyone believes that the high fever has actually brought on Marcos's death, which is far from the case. Instead the despairing, Marcos runs into a man he recognized as the perfidious matchmaker, Gamarra, who asks him what he is doing. When Marcos reveals his plan to hang himself, Gamarra claims to be intent on taking his own life, having misappropriated and then gambled away his master's possessions. He addresses Marcos, "Temiendo esto, tomé este cordel, y me vine aqui donde vn arbol destos, y vos, seran testigos de mi desuentura, y no todos los ojos de la Corte, y si vos venís con esse mismo intento, aqui ay arboles, y cordel para los dos; y diziendo esto, sacó de la faltriquera el cordel. Agradeciendole don Marcos el socorro" [13] "['If you've come with the same intention (to hang yourself as I intend to take my own life) there are plenty of trees and ample rope for the two of us.' As he said these words, he drew rope from his purse. Marcos thanks him for his generosity (111)].

This entire conversation is overheard by a man who can see Marcos, but not his interlocutor. He sees the hanged Marcos, but only an empty noose next to him. The authorities try to ascertain the identity of Gamarra, but to no avail. The story he had told about his master's possessions is not true. From these discrepancies the law officials conclude that the other man must have been the Devil, who had fabricated the multiple lies in order to bring Marcos to the point of suicidal despair.

The second ending indicates that once he contracted the fever he soon died, an utterly miserable man. While this was Marcos's fate, Isidora, we learn, also came to misery, tricked by Agustín and Inés, who absconded on a boat to Naples with the six thousand ducats and everything else that Isidora had stolen from Marcos. Agustín became a soldier, supported by the earnings Inés had made as a courtesan while Isidora ends her days begging alms.

Alvaro finishes the narrative by indicating that the *maravilla* was narrated to him by Isidora and that he told it "para que vean los miserables el

fin que tuvo éste, y no hagan lo mismo, escarmentando en cabeza ajena"
(164) [so that misers can see what a bad end this one had. Maybe they
can learn a lesson from another's experience and not make the same mistakes (112–13)]. Yet the univocally exemplary message Alvaro purports
to offer both before and after his tale becomes highly debatable given
the victimization Marcos suffers as a result of Isidora, the matchmaker,
Agustín, Marcela, and Inés. If he did make a mistake, was it his extreme
frugality or his trust in human nature? The interpretive excess, the instability Zayas embeds within this tale remains unresolved, offering a prime
example of "both writer and reader . . . carried away by the richness of
the concrete instance to the neglect of the concept being illustrated." [14]
Zayas turns Isidora's "moralizing" text into Alvaro's novelistic script, and
into the reader's interpretive adventure.

La más infame venganza (The Most Infamous Revenge)

With the second tale of part II, La más infame venganza, we find excess,
the multiplicity of interpretations, staged both by the characters, the narrator, and the discussants of the sarao itself. Lisarda is the narrator this
time, and she is memorable for her hesitation in complying with Lisis's
injunction to speak ill of men as the victimizers of women. She reveals a
notable degree of distance in her prefatory remarks when, for example,
we are told that she addresses the topic of misandry with great reluctance
given especially the presence of her beloved Juan. As she begins her discourse we are told by the global narrator that she speaks as if her eyes
were saying "más por cumplir con la obligación que por ofenderte (Lisis)
hago esto" (171) [I do this only out of duty and in no way mean to offend
you" (68)]. Next Lisarda voices this same reservation very pointedly, saying to her hostess:

Mandásteme, hermosa Lisis, que fuese la segunda en dar desengaños a las damas,
de que deben escarmentar en sucesos ajenos, para no dejarse engañar de los hombres. Y cierto, que más por la ley de la obediencia me obligo a admitirlo que por
sentir que tengo de acertar. Lo primero porque aún no ha llegado a tiempo de
desengañarme a mí, pues aún apenas sé si estoy engañada, y mal puede quien

no sabe un arte, sea el que fuere, hablar de él, y tengo por civilidad decir mal de quien no me ha hecho mal. Y con esto mismo pudiera disculpar a los hombres; que lo cierto es que los que se quejan están agraviados, que no son tan menguados de juicio que dijeren tanto mal como las mujeres dicen. (69)

[Beautiful Lisis, you commanded that I be the second to disenchant the ladies in such a way that they can learn a lesson from what has happened to others and so they won't let themselves be deceived by men. In truth, I do this more to obey you than from any feeling that I will succeed. First because I've never been disenchanted myself; indeed I don't think I've ever been deceived. One who has had no experience of a thing can scarcely speak of that thing; besides I consider it rude to speak ill of those who have done me no ill. For that reason alone, I could excuse men. What is certain is that men who complain have been aggrieved, for they are not so lacking in judgment as to invent all the evil they tell about women.] (85)

The effect of this forematter is striking since it has an undeniable impact on the prescribed theme of part II, the exposition of the evil that men do to women. Does Lisarda really feel no animosity as she claims, or is she merely saying so in order not to alienate Juan? Is this, in other words, Zayas's way of registering the fact that no discursive situation is neutral, innocent? The silenced men in the group, we know, are understandably dissatisfied with the rules of part II, with its theme and its exclusively female narrators ("todos los hombres mal contentos de que, por no serles concedido el novelar, no podían dar muestra de las intenciones" [12]). Zayas is here underscoring contrastively the legacy of the novella which had been, with very few exceptions, presented from an exclusively male perspective.

We cannot help but notice that for someone who professes not to feel negative about the way men treat women, she succeeds in offering a resoundingly devastating account of the inhuman actions of two men, Juan and Carlos, against two women. If she is in fact lying about her attitude toward men in general in order not to offend Juan, then she seems unaware of the incriminating nature of her narrative. She claims that she can recount the tale "sin agraviar," without offending men, but this seems debatable, to say the least. Later in the narrative she clarifies her position somewhat, claiming there that La más infame venganza is intended to be a lesson for men as much as it is for women in need of disenchantment (90). If this is true, if men are in fact educable, we can not simply dismiss them as irredeemable villains, although the two male protagonists certainly portray themselves as such. The tension created between diegetic characters and extradiegetic context (including tensions existing among the partygoers themselves) reminds us of the manifold psychological motivations, narrative filters, and interpretations at issue in this, and indeed, in all of the *Novelas*.

The particular events in question also involve a brother and sister, Juan and Octavia, and her suitor, Carlos. In spite of his promises and exclamations to the contrary, Carlos has no intention of marrying Octavia because of his greater wealth and also, it seems, his father's attitude: "que entendía no había hasta entonces nacido mujer que igualase a su hijo" (71) [that the woman had not yet been born who was good enough for his son (87)]. In spite of her ignorance regarding the father's attitude, Octavia is cautious, realizing that the greater wealth of Carlos can only mean that he would never consider marrying her. Because of this duplicity exhibited by the relentless Carlos, the (global?) narrator intervenes with the exclamation, "¡Oh, qué de engaños han padecido por esta parte las mujeres, y qué de desengañadas tienen los hombres, cuando ya no tienen remedio! (71) [Oh, how many women have suffered this kind of deception, and how many men keep them deceived until it is too late! (87)]. Thus the inconsistency in Lisarda's claim not to be biased in terms of gender may be seen as consistent but countered at various points in the text by the global narrator's gendered assertions. The reader or auditor cannot know with certainty who utters which commentary since there is no indication of who speaks them (the anonymous global narrator or Lisarda herself). Yet, whether it is Zayas's authorial narrator or Lisarda herself, the discrepancy of views leads once more to excess.

Octavia's unyielding attitude does not deter Carlos from his cynical quest for her virginity. Once he attains it, Carlos initially visits Octavia with such frequency and indiscretion that he acts as though he were the "dueño de la casa" (81). But, as happens so often, for Carlos desire and possession are antithetical terms. He tires of Octavia, rejecting her for a wealthy young woman named Camila whom he marries instead. Devastated by this betrayal, Octavia asks her brother Juan to avenge her, which he does—not by pursuing the deceitful Carlos, but by disguising himself as a woman in order to gain entry to Camila's chamber whereupon he rapes her.

After more than a year of living in a convent at Carlos's suggestion, Camila is persuaded to return home. Yet Carlos refuses to eat or sleep with her, and, as for her own situation, "vivía [como] mártir" (97). This condition deteriorates even further as Carlos decides to poison her so as to eliminate the dishonor of living with a wife who has been defiled by a rival. The poison fails to kill her, however, leaving her instead in a permanently disfigured, "monstrous" form:[15] "No la quitó el veneno luego la vida, mas hinchándose toda con tanta monstruosidad, que sus brazos y piernas parecían unas gordísimas columnas, y el vientre se apartaba una gran vara de la cintura" (97) [The poison didn't kill her immediately; instead it made her whole body swell monstrously: her arms and legs looked like huge pillars and her stomach distended at least a rod from her waistline (108)]. She dies after living bedridden for six months in this lamentable state, while both Carlos and Juan disappear, and Octavia takes her to the convent, becoming wedded to the "verdadero Esposo" (98) rather than the deceitful, earthly Carlos.

For whatever reason, it seems that Lisarda is unwilling to condemn men in her narrative. In describing, for example, Carlos's cynical quest to seduce the idealistic Octavia, she resorts first to the well-known architectural metaphor of a woman's honor as a fortress under seige (Carlos "empezó primero la conquista de este fuerte" [71]; or "qué peligrosa bala para el fuerte" [73]).

Female chastity as architecture and fortress recalls especially Cervantes' exploitation of the metaphor in El curioso impertinente, the intercalated tale in Don Quijote I, 32–35, where the perverted Anselmo, husband of the virtuous Camila, gets his best friend to test his wife's chastity. He loses control of the situation which leads to labyrinthine deception culminating in the deaths of all three characters and the image of his literal house as utterly abandoned. By the coincidence in names and the asymmetry of having the architectural metaphor grafted upon Octavia, Zayas recalls El curioso impertinente contrastively. Octavia is, like her Cervantine predecessor, victimized by a deceitful male. Yet she is not guilty of dishonoring her husband with his best friend; she is not married, and, in addition, she yields to Carlos only after marrying him. As we might expect, he insists that it must be a secret ceremony for the time being.

Lisarda criticizes Octavia for not defending herself more wisely: "Cuan flacas son las mujeres, que no saben perseverar en el buen intento. Y aun por esta parte disculpo a los hombres en la poca estimación que hacen de ellas; mas disculpemos los yerros de amor con el mismo amor" (76) [How weak are those women who cannot persevere in their good intentions, and this is why I excuse men for their low opinion of women. But let us lovingly excuse love's errors (91)]. Lisarda's simultaneous condemnation of women and excuse of men here seems rather perverse.

It appears almost as though Zayas is presenting us with a misogynistic woman, or at the very least, with one who embodies multiple subject-positions, capable of condemning women while portraying their victim-ization; capable also of understanding the charge of inconstancy, the low opinion men attribute to them. It is the position of this remark, which seems strangely out of place at the moment when Octavia yields to Carlos's deception, that shocks us. The remark that women are weak in resisting temptation is a time-worn sermonic observation, but it fails to convince us as Octavia is represented in terms of a fortress under seige. Lisarda's siding with the men, saying that their contempt for women ("la poca estimación que hacen de ellas" [176]) borders on the grotesque. What Zayas does here is to offer "misappropriated *exempla*," grafting ex-emplary *dicta* onto wholly inappropriate contexts.[16] This not only shows the possibilities for excess, but also the potential uselessness of exem-plary discourse, as a successful pedagogical tool. Beyond this interroga-tion of Lisarda's values, of course, such misappropriated exemplary re-marks threaten to derail Lisis's entire exposé of male duplicity.

The extradiegetic commentary of Lisarda continues when she identi-fies her tale as a paradigmatic one—as applicable to male-female relations today as it was in the past. She indicates, moreover, that female beauty should be judged according to virtue rather than physiognomy. This stan-dard of physical beauty runs counter to the standard literary assessments, but is in keeping with the dualism of appearance versus reality talked about so extensively in seventeenth-century theater in terms of titular and inherent nobility. In another revealing remark, Lisarda applauds Octavia's resolve to avenge her honor against the deceitful Carlos. When she learns that Carlos has left her for another woman, in spite of their marriage vows, Octavia enlists the aid of her brother.

Lisarda praises this action, saying that if women took charge of their honor as she does "no hubiera tantas burladas y ofendidas" (90) [there wouldn't be so many women who get seduced and end up aggrieved (102)]. The praise is qualified, however, for Lisarda admits that rather than learning from their mistakes women tend to move on to the next liaison and get further abused. Yet this criticism does not apply either to Octavia (who enters a convent) or to the exemplary Camila (the chaste wife who is raped and dies a protractedly monstrous death).

It seems that no matter how impeccably a woman behaves, she is doomed. And that is why Lisarda says her *desengaño* is as much a lesson for men as it is for women; that they should consider the cruel inequity of their behavior in defense of the so-called honor code. The pervasiveness of this male attitude is registered by Lisarda as she informs her audience that people disagree as to whether Carlos should kill his wife: "Divulgóse el caso por la ciudad, andando en opiniones la opinión de Camila. Unos decían que no quedaba Carlos con honor si no la mataba; otros que sería mal hecho, supuesto que la dama no tenía culpa, y cada uno apoyaba su parecer" (96) [The scandal spread throughout the city and Camila's reputation was on every tongue. Many said that Carlos would be dishonored unless he killed her; others that that would be wrong for she wasn't to blame. They all defended their own opinions (107)].

Although Camila is described as a Christian martyr and presented as being like an "apostle," who lived out her days offering wise advice to her maids, the tale ends with an emphasis not on her laudably paradigmatic martyrdom, but on her unwarranted suffering. Lisarda ends *La más infame venganza* by observing that innocent women are just as subject as evil ones to misfortune: "si esta desdicha la causan los engaños de los hombres o su flaqueza, ellas mismas lo podrán decir, que yo, como he dicho, si hasta agora no conozco los engaños, mal podré avisar con los desengaños" (98) [Whether misfortune is caused by men's deception or by women's weakness only women can decide, for, as I said earlier, I've never known deception and so can scarcely give advice about disenchantment (109)].

Like the endings of the other tales, the conclusion of Lisarda's presentation prompts a variety of responses. Juan says that her presentation was most impressive, and not at all insulting to men or women—apparently not taking personally the perfidy either of his namesake, Juan, or of Carlos, both of whom go unpunished for their actions. Isabel addresses Carlos's treatment of Camila, finding her to be remiss for not having told him about Juan's indecorous advances. To her mind, Carlos would have protected her, bearing in mind the offense that he had committed against Juan's sister and knowing that Juan would stop at nothing as a result. Lisis disagrees with Isabel's analysis saying that if Camila had mentioned the matter to her husband, she would surely have been doomed. Once jealousy is aroused, it can never be eradicated.

Speaking as a believer in the possibility of romantic love, Lisis surprises us by saying that "la fineza del amor es la confianza; que aunque algunos ignorantes dicen que no es sino los celos, lo que tengo por engaño, que el celoso, no porque ama más guarda la dama, sino por temor de perderla, envidioso de que lo que es suyo ande en venta para ser de otro" (99) [the best thing about love is the sense of mutual trust and confidence, although some ignoramuses say jealousy is. I believe they're wrong because a jealous man overprotects his wife not from love but from fear of losing her and also from envy that what is his might belong to another (110)]. What is surprising about this statement is that Lisis enunciates it disapprovingly, she who thrives on generating jealousy between her suitors. No consensus is reached by the storyteller or her auditors on the relative culpability of the characters. And it is precisely such unresolved lack of agreement about what the tale ultimately signifies that points to Zayas's desire to turn exemplarity into excess.

Tarde llega el desengaño (Disenchantment Comes Too Late)

While Lisarda is not disenchanted by the unforgivable behavior of the men in her account, Filis provides in *Tarde llega el desengaño* (II, 4), a tale in which she defends a man who persecutes his innocent wife. But while she seems not to become enlightened by the incident, a principal male character, who hears the narrative within the story itself, is. Thus we have once again a wide disparity of readings generated by the Zayesque tale, and interpretations that are by no means drawn according to the boundaries of gender.

Filis indulges in a lengthy meditation on male-female relationships before beginning her story, and it is a very pointed discussion. She begins by saying that everyone, regardless of class or station, lives by deception. Moreover, she questions whether women are, in fact, deceived or whether they permit themselves to become so. Even without drawing wisdom from ancient exempla, we see every day women who are the victims of great deception. What more disenchantment do we need? Men, according to Filis, should not be blamed for everything—"los hombres [no] deben tener la culpa de todo que se les imputa" (175)—but neither should women. Bad luck is also a factor, according to Filis, who recalls the examples of Camila and Roseleta as two innocent victims who were powerless against their fates, which were caused, in fact, by their husbands. Just when it seems Filis is an advocate of men, however, she turns her discourse around, taking on the perspective of a staunch female apologist. She indicates that women could outdo men if they were given the chance to study warfare and science. Men want to deprive women of education because they are afraid of the power and distinction that their female relations would no doubt attain.

Not only would women not be subject to abuse if they wore swords; men deprive women of arms and letters just as Moors do to the Christians who serve their women, turning them into intellectual "eunuchs" so they can be sure of them: "los hombres de temor y envidia las privan de las letras y las armas, como hacen los moros a los cristianos que han de servir donde hay mujeres, que los hacen eunucos por estar seguros de ellos" (178).

This image of being intellectually neutered by men is a devastating indictment of an oppressively phallocentric society, one that is in keeping with Zayas's concern for the intellectual welfare of women. And to prove its inequity, Filis offers a catalog of intellectually illustrious women, in spite of the educational inequality to which most women are doomed. Included in this list are such figures as Princess Isabel Clara Eugenia of Austria (1566–1633), the Countess of Lemos (d. 1628), lady-in-waiting to Queen Margaret of Austria, governess to the empress of Germany, and grandmother of the Count of Lemos. Included for their prowess in literature are María Barahona, Ana Caro, and Isabel de Ribadeneira. Having vented her emotion concerning the grossly unequal educational opportunities available to women, Filis finally gets down to her story which is based on the thirty-second tale in Marguerite de Navarre's *Heptameron*.

In the model text a woman is unfaithful to her husband in their own home where he discovers her with her lover. As punishment, the husband kills the lover and shaves his wife's head to signal her immodesty. Except for meals she is confined to the chamber in which she committed her infidelity, wherein hangs the skeleton of her dead lover except for his skull, which serves as her drinking cup. In all other respects the lady lives as before, in beautiful surroundings and well cared for. The guest to whom the husband has revealed her story indicates that the husband should forgive her, given both her extreme remorsefulness and the fact that they have no heirs. After giving the matter some thought, the husband agrees, whereupon they are restored to their former marital relationship, being in addition blessed with many fine children as well. Zayas complicates this narrative, rewriting it with a Baroque luridness involving not only gender, but race, class, and the grotesque sadism of the husband.

A man identified as Martín of Toledo laments the absence of his lady, who is also his cousin, a woman whom he looks forward to marrying. Yet this fervent desire is delayed when Martín's ship is blown off course by a terrible tempest, depositing him and his crew on Grand Canary Island. Soon after their arrival, a gentleman named Jaime graciously invites them to stay at his home while they recuperate from their harrowing voyage—an invitation which they willingly accept. The guests are unprepared, however, for the grim spectacle which lies in store for them.

As they are being seated for dinner, Jaime opens a small locked door from which a beautiful but very pale woman named Elena emerges carrying a human skull. At this point, another woman also enters the room; she is black, and described as follows: "si no era el demonio . . . debía ser su retrato" (185) [if she wasn't the devil, she was his very likeness (146)]. Filis's description of this second woman is lengthy and positively bestial in its ugliness, a portrait meant to contrast with the beautiful dress and splendid jewels she wears. We learn from Filis that she had formerly been a slave (along with four white slaves) in Jaime's employ, until she told him that Elena was unfaithful to him with her cousin, whom Jaime had taken in and treated like his own son.

The black woman's words are, however, mendacious; she lies simply to get revenge against Elena's cousin on whom she herself has designs, although he ignores her. Believing her story, Jaime elevates her to Elena's former status, giving her all of his wife's exquisite jewels and gowns, even feeding her from his plate, while Elena is allowed only to grovel under the table for the bones and scraps that are not worthy even of the dogs:

Se sentaron todos; la negra, a su lado, y don Martín y su camarada enfrente, tan admirados y divertidos en mirarla, que casi no se acordaban de comer, notando el caballero la suspensión, mas no porque dejase de regalar y acariciar a su negra y endemoniada dama, dándole los mejores bocados de su plato, y la desdichada belleza que estaba debajo de la mesa, los huesos y mendrugos, que aun para los perros no eran buenos, que como tan necesitada de sustento, los roía como si fuera uno de ellos. (186)

[They all seated themselves, the gentleman beside the negress and don Martín and his companions across the table from them. The two guests were so amazed and distracted by the sight of her that they could hardly eat. Their host noticed their amazement but that didn't make him desist from his continuous and affectionate attentions to his diabolical black lady. He picked out the tastiest morsels from his plate for her while he gave crusts and bones not fit even for a dog to the ill-fated beauty beneath the table. Ravenously she gnawed at them as if she were a dog.] (147)

At this point Jaime offers the history of this hideous spectacle. While he had been in Flanders, he received a message from a lady who noticed him and wanted to meet him, although she refused to identify herself. Telling her messenger that he would comply with the lady's request, Jaime was blindfolded and led on an hour-long journey to the woman's house. Although his blindfold was removed, it made no difference: "me desvendó los ojos; aunque fue como si no lo hiciera, porque todo estaba a oscuras" (191) [she removed my blindfold but to tell the truth it made no difference for everything was in total darkness (150)]. The tryst occurs in the dark, so that Jaime cannot see the lady's face and, when it is concluded, she gives him jewels in exchange for his sexual favors. Such a portrait of a gentleman who finds himself treated like a blindfolded male prostitute no doubt titillated Zayas's readers, male and female. In similar fashion, the sadistic treatment of Elena by her husband and his replacement of her by the black woman as his wife must have been equally scandalous.

Jaime engages in this peculiar trysting for over one month, getting paid each night in money or jewels by the unknown woman lover. His friends, meanwhile, notice this new-found wealth and suspect that he must have become a thief, so in order to disabuse them, he uses a bloody sponge to leave a trail to the lady's house. His efforts yield results: he discovers that she is a beautiful young widow named Lucrecia, princess of Erne. Having found out that he knows her identity, the lady instructs six hench-men to kill Jaime, after which they shoot and stab him, leaving him for dead. Somehow he recovers from his wounds and goes back to Aragón, but he can think only of Lucrecia. During Holy Week he sees a woman who looks so similar to her that he believes that she must have repented of her wrath and come to Spain looking for him. But the woman he sees is Elena, whom he marries and about whom the black woman tells the wicked lie that causes not only her unwarranted suffering, but the death of her innocent cousin as well.

For her part, the black woman becomes mortally ill and as she dies she confesses her lie and Elena's innocence, that it was all fabricated as a result of her unrequited love for Elena's cousin. Jaime stabs her and runs to find Elena to beg her forgiveness, but he is too late. When he discovers that she has died, having attained the "premio de su martirio" (reward for her suffering) he himself goes mad. Martín finally marries his beloved cousin, more convinced than ever of the need to disbelieve wicked servants.

Filis concludes her narration by pointing out the consummate cruelty of men and the fact that "ni con el sufrimiento los vencemos, ni con la inocencia los obligamos" (208) [we have such a bad name among men that we can't change their minds through our innocence, nor through our suffering shall we overcome (163)]. The horrific suffering inflicted by Jaime on his innocent wife is certainly despicable and unwarranted, but by its totalizing nature Filis's judgment falls short of convincing us. For none of this would have happened if the lustful Lucrecia had not seduced Jaime. Even more nefarious and destructive is, of course, the black woman's vicious lie, the immediate cause of Elena's untimely death.

In addition to her function as a study in female evil, Zayas extends this meditation on villany and lust in woman by bestowing the name Lucrecia (a byword for uxorial chastity and self-sacrifice) upon a character of tremendous—and tremendously transgressive—sexual appetites. And while not writing approvingly of her character, Zayas clearly enjoys registering for her reader the great potential that exists in the female imagination and libido, as well as the power of female agency and the ability to realize these monstrous sex drives. It is a bold and racy exposé. Elena is, similarly, the opposite of her classical namesake, Helen of Troy, the devastating beauty who was at the same time horribly divisive and deceitful. This Elena is instead a paragon of chastity and passive suffering.

By the juxtaposition of these two women and by the inversion of their legendary association Zayas underscores with great vehemence the error of typecasting in fiction or in real life. She also indicates the impoverishing gesture involved in assigning one ethical abstraction to a given character, designating one exclusive significance to each narrative as traditional exempla do. If one wants to identify male cruelty toward women as the lesson, then what of the female villains who set the suffering of Elena in motion? On the positive side, the tale convinces Martín more than ever not to trust the words of deceitful servants, and Jaime's ultimate insanity caused by remorse for the way he has treated his wife also mitigates the exclusive message that Filis's derives from the tale. It is once again excess, here in both senses, excess of lust which leads to the sequence of events that culminates in an excess or surplus of meaning.

El traidor contra su sangre (Traitor to His Own Blood)

With El traidor contra su sangre (II, 8) we find a continuation of the interest in polysemy witnessed in the stories thus far, as Francisca assumes the role of narrator. The remarks she makes before beginning her narration are noteworthy because of the narrative's placement as this eighth tale of part II (hence as the eighteenth story of the entire collection).

In spite of the seven desengaños that Francisca has listened to ostensibly within the framework of Lisis's misandrist theme, she is still unconvinced, as are some other partygoers, of the overwhelmingly blameworthy nature of men. Frankly, given the gory and routinely unjustified torture and wife-murder that confronts the auditors it is a striking reaction. And it is a reaction that weakens any reading of Zayas from the exclusive perspective of Lisis's discourse. Because of the numerous contradictions in their discursive positions, all of the female narrators cannot be equated with Lisis, just as her univocal position can not be equated with Zayas's appreciation of multiple subject-positions.

Francisca begins her prefatory remarks by saying, for example, "Que los hombres siempre llevan la mira a engañar a las mujeres, no me persuado a creerlo; que algunos habrá" (296) [I cannot convince myself that men are always trying to deceive women. Of course there are some (273)]. She goes on to condemn male deception but also female gullibility; given all the examples we constantly have before us, how could a woman still be deceived by what men say? Beginning with the claim that not all men are deceptive, Francisca then seems to universalize her negative view of them, thereafter moving first to a condemnation of women for their lack of discernment, and then moving back to a condemnation of men. The problem with men, she concludes, is that they malign women; men publicize the misconduct of bad women, yet if they are good they are slandered nonetheless (298).

Words, in Francisca's estimation, are powerful weapons, capable of destroying human life. In fact it is the misuse of words, malicious gossip (frequently invented by a jealous female), that results in the unfortunate events that befall so many of Zayas's ill-fated heroines.[17] The idiosyncratic, subjectively novelistic lack of referentiality that words can assume is as central to Zayas's literary project as it is to Cervantes'. Francisca ends her somewhat circuitous discourse that presents men and women as more or less blameworthy by saying that her intention is to "probar que hay y ha habido muchas buenas [mujeres], y que han padecido y padecen en la crueldad de los hombres, sin culpa" (298) [prove that there are and have been many good women who, without fault, have suffered and still suffer great cruelty from men (274)].

The story itself certainly bears witness to this precept, yet not without significant complications. We learn that approximately twenty-six years ago there lived a cruel man, Pedro, who had a son and daughter, Alonso and Mencía; and that Pedro refused to let his daughter marry because he wanted her to become a nun, thereby permitting his son to receive all of his father's inheritance. One of the men who attempts courtship is Enrique, a descendant of *cristianos viejos* (old Christians), the grandson of *labradores* (farmers), who is dismissed by Pedro and Alonso as a result of his unacceptably humble origins.

Risking great danger, Enrique falls in love with Mencía, serving her as a steadfastly true lover. However, his devotion to her arouses the jealousy of his former lady (Clavela), who decides to wreak revenge on the happy couple by telling lies to Alonso. Clavela's wicked plan works very effectively, resulting in Mencía's death by stabbing from her crazed brother, and also in the similar yet even more vicious stabbing of the honorable Enrique. In spite of his twenty-two stab wounds, Enrique somehow recovers, becoming a man of the cloth, while Alonso is sentenced in absentia to execution by beheading, although he goes to Naples to become a soldier instead.

While in Italy Alonso falls in love and marries a beautiful fifteen-year-old named Ana, and within nine months has a son by her whom he names Pedro in honor of the grandfather. Although Alonso is very happy with his wife, he suddenly turns against her as his wedding is made known to his wicked father. The father's wrath stems from the fact that Ana is poor rather than being the kind of rich noblewoman he had hoped his son would marry, thereby enriching his estate and lineage. Pedro not only disowns Alonso for this action, but says in addition that he would kill him if he were nearby, just as Alonso had done to his sister Mencía for the same reason.

Aided by an infamous friend named Marco Antonio, a dissolute Italian cleric ("clérigo salvaje" [316]), Alonso beheads Ana, throwing her headless body down a well while he hides her severed head in a cave. Once discovered, the decapitated corpse is taken by the authorities to the plaza to see whether anyone recognizes it, and it is ultimately claimed with great sadness by Ana's grandfather, Fernando de Añasco. Alonso is apprehended and sentenced to death by beheading, and Marco Antonio by hanging. While Marco Antonio confronts his death in a businesslike manner, Alonso is terrified, saying, "¡[Si] supiera qué era morir, no matara!"

(328) ["If I'd known what it was like to die, I never would have killed!" (299)]. He informs the authorities of the head's whereabouts, at which point he swoons realizing from his profound emotion that he had never meant to harm Ana, but had been driven to kill her by his father's rage and Marco Antonio's nefarious advice. When Pedro learns of his son's demise as he is playing cards, his only reaction is to say "Más quiero tener un hijo degollado que mal casado" (329) ["Better a son beheaded than one ill-wedded" (300)].

It would be hard to imagine a more graphic indictment of the destruction wrought by the so-called honor code than what we find in the behavior of Pedro and his son towards Mencía and Ana. The true love of Mencía and Enrique was initially revealed and maligned by Clavela in order to assuage her jealousy, this jealousy being the catalyst for their stabbings by Alonso. The couple is presented, nonetheless, as supernatural, immune to the ugliness of mortality and putrefaction. After being stabbed twenty-two times, Enrique survives his attack, becoming a friar in order to devote himself to God. And, while Mencía dies, she has the unique ability to speak although dead; in addition, her wounds bleed for an entire year, thereby signaling her special status, her extraordinary nature by comparison with the baseness of her brother and father. By these traits that defy nature Mencía and even Enrique are singled out, reminiscent of similar traits exhibited by myriad saints as recorded by their hagiographers. The ability of Ana's head to look beautiful, totally incorruptible after being dead for six months, is equally astounding and calculated to inspire *admiratio* in the tale's auditors and readers. The description of Ana as a "tierna y descuidada corderilla" [tender and unsuspecting lamb] whom Alonso would lead to the *matadero* (slaughterhouse) augments this impression of horror and admiration at the same time.

Zayas clearly means to project both Mencía and Ana as blameless victims of the "system," of the cruel effects that the honor code, taken to its extremes, could bring about. It is not simply *limpieza de sangre*, in Pedro's case with Enrique, ensuring that he not have any *labradores* as relatives. For if one rejects the so-called old Christians, the *cristianos viejos*, one is left with the *cristianos nuevos*, the *conversos* or converts from Judaism, who were viewed as equally problematic. In the figure of Pedro, Zayas dramatizes the social crisis stemming from the concept of blood purity, an insoluble and destructive force in seventeenth-century Spain, one which was repeatedly addressed in the literature of that time.[18]

The case of Ana de Añasco further magnifies the pernicious irrationality of this social code, since she is sacrificed even though she is, as Marco Antonio tells Alonso, his equal in social standing: "demás de ser muy virtuosa y honesta, en calidad no os debe nada, porque su padre tuvo el hábito de Santiago por claro timbre de su nobleza" (320) [besides being virtuous and chaste, she is in no way inferior to your rank. Her father won the habit of the Order of Santiago because of the clear timbre of his nobility (292)]. The question then arises as to whether it is blood lines or wealth or both which constitute nobility, or is it instead the inherent nobility of virtue?

While Pedro seems to be the spokesman for the most hidebound and pernicious form of titular (and monetary) honor, his son is presented in a different light. As Pedro callously receives the news of his only child's death with the words "más quiero un hijo degollado que mal casado," totally convinced of the value of his beliefs, Alonso realizes his grave error. He does not mention the cold-blooded murder of his sister, presumably because he believed Clavela's slanderous portrayal of her as having besmirched the family name by unpardonable promiscuity. Yet with Ana, he clearly sees that the act he committed was, in fact, nothing other than an unjustifiable, indeed senselessly vicious crime prompted by the evil influence of his father and "friend." This irony is augmented when, at the story's conclusion, we learn that Pedro's namesake and grandson, the child of Ana (the woman who was so detested by the elder Pedro), inherits all of the family fortune.

Zayas teases her reader at this point saying that when Francisca had finished her amazing tale no discussion followed because it was so late in the evening. Instead, the partygoers retire immediately to a lavish supper table. The deferred discussion finally begins as both the ladies and gentlemen engage in *diversas y sabias disputas* (diverse and wise debates). It is important to note that the gentleman vote in favor of the ladies, we are told, either out of politeness (fear of reprisals from their own ladies?) *or* because they were genuinely convinced by the truth (330). The outcome of the vote is clear, the motivation(s) for it, however, remain obscure. Unresolved perspectivism reigns once more.

Estragos que causa el vicio (*The Ravages of Vice*)

The last of the twenty *Novelas, Estragos que causa el vicio* (II, 10), is narrated by the hostess of the *sarao*, Lisis herself. The anticipation caused by this final narrative and Lisis's recounting of it is concretized by the fact that all the assembled ladies and gentlemen rise to their feet, bowing politely and standing until the hostess has taken her place in the "seat of disenchantment." Having done so, Lisis claims that she will speak plainly so that her discourse will be transparent, comprehensible to everyone, the ordinary as well as the cultivated audience. She wants to leave no possible margin of error in the interpretation of her message, namely, that "como todos [los hombres] están ya declarados por enemigos de las mujeres, contra todos he publicado la guerra" (412) [because all men are declared enemies of women, I have declared my war against all men (367)]. We see that her will to prescribe interpretation could not be more forcefully articulated. However, she will not succeed given that Zayas communicates through her probably the most incriminating of the twenty tales in terms of gender relations, one involving wicked women and innocent men. The vice indicated in the tale's title is initiated by the women, setting into motion Zayas's bloodiest narrative of all. The validity of her discourse is belied by the facts of the story.

Having indicated in no uncertain terms that she has declared war on men, Lisis then attempts to persuade them not to deceive the ladies. While it is inconsistent and strikingly unstrategic to address them first in a hostile manner, thereafter soliciting their aid and understanding, this is in fact what Lisis does. Yet it is not the only inconsistency in her prefatory remarks to *Estragos que causa el vicio*. Referring now to the gentlemen as "discreet," she proceeds to flatter them in hyperbolic terms: "Claro está que siendo, como sois, nobles y discretos, por mi deseo, que es bueno, habéis de alabar mi trabajo; aunque sea malo, no embote los filos de vuestro entendimiento este parto del pobre y humilde mío" (412) [Of course, being noble and discreet as you are, my wish is for you to praise my work. Even if it's bad, this child of my poor, humble mind will not dull the edges of your mind (368)].

Asking male writers to praise her work "even if it's bad" seems foolish, or at the very least hypocritical. It is also a contradiction in terms of Lisis's stated desire to speak truthfully and plainly. She not only flatters the men, she resorts to servile hyperbole when she says, for instance: "Supuesto que, aunque sea moneda inferior, es moneda y vale algo, por humilde, no la habéis de pisar; luego si merece tener lugar entre vuestro grueso caudal, ya os vencéis y me hacéis vencedora" (413) [While it may be common coin, still it is coin and has some value and shouldn't be trampled because it's humble. If it deserves to find a place among your immense riches, you will win and you will make me a winner (368)]. Is Lisis then a "straight shooter" only in speaking of gender matters? Is she toying with her illustrious male contemporaries? Is this really Zayas intervening as she had in the global prologue to the work, ranging between the poles of self-assurance as a writer of distinguished prose on the one hand and, on the other, insecurity?

If this is really Zayas speaking, which seems a logical deduction, then we see her being as contradictory in the final extradiegetic remarks as she was at the opening moments of her enterprise. She does not speak in a coherent voice, but a contradictory one, just as her narrators and characters do, expressing at times multiple (even unanticipated) subject-positions. She continues her contradictory discourse, speaking now of the "elegance" and "erudition" contained within her prose, a clear contradiction of the claim made in a previous paragraph: "ni en lo hablado, ni en lo que hablaré, he buscado razones retóricas, ni cultas; porque de más de ser un lenguaje que con el extremo posible aborezco, querría que me entendiesen todos, el culto y el lego" (412) [in everything I shall say, I've not sought rhetorical or cultivated style, not only because that's a style I abhor but because I would want everybody, both ordinary and cultured, to understand me" (367)]. In the final analysis, what can be stated for sure is that this is not a voice that speaks with the coherence of a single point of view, an exemplary voice. And the story which follows is similarly problematic.

Like *Mal presagio casar lejos*, *Estragos que causa el vicio* is concerned with nationalism and with cross-cultural differences. In this case, rather than a Spanish female pondering the differences between Portuguese and Spanish men and foreign husbands, a Spanish male, Gaspar, reflects on the differences between Spanish and Portuguese women while undergoing an extraordinary adventure in the service of King Philip III of Spain who is temporarily residing in Lisbon. In a remark whose validity will soon be undermined, Lisis judges Portuguese women to be discreet and cautious in relationships, whereas Spaniards, both male and female, are not: "lo que más pierden las [personas] de nuestra nación, tanto hombres como mujeres es en la ostentación que hacen de los vicios" (414) [where people from my country fall down, men as well as women, is (in) the way they display their vices (369)]. What we will see, however, is the exemplary behavior of Gaspar, which is not only discreet and virtuous, but generous as well, in contrast with the not simply indiscreet, but positively perfidious behavior of two Portuguese women who bring about the downfall of twelve innocent people.

When we first meet Gaspar, he courts a lady, one of four sisters, who live in a large house. Although his affair progresses to his satisfaction, it is cut short as he discovers within the house a youth who has been impaled to death on a hook. It is determined that he has been dead for nearly two weeks, yet is still capable of moaning, which is how Gaspar makes the horrific discovery. Terrified by his discovery, construing it as a warning from God, he determines to sever his ties with these women, after first paying for the burial of the unidentified young man.

While hearing mass one day, he falls in love with a Lusitanian beauty by the name of Florentina, who lives with her beloved stepsister, Magdalena, and brother-in-law, Dionís. Gaspar pursues his lady, yet, we are told that, for reasons of nationalism, the relationship seems doomed to failure: "Como era castellano, no halló en ellos [los portugueses] lo que deseaba, por la poca simpatía que esta nación tiene con la nuestra, que, con vivir entre nosotros, son nuestros enemigos" (420) [Because he was Spanish, he couldn't get anywhere—the Portuguese feel little love for our nation and are our enemies even though they live together with us (374)].

As he dwells on strategies by which he might win the interest and affection of Florentina, Gaspar finds her lying on the ground, bathed in blood. Taking her to his quarters, he summons a priest and a surgeon who ultimately restores her to health in spite of the multiple stab wounds which she has suffered. Having regained her strength, Florentina instructs Gaspar to call the police and go to Dionís's house, where he beholds a scene of unspeakable carnage which Florentina admits was all her doing ("por culpa mía" [426]). Dionís, prior to taking his own life, kills ten members of his household staff (slaves, servants, and pages) as well as his virtuous wife, Magdalena. The position of each body and the place where it was stabbed are all minutely recorded before Florentina proceeds to reveal the cause of this gruesome spectacle, namely, her own illicit desire for Dionís.

"Intricado laberinto" [intricate labyrinth] (434) is the phrase Florentina uses to describe her convoluted deception of the two people who love her most in the world, her sister and brother-in-law. First she declares her love to Dionís, who claims that he loves her as well. This leads to a four-year relationship of which Magdalena is unaware. Florentina not only enjoys a forbidden love, she displaces Magdalena even, it seems, in terms of domestic authority: "Yo mandaba en [la casa]. Lo que yo hacía era lo más acertado; lo que mandaba, lo obedicido. Era dueño de la hacienda, y de cuya era. Por mí se despedían y recibían los criados y criadas, de manera que doña Magdalena no servía más de hacer estorbos a mis empleos (439) [I was queen of the household. Everything I did was right, my every command was law. I was mistress of the whole estate as it was mine. Servants were hired and fired by my will and doña Magdalena came to be simply an obstacle to my desires (388)].

Because she views Magdalena as an impediment, Florentina determines to kill her, convinced by an evil maid of the necessity of doing so. Offering a biblical example, the maid instructs Florentina to kill Magdalena just as David killed Uriah, after which the maid assures her mistress that she can repent of her sin: "que por la penitencia se perdona el pecado, y así lo hizo el santo rey" (442) [for sin is forgiven through penitence and that's how the holy king did it (390)]. The murder of the faithful Magdalena is provoked as the maid tells Dionís that she sleeps with an eighteen-year-old servant who works in the house. This fiction is deceptively staged for the purpose of convincing Dionís of his wife's infidelity and he kills her, having fallen prey to this *engaño a los ojos*. After this lamentable event, the maid confesses her collaborative deception to Dionís who kills her first and then himself, unable to live with the guilt of having killed eleven innocent people.

The author of the carnage, Florentina, shocks Gaspar by her account, after which he suggests that she take up a religious vocation in the convent, where she would be immune from further calamity. The king grants a pardon to Florentina for her guilt in the matter, thus liberating her to inherit everything from the stepsister and brother-in-law who had loved her so dearly. We learn that she takes up residence in one of the most sumptuous convents in Lisbon, and that her great inheritance provides her with a rich dowry to do so. Lisis ends by indicating that "hoy vive santa y religiosísima vida, carteándose con Gaspar, a quien, siempre agradecida, no olvida" (450) [today she still lives a saintly and devout life. She writes to Gaspar, never forgetting her gratitude to him (396)].

If exemplarity is Lisis's object, to prove that women are the victims of men, what results instead is a notable excess or obscurity from this final *Novela*, in spite of her claim ("bien ventilada me parece que queda, nobles y discretos caballeros, y hermosísimas damas . . . la defensa de las mujeres" [452]) [I think the defense of women has been thoroughly aired (398)]. Claims made to the contrary, it is the Portuguese who reveal themselves to be indiscreet in affairs of the heart. If the impaled corpse Gaspar finds buried in the house of the four sisters arouses some suspicion, the behavior of Florentina and her maid offer prime examples of their debauchery. Dionís is reprehensible as well, carrying on a four-year affair with his sister-in-law in his house, as he utterly neglects his own virtuous wife. If Gaspar, meanwhile, can be criticized for anything it is that he helps Florentina escape any judicial action, allowing her instead to enjoy the pleasures of sumptuous convent life. Although it seems difficult to excuse, indeed irrational, this weakness is attributable to his fondness for a woman who has destroyed so many lives. Lisis's claim that Florentina leads a "saintly" life seems hard to accept, to say the least.[19]

Except for this notable error of judgment, however, Gaspar has behaved impeccably in his dealings with women, and even in his decorous and generous treatment of the unidentified corpse of the young man. He is an exemplar of virtue and discretion, and Lisis's opinion to the contrary, he is Spanish, while the worst offenders are Portuguese. And Lisis's claim that this tale proves men are the mortal enemies of women, of course, strains the imagination. The other male figures of the tale (with one exception) are virtuous: the servants, for example, and Dionís, who kills his innocent wife because Florentina and her maid create a fiction for the purpose of convincing him that his wife is engaged in an adulterous liaison.

What Zayas illustrates here and throughout her collection is the impoverishing nature of unidimensional characters meant to serve as predictable ethical or ideological abstractions. To this end, Lisis functions as a foil.[20] In this age of modern subjectivity with its appreciation of the "intricate labyrinth" of the human psyche, Zayas figures obscurity as the only solution to the representation of the human condition.[21] She understands the inescapably "excessive" nature of the early modern example. Any degree of specificity, any reference to historical particulars—or to fictional ones—necessarily leads to excess, distracting the reader from the generalization the example ostensibly seeks to illustrate. By her writing, Zayas stages the shift from Renaissance exemplarity to Baroque excess.

Epilogue: Who Is Fabio?

Etymologically, *lisis* means "solution," but also its opposite, "dissolution," a direct translation (and transliteration) from the Greek λύσις. This name is very appropriate, figuring the overall aporia generated by Zayas's text since the concluding remarks offered by and about the hostess of the extended soirée in the epilogue that follows the twentieth tale are anything but conclusive. In fact, they serve to obscure definitively her ideological status as Zayas's official voice on gender relations. If we consider Lisis's words and actions in the concluding pages, we find an unresolvedly ambivalent assessment of men, of women, and of their potential for productive interaction.

In these final pages she admits that "hay hoy más mujeres viciosas y perdidas, que ha habido jamás; mas no que falten tan buenas que no exedan el número de las malas" (454) [there are in this day and age, more loose and vicious women than there have ever before been, but that doesn't mean that there aren't more good women than bad (399)]. Remarks such as this offer a strikingly weak endorsement for someone who has dictated, as the global theme of part II, that man is the unredeemed victimizer of blameless woman.

In terms of the hopelessness of changing male attitudes, Lisis also wavers in her discourse. At times she views them as a lost cause, while at others she exhorts them to act nobly in their relations with women —thereby acknowledging that they are educable, hence redeemable. If her expressed project is to denigrate men as relentless victimizers, she contradicts herself by acknowledging, as she does here, the possibility of enlightened male behavior. Shortly after explaining that there are more wicked women than there used to be in the world, she reflects a belief in the possibility of equitable male behavior: "Estimad y honrad las mujeres y veréis cómo resucita en vosotros el valor perdido" (456) [Respect and honor women and you will see how your lost valor returns (401)].

Not only do comments such as these seriously call into question Lisis's stated objective in praising women and denigrating men, she even resorts to faulty reasoning, as when she indicates that if a woman is bad, she should, nonetheless, be treated well because there are so many good women in the world: "[No] es caballero, ni noble, ni honrado el que dice mal de las mujeres, aunque sean malas, pues las tales se pueden librar en virtud de las buenas" (457) [The man who speaks ill of women is not a gentleman; he's not noble; he's not honorable. Even if a woman is bad, she is redeemed by the virtue of the good woman (401)].

Again, this position makes no sense given the exemplary project she has articulated in such outspoken terms. In a similarly awkward manner she says that the bad women depicted in a number of the tales aren't women at all, being rather "monsters."[1] Finally, she even includes the observation that there are good and bad women, just as there are good and bad men in the world. In other words, Zayas "writes in" every conceivable opinion about men, women, and their potential for harmonious interaction.

The only way to read this polysemy is that she is aware of different types of readers and of multiple subject-positions. As such, the misogynist, misandrist, pious, and status quo readers, as well as the sensationalist thrill seekers addicted to the gory and sordid relatos de sucesos, can all find personal fulfillment. By conceiving her book in this polymorphous manner, Zayas not only acknowledges the complexity of human subjectivity; she provides a highly successful marketing strategy which clearly contributed to her status as a best-selling author.

Recent scholarship devoted to Zayas as a surprisingly early proponent of the feminist cause has focused on Lisis's apparently last-minute decision to enter a convent instead of marrying Diego, as everyone expected she would do. This retreat to the female community of convent life is read as concrete proof of Lisis's (and probably Zayas's) definitive rejection of male-dominated society. Yet, what about the inevitable male presence of the father confessor, whose authoritarian presence in convent life is undeniable?[2]

Lisis's idealized conventual society, which she explicitly equates with freedom from male abuse while representing a sisterhood of partygoers actually bears little resemblance to daily convents, which Miraló Vigil describes in the following terms: "En parte eran centros de vida religiosa, en parte guarderías de niñas pequeñas, internados de señoritas, locales para las sin casar, refugios de viudas, residencias de ancianas, hostales. . . . Eran como aparcamientos de mujeres" [They were partly centers of religious life, part childcare centers for little girls, places of internment for young girls, places for spinsters, widows, residences for the elderly, hostels. They were like parking lots for women.] [3] While the convent is populated exclusively by women, its attractiveness predominantly as a place of refuge from men for an aristocrat like Lisis seems questionable for more than a provisionally brief time.

Perhaps Zayas situates Lisis in the convent as an acceptably respectable place for someone who has just rejected her fiancé, and for someone whose discourse has, at times, offered such a stern indictment of the status quo male order. Yet this suggested form of closure is soon disrupted, for shortly after painting this liberatingly utopian female space, Zayas herself definitively unravels its teleological importance for Lisis. She effects this unexpected shift in her very last paragraph, which reads as follows:

Ya, ilustrísimo Fabio, por cumplir lo que pediste de que no diese trágico fin a esta historia, la hermosísima Lisis queda en clausura, temerosa de que algún engaño la desengañe, no escarmentada de desdichas propias. No es trágico fin, sino el más felice que se pudo dar, pues codiciosa y deseada de muchos, no se sujetó a ninguno. Si os duran los deseos de verla, buscadla con intento casto, que con ello la hallaréis tan vuestra y con la voluntad tan firme y honesta, como tiene prometido, y tan servidora vuestra como siempre, y como vos merecéis; que hasta en conocerlo ninguna le hace ventaja." (461)

[Now, illustrious Fabio, to comply with your request that I not give a tragic end to this story, the beautiful Lisis lives in the cloister, still fearful that some deception might disenchant her because she did not learn directly from her own misfortune. This end is not tragic but rather the happiest one you can imagine for, although courted and desired by many, she did not subject herself to anyone. If you still wish to see her, seek her with chaste intent and you will find her at your service, with loyal and honorable good will as she has promised. As always, your humble servant as befits your merits, and even in acknowledging that, no woman excels her.] (488)

This is the first indication we have of Fabio's existence, and it is certainly a precipitous one, coming as it does in the final paragraph of her nine-hundred-page work. He is mysterious, in addition, because he is only described by the vague qualifier "illustrious," with no more detail of any kind as to his personal identity. The fact that he has requested a "happy outcome" for Lisis is also problematic, suggesting that Lisis's existence is indeed fictional, in spite of claims to the contrary. From this outcome Montesa Peydro concludes that it is an autobiographical clue that definitively identifies Lisis as figuring Zayas herself who, according to him, retreated to a convent to live out her final days. This is pure speculation, however, since nothing is known about Zayas's life after the publication of part II.[4]

Ruth El Saffar advances a different hypothesis, based not on this postscript naming of Fabio, but on an enigmatic reference contained in a ballad sung by Lisis between I, 9, and I, 10:

Celos tengo, y pues los celos
    son del infierno semilla,
    nacer penas en el alma
    no es muy mucha maravilla.
    ¡Ay del pecho que en tal fuego
    se abrasa y se precipita!
    ¡Y ay de aquel que su remedio
    sólo en la muerte se cifra!
    Morir quien es desdichado
    no es muerte, piedad sería;
    más la cruel muerte huye
    de los que tienen desdichas.
    Son tantas las que padezco,
    que soy la desdicha misma:
    la vida en mí es triste muerte,

muerte es mi cansada vida.
Mas si Fabio es vida y cielo,
¿de qué te espantas, Marfisa,
que oiga el cielo las penas
y dé la muerte la vida?
Así llora Marfisa,
cuando los campos vierten alegría. (400)

[Jealous I am and since jealousy/is the very seed of hell,/it's no great wonder/that it sows sorrow in the soul,/Alas for the heart burned/and bedeviled by such a flame!/And alas for the poor soul/whose only relief lies in death!/For the unfortunate lover to die/is not really death but mercy;/but cruel death flees/from those who are unfortunate./The misfortunes I suffer are so great/that I am misfortune personified;/life for me is living death./But if Fabio is both life and heaven,/why do you, Marfisa, fear/that heaven will hear your sorrows,/that life will grant you death?/While nature overflows with gladness,/only Marfisa weeps.] (294–95)

On the basis of this onomastic reference El Saffar logically wonders:

Who is Marfisa? Who is Fabio? The fact that nothing in what Lisis appears to be experiencing suggests that "Marfisa" and "Fabio" are figures for her and Don Diego, leaves the door wide open, once again, for the possibility that Zayas' work has a riddle quality designed to be understood by a specific, historical reader. Hovering unseen over the entire collection may be another pair of lovers, between whom our text moves as a message only they can decode.[5]

The fact that Fabio discloses interest on the part of "many" for Lisis's affection is also significant, pointing potentially to not one but possibly many unrepresented realities (erotic and otherwise) in the *Novelas*, since we know only of Diego's courtship of her. While the disconsolate Diego becomes a soldier, subsequently losing his life in the service of his country, and while Juan goes mad, dying as a result of remorse for his disloyalty toward Lisis and Lisarda's final rejection of him, we are left to ponder whether perhaps Lisis has only sought temporary refuge in the convent as a way of disengaging herself from Diego, interested instead in Fabio (or perhaps one of her other numerous suitors) to whom she will soon turn her attention.

These disturbing questions remain unanswered, thus projecting an impression of open-endedness or at the very least of unstable closure for the work. We as readers are caught totally off guard and Zayas offers us no solutions. As such, Foucault's description of the early modern period as a time when signs "interact with themselves in a perpetual state of decomposition and recomposition" seems particularly relevant here.[6] Zayas's text is paradigmatic of this perception of reality. The global debate over the sexes and their relative merits, over the honor code, the public persona of Lisis—her ideological stance—as opposed to her private affairs, persist unresolved. The reader remains subject to, and the subject of, Zayas's labyrinth.

Notes

Preface

1. See William Kerrigan and Gordon Braden, *The Idea of the Renaissance* (Baltimore: Johns Hopkins University Press, 1989); and Margreta de Grazia, "The Ideology of Superfluous Things: *King Lear* as Period Piece," in *Subject and Object in Renaissance Culture*, ed. Margreta de Grazia, Maureen Quilligan, and Peter Stallybrass (Cambridge, England: Cambridge University Press, 1996), pp. 17–42.

2. Larry McCaffrey, *The Metafictional Muse* (Pittsburgh: University of Pittsburgh Press, 1982), p. 264.

3. Linda Hutcheon, *A Poetics of Postmodernism* (New York: Routledge, 1988), p. 11.

4. Rosalind Krauss, "Poststructuralism and the 'Paraliterary,'" *October* 13 (1980): 37.

5. Ihab Hassan, "On the Problem of the Postmodern," *New Literary History* 20 (1988): 23.

6. Cited in René Wellek, *Concepts of Criticism* (New Haven, Conn.: Yale University Press, 1963), p. 116.

7. William Clamurro, "Ideological Contradiction and Imperial Decline: Toward a Reading of Zayas' *Desengaños amorosos*," *South Central Review* 5 (1988): 46.

8. "¿De qué pensáis que procede el poco ánimo que hoy todos tenéis, que sufrís que estén los enemigos dentro de España, y nuestro Rey en campaña, y vosotros en el Prado y en el río, llenos de galas y trajes femeniles, y los pocos que le acompañan, suspirando por las ollas de Egipto? De la poca estimación que hacéis de las mujeres, que a fe que, si las estimarais y amárades, como en otros tiempos se hacía, por no verlas en poder de vuestros enemigos, vosotros mismos os ofreciérades, no digo yo [a] [ir] a la guerra y a pelear, sino a la muerte, poniendo la garganta al cuchillo, como en otros tiempos, y en particular en el del rey don Fernando el Católico se hacía, donde no era menester llevar los hombres

por fuerza, ni maniatados, como ahora (infelicidad y desdicha de nuestro católico Rey), sino que ellos mismos ofrecían sus haciendas y personas: el padre, por defender la hija; el hermano, por la hermana; el esposo, por la esposa, y el galán por la dama" (455).

9. This opinion runs counter to Huarte de San Juan's influential *Examen de ingenios* (1575) where he writes in accord with Galen: "El hombre que se hace de cimiente de mujer no puede ser ingenioso ni tener habilidad, por la mucha frialdad y humedad de este sexo. Por donde es cierto que en saliendo el hijo discreto y avisado, es indicio infalible de haberse hecho de la simiente de su padre. Y si es torpe y necio, se colige haberse formado de la simiente de su madre" (Juan Huarte de San Juan, *Examen de ingenios para las ciencias*, ed. Martín de Burgos [Madrid: Atlas, 1953], p. 515). [The man who is engendered from the seed of a woman can be neither clever nor capable, as a result of the cold and wet nature of females. For this reason it is clear that if a child is of good judgment, he is obviously the product of his father's seed. And if he is awkward and foolish, we can assume that he was formed from the seed of his mother] (my trans.).

10. Beyond the lyric she embeds within her novellas, Zayas wrote a considerable number of poems that have survived. She wrote for the stage as well, although only one of her plays survives, *La traición en la amistad*. For an interesting recent study of her satirical verse see Lía Schwartz Lerner, "La mujer toma la palabra: Voces femeninas en la sátira del siglo XVII," in *Images de la femme en Espagne au XVIe et XVIIe siècles*, ed. Agustin Redondo (Paris: Presses de la Sorbonne Nouvelle, 1994), pp. 381–90.

11. For an interesting discussion of labyrinths and their literary representation see Penelope Doob, *The Idea of the Labyrinth from Classical Antiquity Through the Middle Ages* (Ithaca, N.Y.: Cornell University Press, 1990).

Chapter 1. Spectacle and Surveillance

Note to epigraph: Words spoken by a Jew in Lope de Vega, *El niño inocente de la Guardia*, ed. Anthony J. Farrell (London: Tamesis Books, 1985), pp. 59–60.

1. Michel Foucault, *Discipline and Punish*, trans. A. M. Sheridan (New York: Vintage, 1979), p. 88.

2. J. H. Elliott, *Imperial Spain, 1469–1717* (New York: New American Library, 1966), p. 220. Mary Elizabeth Perry offers a similar evaluation in her essay which characterizes the sociopolitical climate during the time in which Zayas wrote: "The Inquisition carried out strategies at least as concerned with political and social order as with theological issues." "Crisis and Disorder in the World of María

de Zayas y Sotomayor," in *María de Zayas: The Dynamics of Discourse*, ed. Amy R. Williamsen and Judith A. Whitenack (Madison, N.J.: Farleigh Dickinson University Press, 1995), p. 28.

3. For an analysis of the Inquisition and its impact on daily life in Spain see Edward Peters, *Inquisition* (New York: Free Press, 1988), pp. 189–90.

4. For a discussion of the term see Marina S. Brownlee and Hans Ulrich Gumbrecht, *Cultural Authority in Golden Age Spain* (Baltimore: Johns Hopkins University Press, 1995), esp. pp. ix–xvii.

5. Antonio de Guevara, *Menosprecio de corte y alabanza de aldea*, ed. M. Martínez de Burgos (Madrid: Clásicos Castellanos, 1928), pp. 30–36. These passages are cited in an important essay by Joseph Silverman, "On Knowing Other People's Lives, Inquisitorially and Artistically," in *Cultural Encounters: The Impact of the Inquisition in Spain and the New World*, ed. Mary Elizabeth Perry and Anne J. Cruz (Berkeley: University of California Press, 1991), p. 167.

6. Perry accurately conveys the obsession with genealogical purity and its increasing intensity as follows: "The centuries-long pattern of intermarriage between Christians and *conversos* became less tolerable as forcible baptisms of Jews and Muslims led to increasing concern with apostasy. By the middle of the sixteenth century, royal and clerical appointments required proof of genealogical purity, and *Libros verdes* published genealogies of leading families that revealed in many of them the 'taint' of *converso* blood." "Crisis and Disorder," p. 29.

Américo Castro's work on the impact of *limpieza* for Golden Age literature is still very illuminating. See especially his *De la edad conflictiva: Crisis de la cultura española en el siglo XVII*, 4th ed. (Madrid: Taurus, 1976).

The stigma of being non-Christian, especially Jewish or Muslim, extended back to the Middle Ages in Spain. For an illuminating treatment of it, see Louise Mirrer, *Women, Jews, and Muslims in the Texts of Reconquest Castile* (Ann Arbor: University of Michigan Press, 1996), and her "Representing 'Other' Men: Muslims, Jews, and Masculine Ideals in Medieval Castilian Epic and Ballad," in *Medieval Masculinities: Regarding Men in the Middle Ages*, ed. Clare Lees (Minneapolis: University of Minnesota Press, 1994), pp. 169–86.

7. Patricia Meyer Spacks, *Gossip* (New York: Knopf, 1985), pp. 10–11.

8. E. C. Riley captures the unexemplary position occupied by this literary form when he explains that "The word 'novela,' as well as being interchangeable with words like 'patraña,' or 'deceitful fiction,' must have conjured up for the public the names of Boccaccio and Bandello and other 'novellieri' well known in Spain, bywords for salaciousness." In *Cervantes's Theory of the Novel* (Oxford: Clarendon Press, 1962), p. 102. For an informative treatment of the theory and practice of the *novela* form, see Walter Pabst, *La novela corta en la teoría y en la creación literaria*

(Madrid: Gredos, 1972) and for an illuminating discussion of the seventeenth-century Spanish novella in particular, see Evangelina Rodríguez, *Novelas amorosas de diversos ingenios del siglo XVII* (Madrid: Castalia, 1987), pp. 9–81. In the context of the neo-Aristotelian controversy over the writing of *novela* fiction in Spain, see Marina S. Brownlee, *The Poetics of Literary Theory: Lope de Vega's "Novelas a Marcia Leonarda" and Their Cervantine Context.* Madrid: Porrúa, 1981.

9. Américo Castro's classic study, *De la edad conflictiva*, is still indispensable. In more general anthropological terms, see Mary Douglas, *Purity and Danger: An Analysis of the Concepts of Pollution and Taboo* (London: Routledge, 1966).

10. Guido Ruggiero, *Binding Passions: Tales of Magic, Marriage, and Power at the End of the Renaissance* (New York: Oxford University Press, 1993), p. 60.

11. Many contributions to the study of Zayas's work have appeared since the 1970s. In addition to numerous fine essays produced in recent years, a number of monographic studies have been very influential: among the most notable are the 1972 dissertation by Kenneth Stackhouse, "Narrative Roles and Style in the *Novelas* of María de Zayas y Sotomayor" (Ph.D. diss., University of Florida); Irma Vasileski, *María de Zayas y Sotomayor: Su época y su obra* (New York: Plaza Mayor, 1972); Alessandra Melloni, *Il sistema narrativo di María de Zayas* (Turin: Quaderni Ibero-Americani, 1976); Hans Felten, *María de Zayas y Sotomayor: Zum Zusammenhang zwischen moralistischen Texten und Novellenliteratur* (Frankfurt: Klostermann, 1978); Sandra Foa, *Feminismo y forma narrativa: Estudio del tema y las técnicas de María de Zayas y Sotomayor* (Valencia: Albatros, 1979); and the collection of essays edited by Amy R. Williamsen and Judith A. Whitenack, *María de Zayas: The Dynamics of Discourse* (Madison, N.J.: Fairleigh Dickinson University Press, 1995).

12. See Agustín de Amezúa, ed. *Novelas amorosas y ejemplares de Doña María de Zayas* (Madrid: Aldus, 1948), p. xxxi.

13. See in this connection the introduction to the *Parte segunda del sarao y entretenimiento honesto*, by Alicia Yllera (Madrid: Cátedra, 1983), pp. 82–93, for a long bibliography of translations into French, English, German, Dutch, and Slavic languages.

The fact that the first publication of the second ten stories in 1647 is entitled *Parte segunda del sarao y entretenimiento* (rather than *Parte segunda de las novelas amorosas y ejemplares*) appears to allude to the fact that Zayas initially called her work *Honesto y entretenido sarao* (this is the title indicated by the document of approval and right to publication, written in 1637). The title was changed soon after, presumably because she thought it more appealing (perhaps more transgressive) to *Novelas amorosas y ejemplares*. As of 1659, when the two collections began to appear together, the title became (and remained) *Primera y segunda parte de las novelas amorosas y ejemplares de Doña María de Zayas y Sotomayor.* The two collections continued to be published together until the end of the nineteenth century.

14. Of the scant biographical details that are known, Anne Cruz writes, "she was close to her father, an infantry captain and caballero de Santiago, as well as to the writers Juan Pérez de Guzmán and Alonso de Castillo Solórzano, whose novels proved highly influential in her own writing. The Catalan writer Francesc Fontanella mocked her in his "Vexamen" for seeming like a man, yet lacking a sword beneath her *saya*." In "Feminism, Psychoanalysis, and the Search for the M/Other in Early Modern Spain," *Indiana Journal of Hispanic Literature* 8 (1996): 43. This summary is informative, yet it omits reference to her close relationship to Ana Caro. Castillo Solórzano refers to this close friendship in *La garduña de Sevilla*: "Acompáñala en Madrid doña Ana Caro de Mallén, dama de nuestra Sevilla," ed. Federico Ruiz Morcuende (Madrid: Espasa-Calpe, 1957), p. 67. Of this, M. Serrano Sanz writes: "Tuvo estrecha amistad con doña María de Zayas, y aun parece vivió en su compañía." Cited from *Apuntes para una biblioteca de escritoras españolas,* (Madrid: 1903–5), 1:177–79.

15. "¡Oh! dulces Hipocrémides hermosas, / las espinas pangegeas / aprisa desnudad, y de las rosas / tejed ricas guirnaldas y trofeos / a la inmortal doña María de Zayas, / que sin pasar a Lesbos ni a las playas / del vasto mar Egeo / que hoy llora el negro velo de Teseo / a Safo gozará Millenea," (Lope de Vega, *Laurel de Apolo: Colección de obras sueltas, assí en prosa como en verso de Frey Lope Félix de Vega Carpio* (Madrid: Antonio de Sancha, 1776), p. 165.

Eleven laudatory poems by men and women in praise of María de Zayas are included in Amezúa's edition of the *Novelas amorosas y ejemplares*, pp. 7–19. This volume contains the first ten stories, and his second volume, entitled *Desengaños amorosos* (Madrid: Aldus, 1950), contains stories eleven through twenty. All citations to Zayas's stories refer to these two volumes, indicated as I and II, respectively.

16. Castillo Solórzano also refers to her as a "sibyl" in a sonnet included by Amezúa in his edition (I, pp. 8–9). Reflecting on the many poems written in praise of Zayas, Amezúa adds, rather chauvinistically, that she was, in all probability, ugly: "Fea o hermosa (más bien lo primero, ya que en las poesías que sus admiradores escribieron en laudo suyo nadie la celebró nunca por bella, unánime silencio muy sospechoso" . . .) (II, xxii).

17. She writes in no uncertain terms that books "llenos de sutilezas se venden, pero no se compran, porque la materia no es importante o es desabrida" (*Novelas*, Amezúa, ed., p. 23). All quotations from *Novelas* will be from this edition, unless otherwise noted.

18. Foucault, *Discipline and Punish*, p. 129.

19. Judith Butler, *Gender Trouble: Feminism and the Subversion of Identity* (New York: Routledge, 1990), p. 13.

20. A particularly fine study that underscores the historical specificity of gender is Nancy Armstrong's *Desire and Domestic Fiction: A Political History of the Novel* (Oxford: Oxford University Press, 1987). Armstrong cogently remarks: "So long as we assume that gender transcends history, we have no hope of understanding what role women played—for better or worse—in shaping the world we presently inhabit" (8).

21. A welcome exception to this trend is the collection of essays edited by Amy Williamsen and Judith Whitenack entitled *María de Zayas: The Dynamics of Discourse*, which brings together a variety of perspectives on Zayas, demonstrating the richness of her writing.

22. Melveena McKendrick, *Woman and Society in the Spanish Drama of the Golden Age* (Cambridge, England: Cambridge University Press, 1974), p. 23.

23. Paul Julian Smith, "Writing Women in Golden Age Spain: Saint Teresa and María de Zayas," *Modern Language Notes* 102 (1987): 238.

24. Valerie Traub, M. Lindsay Kaplan, and Dympna Callaghan, eds., *Feminist Readings of Early Modern Culture* (Cambridge, England: Cambridge University Press, 1996), p. 6.

25. See, for example, Matthew Stroud, *Fatal Union: A Pluralistic Approach to the Spanish Wife-Murder "Comedias"* (Lewisburg, Pa.: Bucknell University Press, 1990), pp. 13ff.

26. In *Sea Changes: Essays on Culture and Feminism* (London: Verso, 1986), pp. 28–29, Cora Kaplan makes the important point: "Critics of twentieth-century popular romantic fiction for women are inclined to assume that women readers identify solely with the dominant female subject represented in the text, that of the exalted heroine." However, "fantasy can entail the pleasure of undermining a fixed subject position for the reader or consumer through the experience of textual pleasure as well as identification with available subject positions in the text."

27. See Roger Chartier, "The Practical Impact of Writing," in *A History of Private Life*, vol. 3, *Passions of the Renaissance*, (Cambridge, Mass.: Harvard University Press, 1989), pp. 112–15. For the case of Spain, see Fernando J. Bouza Alvarez, *Del escribano a la biblioteca: La civilización escrita europea en la alta edad moderna (siglos XV–XVII)* (Madrid: Síntesis, 1992).

28. "Quizá, si ella nos escuchase ahora, podría defenderse alegando que la sensualidad y lascivia de una obra no están en sí mismas, sino en la intención que se pone: que ella nunca canonizó el vicio, antes bien mostró patentes sus estra-

gos y consecuencias con finalidad moral; que no hay regodeo moroso ni culpable deleitación en estas situaciones; y que asi también hubieron de entenderlo los confesores de las innúmeras doncellas y personas de conciencia severa que en los siglos XVII y XVIII devorarían estas novelas (tan reiteradamente impresas), sin que ni ellos ni la Inquisición pusieran a su lectura la más mínima traba; y, por último, que como pueden darse desnudos púdicos en las pinturas, también cabe admitir la escena libre o atrevida literaria cuando es consecuencia lógica de la acción y no se busca de propósito" (Amezúa ed., vol. I, xxxii). [Perhaps if she could hear us now, she could defend herself by claiming that the sensuality and lasciviousness in a work are not necessarily gratuitous, but rather, depend on the author's intent: she never celebrated vice; to the contrary, she dramatized its destructive tendencies and consequences in order to teach morality. There is no perversity or objectionable pleasure in these stories, as the confessors of innumerable young ladies and upstanding citizens who read these novellas that were reprinted so many times in the seventeenth and eighteenth centuries without any objections from the Inquisition attest. Just as one can represent modest nudes in paintings, one can include daring literary representations when they are the logical outcome of the action at hand rather than gratuitous sensationalism] (my trans.).

29. Perry and Cruz, *Cultural Encounters*, ix. In this connection see also Elliott, *Imperial Spain*; Henry Kamen, *Inquisition and Society in Spain* (New York: Mentor Books, 1965); and Edward Peters, *Inquisition*.

30. "An 'appetite for nobility' prevented the middle class from developing into confident independence, for its members preferred to use their wealth to buy the noble status that men such as the father of María de Zayas enjoyed. Like Fernando de Zayas y Sotomayor, they wanted to have the privileges of nobility: many tax exemptions, membership in one of the three powerful military orders, status to disdain manual labor, and license to engage in nonproductive displays of wealth in costume and retinue that sumptuary laws forbade" (Perry, "Crisis and Disorder," p. 25).

Little is known about the actual details of Zayas's life, as Irma Vasileski reflects in what is perhaps the most extensive biographic profile of the writer: "Doña María nació en Madrid y fue bautizada en la parroquia de San Sebastián el 12 de septiembre de 1590. Esta inscripción bautismal es el único documento con visos de autenticidad que conservamos de la que Juan Pérez de Montalbán llamó 'décima musa' y que es quizá la más ilustre de las escritoras madrileñas. Sus padres fueron doña María de Barasa y don Fernando de Zayas y Sotomayor, caballero noble que alcanzó el hábito de Santiago en 1628. El linaje del padre de doña María se encuentra con otros datos sobre los cargos que desempeñó en los archivos de la Orden de Santiago, de la que fué oficial. Concerniente el apellido de doña María, Estaquio Fernández de Navarrete asegura que éste revela la elevada posición social de la familia, y que únicamente, debido a esa posición, le fue posible a doña María a dedicarse a la literatura, ya que la remuneración recibida por los autores de la época no era suficiente para sostenerse económicamente. No ha sido posible localizar ningún dato que revele si doña María contrajo matrimonio o si murió soltera, y todavía existe duda sobre la fecha de su muerte. Debido a la abundancia del apellido Zayas en las familias madrileñas de la Corte, y al hecho de que los libros parroquiales registran dos partidas de defunción bajo el nombre de María de Zayas, una el 19 de enero de 1661, y otra, de 26 de septiembre de 1669, no puede asegurarse cuál pertenece a la escritora, aun en el caso incierto de que una de ellas pueda atribuírsele" ("Doña María was born in Madrid and baptized in the parish of San Sebastián on September 12, 1590. The baptismal record is the only surviving authentic document of the woman who Juan Pérez de Montalbán called the 'tenth muse,' the woman who is perhaps the most illustrious female author from Madrid. Her parents were doña María de Barasa and don Fernando de Zayas y Sotomayor, a nobleman who was awarded the habit of the Order of Santiago in 1628. The lineage of doña María's father is included along with other information regarding the duties he carried out in his capacity as an official in the archives of the Order of Santiago. With reference to doña María's surname, Estaquio Fernández de Navarrete notes that it indicates the family's high social rank and that only as a result of it was it possible for doña María to devote herself to literature since the money made by authors of the period was insufficient to live on. No information has been found that indicates whether doña María ever married, and there still exists confusion about the date of her death. Due to the fact that a number of families in Madrid bore the surname of Zayas, and that parish records note the death of Zayas on January 19, 1661, and also on September 20, 1669, it is not possible to determine which date can be attributed to her" (*María de Zayas*, pp. 11–12).

31. Lynn Hunt, ed., *The Invention of Pornography: Obscenity and the Origins of Modernity, 1500–1800* (New York: Zone Books, 1993), p. 341. See also Jean Marie Goulemot, "Literary Practices: Publicizing the Private," in *A History of Public Life*, vol. 3, *Passions of the Renaissance*, pp. 363–95.

32. Walter Ong, *Orality and Literacy: The Technologizing of the Word* (London: Methuen, 1982), pp. 111–12, 159–60.

33. Luce Irigaray, *Speculum de l'autre femme* (Paris: Minuit, 1974), p. 177.

34. Catherine Gallagher, "Who Was that Masked Woman? The Prostitute and the Playwright in the Comedies of Aphra Behn," *Women's Studies* 15 (1988): 27.

35. For Behn's biography, see Maureen Duffy, *The Passionate Shepherdess: Aphra*

Behn 1640–89 (London: Jonathan Cape, 1977). On Zayas's sketchy biography, see Amezúa's introduction, *Novelas*, vol. 1.

36. Quoted by Josephine Roberts in "An Unpublished Literary Quarrel Concerning the Suppression of Mary Wroth's *Urania,*" *Notes and Queries* 222 (1977): 533.

37. Patsy Boyer, trans., *The Enchantments of Love: Amorous and Exemplary Novels* (Berkeley: University of California Press, 1990), p. 1. Unless otherwise indicated, English translations of the text of the *Novelas* are from this edition.

38. Ann R. Jones, "City Women and Their Audiences: Louise Labbé and Veronica Franco," in *Rewriting the Renaissance: The Discourses of Sexual Difference*, eds. Margaret Ferguson, Maureen Quilligan, and Nancy J. Vickers (Chicago: University of Chicago Press, 1986), p. 304.

39. See Emilie Bergmann, "The Exclusion of the Femenine in the Cultural Discourse of the Golden Age: Juan Luis Vives and Luis de León," in *Religion, Body, and Gender in Early Modern Spain*, ed. Alain Saint-Saëns (San Francisco: Mellen Research University Press, 1991), pp. 124–36. See also Erika Rummel's introduction to her edition of selected Erasmian dialogues, *Erasmus on Women* (Toronto: University of Toronto Press, 1996), pp. 3–14.

40. Julio Jiménez, ed., "Navidades de Madrid y noches entretenidas, en ocho novelas," Ph.D. diss., Northwestern University, 1974, p. 46. Translation mine.

41. Miguel de Cervantes Saavedra, *The Adventures of Don Quixote*, trans. J. M. Cohen (Harmondsworth: Penguin Books, 1981), p. 25. The Spanish is "hijo seco, avellanado, antojadizo." Martín de Riquer, ed., *Don Quijote de la Mancha* (Barcelona: Juventud, 1968), p. 19. All references to the Spanish are to this edition.

42. For recent perspectives on the problematics of the Baroque period, the term, and its usage, see Edward H. Friedman, ed., *"Otro cantará": Approaches to the Spanish Baroque*, special Issue of the *Indiana Journal of Hispanic Literatures* 1 (1992); John R. Beverley, "On the Concept of the Spanish Literary Baroque," in *Culture and Control in Counter-Reformation Spain*, ed. Anne J. Cruz and Mary Elizabeth Perry (Minneapolis: University of Minnesota Press, 1992), pp. 216–30; and José Antonio Maravall, "From the Renaissance to the Baroque: The Diphasic Schema of a Social Crisis," in *Literature among Discourses*, ed. Wlad Godzich and Nicholas Spadaccini (Minneapolis: University of Minnesota Press, 1986), pp. 3–40.

43. *El comendador Mendoza.*

44. Ludwig Pfandl, *Historia de la literatura nacional española en la Edad de Oro*, trans. Rubió Balaguer (Barcelona: Sucesores de Juan Gili, 1933), p. 370. Likewise, Otis Green refers to a number of her stories as "pornographic." See his *España y la tradición occidental*, trans. C. Sánchez Gil (Madrid: Gredos, 1969), vol. 4, p. 164.

45. Matthew Stroud, *Fatal Union: A Pluralistic Approach to the Spanish Wife-Murder "Comedias"* (Lewisburg, Pa.: Bucknell University Press, 1990), p. 14.

46. Antonio Maravall, *Culture of the Baroque in Spain: Analysis of A Historical Structure*, trans. Terry Cochran (Minneapolis: University of Minnesota Press, 1986), p. 163.

47. Peters discusses this (*Inquisition*, pp. 126–27), and Levisi notes the fact that Zayas's sadism has much in common with saints' lives, "estas heroinas son presentadas como santas y mártires, incluso cuando se describen sus momentos finales" (Margarita Levisi, "La crueldad en los *Desengaños amorosos* de María de Zayas," in *Estudios literarios . . . dedicados a Helmut Hatzfeld* (Barcelona: Hispam, 1974), p. 453). More recently, and on the relation of violence to the emergence of the Modern subject, see Francis Barker, *The Tremulous Private Body* (Ann Arbor: University of Michigan Press, 1995), as well as Nancy Armstrong and Leonard Tennenhouse, eds., *The Violence of Representation* (London: Routledge, 1989).

48. "Come non sentirsi infatti assai felici di non essere vittime di una eguale autorità maschile abusiva e sfrenata, gravida di ottusa incomprensione per i problemi delle donne?" (*Il sistema narrativo*, p. 97). Melloni finds an additional, radically different yet convincing reason for the popularity of Zayas's literature, namely the material it supplies to the imagination—e.g., for *el galanteo*; courting, flirting-poems, pretexts, love letters, which could serve as models for the reader in his or her own amorous pursuits.

49. María Zayas, *Parte segunda del sarao y entretenimiento honesto [Desengaños amorosos]*, ed. Alicia Yllera (Madrid: Cátedra, 1983), p. 53. In addition to Amezúa, who reads the *Novelas* as exemplary in spite of their often scabrous subject matter (II: xiiiff.), see also Marcia Welles, "María de Zayas y Sotomayor and Her *Novela Cortesana*: A Re-evaluation," *Bulletin of Hispanic Studies* 55 (1978): 301–10.

50. See Kenneth Stackhouse, "Verisimilitude, Magic and the Supernatural in the *Novelas* of María de Zayas y Sotomayor," *Hispanófila* 62 (1978): 65–76.

51. On the notion of "literature of immediacy" and its importance in Golden Age picaresque, see Harry Sieber, "The Romance of Chivalry in Spain from Rodríguez de Montalvo to Cervantes," in *Romance: Generic Transformation from Chrétien de Troyes to Cervantes*, ed. Kevin Brownlee and Marina S. Brownlee (Hanover: University Press of New England, 1985), pp. 203–19.

52. See Boyer, "Toward a Baroque Reading of 'El verdugo de su esposa,'" in *María de Zayas: The Dynamics of Discourse*, pp. 52–71. The quotation is from Boyer, *The Enchantments of Love*, p. xxv.

53. Several recent studies treat this issue in a variety of insightful ways. See, for example, Sandra Foa, *Femenismo y forma narrativa: Estudio del tema y las técnicas de María de Zayas y Sotomayor* (Valencia: Albatros, 1979); Patricia Grieve, "Em-

broidering with Saintly Threads: María de Zayas Challenges Cervantes and the Church," *Renaissance Quarterly* 44 (1991): 86–105; Elizabeth Ordóñez, "Woman and Her Text in the Works of María de Zayas and Ana Caro," *Revista de estudios hispánicos* 19 (1985): 3–15.

54. In a similar vein, and by way of introduction to her tale *Tarde llega el desengaño (Too Late Undeceived)*, Filis states that neither all men are to blame, proceeding from this assertion to a rather pointed criticism of female vanity as a pointless pursuit: "Si no se dieran tanto a la compostura, afeminándose más que Naturaleza las afeminó, y como en lugar de aplicarse a jugar las armas y a estudiar las ciencias, estudian en criar el cabello y matizar el rostro, ya pudiera ser que pasaran en todo a los hombres" (176) [If instead of studying how to arrange their hair and make up their faces, they applied themselves to learning and to the art of bearing arms, it might well be that they would excel men in every way (140)].

55. Bryan S. Turner, introduction to *Baroque Reason: The Aesthetics of Modernity*, by Christine Buci-Glucksmann, trans. Patrick Camiller (London: Sage, 1994), p. 22.

56. Susan Paun de García, "Zayas as Writer: Hell Hath No Fury," in *María de Zayas: The Dynamics of Discourse*, p. 43.

57. Hans Robert Jauss, *Toward an Aesthetic of Reception*, trans. Timothy Bahti (Minneapolis: University of Minnesota Press, 1982), p. 82.

58. Susan Griswold, "*Topoi* and Rhetorical Distance: The Feminism of María de Zayas," *Revista canadiense de estudios hispánicos* 14 (1980): 113.

59. See in this regard Toril Moi, "Marginality and Subversion," in her *Sexual/Textual Politics* (London: Routledge, 1985), pp. 166 ff.

Chapter 2. Baroque Subjects

Note to epigraph: Mikhail Bakhtin, "Epic and Novel" in *The Dialogic Imagination*, ed. Michael Holquist, trans. Caryl Emerson and Michael Holquist (Austin: University of Texas Press, 1981), p. 15.

1. Edward H. Friedman, *The Antiheroine's Voice*, pp. 213, 5.

2. John Beverley, "On the Concept of the Spanish Literary Baroque," p. 227.

3. Linda Hutcheon, *A Poetics of Postmodernism*, pp. 1–2.

4. For additional reflections on the postmodern mentality and its expression see Charles Jencks, *The Language of Postmodern Architecture* (London: Academy, 1977).

5. John D. Lyons, *Exemplum: The Rhetoric of Example* (Princeton, N.J.: Princeton University Press, 1989), p. 3.

6. Roman Jakobson, "The Metaphoric and Metonymic Poles," in *Fundamentals of Language*, ed. Morris Halle (Paris: Mouton, 1971), p. 92.

7. Alban K. Forcione, "Afterword: Exemplarity, Modernity, and the Discriminating Games of Reading," in *Cervantes's "Examplary Novels" and the Adventure of Writing*, ed. Michael Nerlich and Nicholas Spadaccini (Minneapolis: Prisma, 1989), p. 333.

8. For two interesting publications on the picaresque and its impact, see Peter N. Dunn, *Spanish Picaresque Fiction: A New Literary History* (Ithaca: Cornell University Press, 1993), and Giancarlo Maiorino, ed., *The Picaresque: Tradition and Displacement* (Minneapolis: University of Minnesota Press, 1996).

9. Vicente Espinel, *Marcos de Obregón*, 2 vols., ed. María S. Carrasco Urgoti (Madrid: Castalia, 1972), 1: 230.

10. José Antonio Maravall, "From the Renaissance to the Baroque," p. 23.

11. Elliott, *Imperial Spain*, pp. 254–55. See also his "Self-Perception and Decline in Early Seventeenth-Century Spain," *Past and Present: A Journal of Historical Studies* 20 (1961): 41–61.

12. Henry Kamen, *The Iron Century* (New York: Praeger, 1971), p. 389.

13. Anthony J. Cascardi, "The Subject of Control," in *Culture and Control in Counter-Reformation Spain*, p. 246.

14. Louis Althusser, "Ideology and Ideological State Apparatuses (Notes Toward an Investigation)," in *Lenin and Philosophy and Other Essays*, trans. Ben Brewster (New York: Monthly Review Press, 1971); and Michel Foucault, "The Subject of Power," in *Art After Modernism: Rethinking Representation*, ed. Brian Wallis (New York: Museum of Contemporary Art, 1984), pp. 417–32.

15. Paul Smith, *Discerning the Subject* (Minneapolis: University of Minnesota Press, 1988), p. xxxv.

16. See Anika Lemaire, ed., *Jacques Lacan*, trans. David Macey (London: Routledge, 1977).

17. Catherine Belsey, "Constructing the Subject," in *Feminisms: An Anthology of Literary Theory and Criticism*, ed. Robyn R. Warhol and Diane Price Herndl (New Brunswick, N.J.: Rutgers University Press, 1991), p. 598.

18. Thomas Laqueur, *Making Sex: Body and Gender from the Greeks to Freud* (Cambridge, Mass.: Harvard University Press, 1990), p. 8.

19. On the parameters of feminism in the European Renaissance, see Constance Jordan, *Renaissance Feminism: Literary Texts and Political Models* (Ithaca, N.Y.: Cornell University Press, 1990), p. 9.

20. Laura Brown, "Amazons and Africans: Gender, Race and Empire in Daniel Defoe," in *Women, "Race," and Writing in the Early Modern Period*, ed. Margo Hendricks and Patricia Parker (London: Routledge, 1994), p. 136.

21. Zayas's short prose is punctuated by intercalated verse at numerous junctures in the text. And in this mixture of prose and verse she is representative of a whole vein of Spanish *novela corta* writing. The effect of the *prosimetrum* form is to distance the reader from the diegetic level of the text, to create a distance by which the text functions as stylized artifact. In an observation made with reference to Menippean satire, but equally applicable to novelistic prose of the kind Zayas produces, Julia Kristeva notes the distancing effect caused by the multiple styles, tones, and axiologies that come into conflict when a writer mixes verse with prose. See her *Desire in Language*, trans. Thomas Gora, Alice Jardine, and Leon S. Roudiez (New York: Columbia University Press, 1980), p. 83. It is also worth noting that by mixing prose and verse, Zayas further blurs the claim to the unadorned "historical accuracy" of her narratives.

22. Not only Zayas but her personal friend, the equally celebrated writer Ana Caro, was referred to as a literary "sibyl." In *La garduña de Sevilla* Alonso de Castillo Solórzano conveys the association of these women—as friends and outstanding authors: "En estos tiempos luce y campea con felices lauros el ingenio de doña María de Zayas y Sotomayor, que con justo título ha merecido el nombre de Sibila de Mardid, adquirido por sus admirables versos, por su felice ingenio y gran prudencia, habiendo sacado de la estampa un libro de diez novelas, que son diez asombros para los que escriben deste género, pues la meditada prosa, el artificio dellas y los versos que interpola, es todo tan admirable, que acobarda las más valientes plumas de nuestra España. Acompáñala en Madrid doña Ana Caro de Mallén, dama de nuestra Sevilla, a quien se deben no menores alabanzas, pues con sus dulces y bien pensados versos suspende y deleita a quien los oye y lee" (66–67). Because of the coincidence of the name Ana in addition to the sybilline association, it seems plausible to read the Ana and Violante of this tale as versions of Caro and Zayas.

23. For a discussion of shoes as sexual experience (referring mainly to *Lazarillo de Tormes*'s fourth *tratado*), see Harry Sieber, *Language and Society in "La vida de Lazarillo de Tormes"* (Baltimore: Johns Hopkins University Press, 1978), pp. 45–58; and Janis A. Tomlinson and Marcia Welles, "Picturing the Picaresque: Lazarillo and Murillo's Four Figures on a Step," in *The Picaresque: Tradition and Displacement*, pp. 66–85.

24. Indeed, the goriness was so predictable and powerful that this body of plays led to historical distortion whereby "a handful of seventeenth-century wife-murder plays used to be taken as evidence that wife-murder was the common pastime of real-life Spanish husbands obsessed with a barbaric honor code, and then read back as dramatic propaganda *for* the code" (McKendrick, *Women and Society*, p. 200).

25. Angela Carter writes about victimized females, and sensationalist violence against them in relation to the Marquis de Sade, yet in a way that illuminates a reading of Zayas. See her *The Sadeian Woman and the Ideology of Pornography* (New York: Pantheon, 1979), p. 23. Her rewriting of classic fairy tales from a feminist perspective that takes into account the diversity of female agency is also relevant in connection with Zayas's enterprise. See *The Bloody Chamber* (New York: Penguin, 1992).

26. For a discussion of convent life see Electra Arenal and Stacey Schlau, *Untold Stories: Hispanic Nuns in Their Own Works*, trans. Amanda Powell (Albuquerque: University of New Mexico Press, 1989); and Mariló Vigil, "Conformismo y rebeldía en los conventos femeninos de los siglos XVI y XVII," in *Religiosidad feminina: Expectativas y realidades (ss. VIII–XVIII)* (Madrid: Asociación Cultural Al-Mudayna, 1991), pp. 165–85.

27. To be sure, voyeurism is not an invention of the early modern period, nor is its literary representation. Such moments find expression in earlier literature, for example in the *Decameron* (II, 9), or in the various accounts of the fairy Mélusine who becomes victimized by her husband's forbidden gaze. But unlike the type of public reading entailed by the Boccaccian text or the medieval romance, Zayas's stories are intended for individual, private reading, despite the frame narrative. The effect of the voyeuristic environment becomes much more transgressive as one individual (the reader) personally spies on another.

28. Paul Julian Smith, "Writing Women in Golden Age Spain: Saint Teresa and María de Zayas," *Modern Language Notes* 102 (1987): 238.

29. Natalie Zemon Davis, "Boundaries and the Sense of Self in Sixteenth-Century France," in *Reconstructing Individualism: Autonomy, Individuality, and the Self in Western Thought*, ed. Thomas C. Heller, Morton Sosna, and David Wellbery (Stanford, Calif.: Stanford University Press, 1986), p. 61.

30. Margarita Nelken, for example, writes of the friendship of Caro and Zayas that: "A doña Ana Caro dióle fama, tanto como su talento, su amistad con doña María de Zayas y Sotomayor." See *Las escritoras españolas* (Barcelona: Labor, 1930), p. 151.

31. Not only is this the third description of woman as an "angel" in a Zayasian catalogue which includes many more references, but it constitutes a topos along with the polar opposite image of woman as a demonic creature. Speaking of this polarity in the context of female authorship in general, Sandra Gilbert and Susan Gubar ask a probing question that has considerable relevance for all women authors: "If the vexed and vexing polarities of angel and monster, sweet dumb Snow White and fierce mad Queen, are major images literary tradition offers women, how does such imagery influence the ways in which women attempt the pen?"

(Sandra M. Gilbert and Susan Gubar, *The Madwoman in the Attic* [New Haven, Conn.: Yale University Press, 1979], p. 46).

32. Amy R. Williamsen, "Challenging the Code: Honor in María de Zayas," in *María de Zayas: The Dynamics of Discourse*, p. 143.

33. According to Yllera (61), only II, 1, bore a title at the time of the initial publication of Part II in 1647. The remaining *desengaños* were not assigned titles until the 1734 Barcelona edition, which means that the titles should not be ascribed to Zayas, and that they may not necessarily foreground the dimensions of the text that Zayas intended.

34. Elizabeth Ordóñez, "Woman and Her Text," p. 4.

35. Amy Katz Kaminsky notes the need to distinguish the *Maravillas* of part I from the *Desengaños* of part II. If the two parts are read as one integral work, the power of part II is diminished. "Dress and Redress: Clothing in the *Desengaños amorosas* of María de Zayas y Sotomayor," *Romanic Review* 79 (1988): 377–91.

36. Marcia L. Welles, "María de Zayas y Sotomayor and Her 'Novela Cortesana,'" p. 307.

37. That Zayas offers us a novelistic world is clear from all the competing discourses which lack resolution in her work. As such, she projects the same type of "transcendental homelessness" which Anthony Cascardi names as the literary environment projected by *Don Quijote*. He writes: "Lukács places the origins of the novel in Cervantes' *Don Quijote* on the edge of a great upheaval of values. On the one hand, Cervantes appears as the faithful Christian and loyal patriot, a steadfast believer in the values of traditional society; yet on the other hand his protagonist is set in a world that no longer recognizes the purpose of heroic action and that has come to doubt the value of literature as a source of ethical instruction and cultural renewal" (*The Subject of Modernity* [Cambridge, England: Cambridge University Press, 1992], pp. 72–73). For the parameters of romance see Northrop Frye, *The Secular Scripture: A Study of the Structure of Romance* (Cambridge, Mass.: Harvard University Press, 1976); and *Romance: Generic Transformation from Chrétien de Troyes to Cervantes*, ed. Kevin Brownlee and Marina S. Brownlee.

38. For the importance of claiming historical veracity, see Henry Ettinghausen, "The Illustrated Spanish News: Text and Image in the Seventeenth-Century Press," in *Art and Literature in Spain: 1600–1800. Studies in Honor of Nigel Glendinning*, ed. Charles Davis and Paul Julian Smith (London: Tamesis, 1993), pp. 117–33.

On the importance of projecting the appearance of truth see also John D. Lyons, "Belief and Representation in a Renaissance Novella," in *The Dialectics of Discovery: Essays on the Teaching and Interpretation of Literature Presented to Lawrence Harvey*, ed. John D. Lyons and Nancy J. Vickers (Lexington, Ky.: French Forum,

1984), pp. 83–92; and William Nelson, *Fact or Fiction? The Dilemma of the Renaissance Storyteller* (Cambridge, Mass.: Harvard University Press, 1973).

39. On the representation of lesbian desire in the early modern period see Valerie Traub, "The (In)Significance of 'Lesbian' Desire in Early Modern England," in *Erotic Politics: Desire on the Renaissance Stage*, ed. Susan Zimmerman (New York: Routledge, 1992), pp. 150–69.

40. See the discussion of *Mal presagio* above, pp. 42–52.

41. This behavior corroborates Goytisolo's observation that in Zayas "se ama lo que no se posee; una vez obtenido el ser amado, el amor, inevitablemente se desvanece" (Juan Goytisolo, "El mundo erótico de María de Zayas," in *Cuadernos de Ruedo Ibérico*, 39–40 [1972], p. 73).

42. In "La visión artística de María de Zayas," (*Estudios sobre el siglo de oro en homenaje a Raymond R. MacCurdy*, ed. Alfred Rodríguez [Madrid: Cátedra, 1983], pp. 253–63), Patsy Boyer suggests that Aminta and other avenging females are punished for their male pattern vengeance by the incapacity to bear children.

43. This story is a rewriting of Lope's *Las fortunas de Diana*, one of his four *Novelas a Marcia Leonarda*. See the comparative analysis of the two stories by Ricardo Senabre Sempere, "La fuente de una novela de doña María de Zayas," *Revista de filología española* (1963): 163–72.

44. As Marcel Bataillon observes: "[Cervantes] había descubierto veneros típicamente españoles de la novela corta: uno de ellos, el de la vida picaresca o apicarada contemplada con indulgente sonrisa (*Rinconete, La ilustre fregona*); otro, el de las aventuras de cristianos entre los turcos (*El Cautivo* del *Quijote, El amante liberal*" ("La desdicha por la honra: Génesis y sentido de una novela de Lope," *Nueva Revista de filología hispánica* 1 [1947]: 16).

La gran sultana and *Los baños de Argel* (two of Cervantes' *Ocho comedias inéditas*, published in 1614) further illustrate his enduring fascination with the *novela morisca*, as does the *Quijote*, part 1, chapter 5, where Don Quixote imagines himself to be the Abencerraje, and Dulcinea *la hermosa* Jarifa.

45. Patsy Boyer, "Toward a Baroque Reading," p. 55.

46. "Era el príncipe de hasta veinte años, y de más de ser muy galán, tan noble de condición y tan agradable en las palabras, que por esto, y por ser muy valiente y dadivoso, era muy amado de todos sus vasallos. Era ansimismo tan aficionado a favorecer a los cristianos, que si sabía que alguno los maltrataba, los castigaba muy severamente" (386) [The prince was twenty, a very gallant, noble, and soft-spoken man. He was well loved by all his subjects because of these fine qualities and because of his courage and generosity. Xacimín also tended to favor Christians and, when he found out that they were being mistreated, he would punish them severely (284)].

47. On the extreme presentation of the Moor in literature either as idealized or demonic Other, see Israel Burshatin, "The Moor in the Text: Metaphor, Emblem, and Silence," *Critical Inquiry* 12 (1985): 98–118, and "The Docile Image: The Moor as a Figure of Force, Subservience, and Nobility in the *Poema de Mio Cid*," *Romance Qurterly* 31 (1984): 269–80.

48. "María de Zayas y Sotomayor and Her *Novela Cortesana*," p. 302.

49. "Writing Women in Golden Age Spain," p. 237.

50. Valerie Traub, M. Lindsay Kaplan, and Dympna Callaghan, eds., *Feminist Readings of Early Modern Culture* (Cambridge, England: Cambridge University Press), p. 6.

51. On the status quo of patriarchal rule, see A. Domínguez Ortiz, *El antiguo régimen: Los reyes católicos y los Austrias* (Madrid: Alianza, 1973), p. 195.

52. Carol Neeley, "Constructing the Subject: Feminist Practice and the New Renaissance Discourses," *English Literary Studies* 18 (1988): 13.

53. George Mariscal, *Contradictory Subjects: Quevedo, Cervantes, and Seventeenth-Century Spanish Culture* (Ithaca, N.Y.: Cornell University Press, 1991), pp. 32–33.

54. Jewels are a medium of both autonomy and attraction, as Amy Katz Kaminsky notes in her insightful study "Dress and Redress: Clothing in the *Desengaños amorosos* of María de Zayas y Sotomayor."

Chapter 3. Reading Magic

Note to epigraph: S. H. Steinberg, *Five Hundred Years of Printing* (Harmondsworth: Penguin, 1974), p. 11.

1. "Leisure and Sociability: Reading Aloud in Early Modern Europe," in *Urban Life in the Renaissance*, ed. Susan Zimmerman (Newark: University of Delaware Press, 1989), p. 103.

2. Edward Baker, "Breaking the Frame: Don Quijote's Entertaining Books," *Cervantes* 16 (1996): 26.

3. Roland Barthes, *The Pleasure of the Text*, trans. Richard Miller (New York: Hill and Wang, 1975), p. 62.

4. Michel de Montaigne, *Essais*, ed. Pierre Villey (Paris: Presses Universitaires de France, 1978), 2: 36. The translation is from *The Complete Works of Montaigne*, trans. Donald Frame (Stanford, Calif.: Stanford University Press, 1967), pp. 135–36.

5. *The Tempest* in *The Riverside Shakespeare*, ed. G. Blakemore Evans (Boston: Houghton Mifflin, 1974), 1.2. 109–10.

6. Jean Marie Goulemont, "Literary Practices: Publicizing the Private." p. 385.

7. While pornography is perceived and defined in many different ways, Angela Carter's working definition offers a useful basic approach: "Pornography involves an abstraction of human intercourse in which the self is reduced to its formal elements. In its most basic form, these elements are represented by the probe and the fringed hole, the twin signs of male and female in graffiti, the biological symbols scrawled on the subway poster and the urinal wall, the simplest expression of stark and ineradicable sexual differentiation, a universal pictorial language of lust—or, rather, a language we accept as universal because, since it has always been so, we conclude that it must always remain so." *The Sadeian Woman*, p. 4.

Pointing to the reductionism that pornography implies, Carter adds a few pages later that: "No bed, however unexpected, no matter how apparently gratuitous, is free from the de-universalizing facts of real life. We do not go to bed in simple pairs; even if we choose not to refer to them, we still drag there with us the cultural impedimenta of our social class, our parents' lives, our bank balances, our sexual and emotional expectations, our whole biographies—all the bits and pieces of our unique existences" (9).

For additional perspectives on pornography in early modern times see, Lynn Hunt, ed., *The Invention of Pornography*.

8. Giovanna Formichi, "Saggio sulla bibliografia della novella spagnuola seicentesa," in *Lavori ispanistici*, series 3 (Florence: Università degli Studi, 1973), p. 43.

9. On the sensationalist tabloid literature of the day, see Henry Ettinghausen, "The Illustrated Spanish News"; his "Sexo y violencia: Noticias sensacionalistas en la prensa española del siglo XVII," *Edad de Oro* 12 (1993): 95–107; his "The News in Spain: *Relaciones de sucesos* in the Reigns of Philip III and IV," 1–20; and in *Noticias del siglo XVII: Relaciones españolas de sucesos naturales y sobrenaturales*, ed. Henry Ettinghausen (Barcelona: Puvill, 1992); and Agustín Redondo, "Les 'relaciones de sucesos' dans l'Espagne du Siècle d'Or: Un moyen priviligié de transmission culturelle," *Cahiers de l'UFR d'Etudes Ibériques et Latino-Americaines* 7 (1989): 55–67.

10. Ettinghausen, "Sexo y violencia," p. 107.

11. Benedict Anderson, *Imagined Communities: Reflections on the Origin and Spread of Nationlism*, rev. ed. (London: Verso, 1991), p. 34.

12. Elizabeth Eisenstein, "Some Conjectures About the Impact of Printing on Western Society and Thought," *Journal of Modern History* 40 (1968): 42.

13. S. H. Steinberg, Five Hundred Years of Printing (Harmondsworth, England: Penguin, 1974), p. 11.

14. Joan Kelly-Gadol, "Did Women Have a Renaissance?" in *Becoming Visible:*

Women in European History, ed. Renate Bridenthal and Claudia Koonz (Chicago: University of Chicago Press, 1984), pp. 19–50.

15. Ettinghausen, "The Illustrated Spanish News," p. 118.

16. Elizabeth Grosz, *Volatile Bodies: Toward a Corporeal Feminism* (Bloomington: Indiana University Press, 1994), p. vii.

17. The sorceress Logistilla in Ariosto's *Orlando furioso*, with her cross-referenced book of spells, offers a prime example of the book's magical power in canto 15, lines 13–14, when she gives Astolfo "Un bello et util libro . . . / Che per suo amore avesse ogn'ora allato./Come l'uom riparar debba agl'incanti/Mostra il libretto che costei gli diede;/Dove ne tratta o più inanti,/Per rubrica e per indice si vede." [a fine useful book which he was to cherish and keep by him at all times./This book she gave him listed all the antidotes to magic; it had an index guiding the reader back and forth through the pages to find the right passage]. (*Orlando furioso*, ed. Giovanni Nencioni [Florence: Sansoni, 1970]; *Orlando furioso*, trans. Guido Waldman [Oxford: Oxford University Press, 1974]).

18. We find the Devil of the Christian tradition in two stories (*El desengaño amando y premio de la virtud* and *El jardín engañoso*), a pair of demonic rings (*El desengaño amando y premio de la virtud*), a false necromancer (*El castigo de la miseria*), a true necromancer (*La inocencia castigada*), a number of miracles performed by the Virgin Mary, as well as a few feigned ghost episodes.

19. C. Suárez de Figueroa, *Varias noticias importantes a la humana comunicación*, fol. 234. He writes about this new technology of the book and its implications for society in his *Plaza universal de todas ciencias y artes* (Madrid, 1615). See also in this connection, Antonio Maravall, *Antiguos y modernos: La idea del progreso en el desarrollo inicial de una sociedad* (Madrid: Sociedad de estudios y publicaciones, 1966), and his "La imagen de la sociedad expansiva en la conciencia castellana del siglo XVI," in *Hommage à Fernand Braudel* (Toulouse: Privat, 1973).

20. Roger Chartier, "The Practical Impact of Writing," p. 137.

21. Fernando Bouza Alvarez, *Del escribano a la biblioteca: La civilización escrita europea en la alta edad moderna (siglos XV–XVII)* (Madrid: Síntesis, 1992), p. 137.

22. Steinberg, *Five Hundred Years of Printing*, p. 11.

23. Quoted by D. W. Cruickshank in his "Literature and the Book Trade in Golden Age Spain," *Modern Language Review* 73 (1978): 808.

24. E. M. Wilson, "Nuevos documentos sobre las controversias teatrales: 1650–81," in *Actas del Segundo Congreso Internacional de Hispanistas* (Nimega: Instituto Español de la Universidad de Nimega, 1967), p. 161.

25. Many authors allude to the low aesthetic standards of the *vulgo*. For a good discussion of this readership see Riley, pp. 107 ff.

26. Maravall, *Culture of the Baroque*, p. 90.

27. Salvador Montesa Pedro, *Texto y contexto de la narrativa de María de Zayas* (Madrid: Dirección general de la Juventud y Promoción Sociocultural, 1981), p. 298.

28. As Walter Reed observes, "The novel is distinctive in the prominence and autonomy it gives to forms which are unliterary or uncanonical. . . . The novel explores the difference between the fictions which are enshrined in the institutions of literature and the fictions, more truthful historically or merely more familiar, by which we lead our daily lives." Walter L. Reed, *An Exemplary History of the Novel: The Quixotic versus the Picaresque* (Chicago: University of Chicago Press, 1981), pp. 4–5.

29. Registering the challenging nature of Zayas's prose style, Paul Julian Smith speaks of it insightfully, as being highly rhetorical, in spite of her claim that it is "simple" and "unaffected": "the constant concern for the effect of her writing on an audience . . . is itself a rhetorical posture. Indeed, the desire to change men's minds and impose one's will on the public is the traditional aim of rhetoric, the art of eloquent persuasion. Zayas thus attempts to dislodge men from the positions of power, both social and stylistic. But she can only do so by adopting those same weapons used by men against women: biological essentialism and linguistic mastery." *The Body Hispanic: Gender and Sexuality in Spanish and Spanish American Literature* (Oxford: Clarendon Press, 1989), p. 32.

With similar lucidity, a few pages later Smith exposes the contradictory double standard frequently expressed by male critics: "the same men who praise Zayas for her simplicity and naturalness chide her for the inclusion of irrelevant detail and the failure to conform to grammatical precept" (38).

30. Cruickshank, "Literature and the Book Trade," pp. 812–13.

31. Welles, María de Zayas," p. 302.

32. Francisco Lugo y Dávila, *Teatro popular: novelas morales* in the Colección Selecta de Antiguas Novelas Españolas (Madrid: Libreros de la Viuda de Rico, 1906), I, pp. 23–24.

33. Kenneth Stackhouse, "Verisimilitude, Magic and the Supernatural," pp. 71–72.

34. Suárez de Figueroa, *Plaza universal de todas*, fol. 54.

35. Hugh Trevor-Roper, *The European Witch Craze of the Sixteenth and Seventeenth Centuries* (New York: Harper and Row, 1967), pp. 90–192. See also Julio Caro Baroja, "Witchcraft and Catholic Theology," in *Early Modern European Witchcraft*, ed. Bengt Ankarloo and Gustav Henningsen (Oxford: Clarendon Press, 1990), pp. 19–43; Francisco Rico, "Brujería y literatura," in *Brujología: Ponencias y comunicaciónes del primer congreso español de brujología, celebrado en San Sebastián, septiembre de 1972* (Madrid: Seminarios, 1975), pp. 97–117; and María Helena

Sánchez Ortiz, "Sorcery and Eroticism in Love Magic," in *Cultural Encounters*, pp. 58–92.

36. Edwin B. Place, *María de Zayas: An Outstanding Woman Short-Story Writer of Seventeenth-Century Spain* (Boulder: University of Colorado Studies, vol. 13, 1923), p. 37.

37. As Ros Ballaster explains a propos the act of reading and its seductive function: "The telling of a story of seduction is also a form of seduction. The struggle for control over the identification and interpretation of amatory signs between male and female protagonists which is enacted on the level of content can be taken as a metaphorical substitution for the struggle for epistemological authority between male and female readers on the level of form" (*Seductive Forms: Women's Amatory Fiction from 1684 to 1740* [Oxford: Clarendon Press, 1992], p. 24). It should be added, however, that in the case of Zayas, the male/female response on the part of the inscribed storytellers and listeners is not at all neatly defined in terms of gender.

38. See Kamen and Elliott for a discussion of the controversial aspects of the nobility and its abuses.

39. On this point I disagree with Judith Whitenack's assessment in her otherwise fine and illuminating study: "María de Zayas created a series of nearly one-dimensional characters—virtuous women contrasted with evil men and their despicable female cohorts." "A Lost Seventeenth-Century Voice: Leonor de Meneses and *El desdeñado más firme*," *Journal of Hispanic Philology* 17 (1992): 37.

40. "Verisimilitude, Magic, and the Supernatural," p. 68. Stackhouse offers an interesting inventory to prove his point: "Lucrecia learned her arts in Italy. Juana and the student from Alcalá fail because they neglect to make the necessary pact with Satan. Zayas appeals to her reader's nationalism to make this point: 'Hay en Nápoles en estos enredos y supersticiones tanta libertad que públicamente usan sus invenciones, haciendo tantas y con tales apariencias de verdades, que casi obligan a ser creídas . . . ; como no hay el freno de la Inquisición, y los demás castigos no les amedrantan . . .' (I, 238–39). Among the Moors diabolical magic is even more frequent, '. . . que como ajenos a nuestra católica fe, no les es dificultoso, con apremios que hacen al demonio' (II, 123). In Northern Europe, Zayas writes, the Devil often deals with men of high degree to gain political power. In *La perseguida triunfante* Satan chooses the crown prince of Hungary as his protégé (II, 372). On the other hand, when Spaniards engage in magic, they at best appear as ridiculous as the miser Marcos in *El castigo de la miseria* who is duped into believing a spell will reveal the whereabouts of his wife. At the worst, they find themselves in a situation comparable to that of Don Alonso in *La inocente castigada*, whisked away by the Inquisition, never to be heard from again (II, 130)" (68).

41. That Zayas loves to play with onomastic associations is evident. She recalls the legendary, exemplary Lucretia in *El jardín engañoso*, whereas in *El desengaño amando* she is a witch and in *Tarde llega el desengaño* she is a lascivious, vindictive lover. We have already encountered the grotesquely libidinous Beatriz in *El prevenido engañado*, while in *La perseguida triunfante* she is, true to her name, "the blessed one." Meanwhile, Teodosia behaves like anything but "a gift of the gods" in *El jardín engañoso*. In like fashion, Isidora etymologically "the gift of Isis," could not be further removed in *El castigo de la miseria* from the goddess of bountifulness and fertility.

42. In *The Culture of The Baroque*, Maravall makes an interesting observation regarding Zayas's geographical scope, and more broadly the depiction of urban geography in the period: "The voluminous quantity of literature in the seventeenth century was produced and consumed in . . . baroque urban centers. This very literature reflected the indisputable predominence of the urban ambience: almost all of Pérez de Montalbán's series of novels have Spanish cities as the settings for their plots; the geography of twenty of María de Zayas' novels encompasses perhaps all the important cities of the Hispanic world" (105).

43. Whitenack, drawing a contrast between Zayas and Carvajal, makes an important point, noting in Carvajal "a rare pattern of female friendship and 'solidarity' (not at all the case with Zayas)." "A Lost Seventeenth-Century Voice," p. 21.

44. In a thought-provoking observation, Ordóñez posits a relationship between the images of confinement and entrapment that occur in Zayas and her self-image as a female writer trapped by male authorial traditions: "As Gubar and Gilbert have observed in the British gothic tradition: 'imagery of entrapment expresses the woman writer's sense that she has been dispossessed precisely because she is so thoroughly possessed.' . . . Anxieties about spatial confinement may encode, then, anxieties about authorship in textual traditions similarly restrictive to women" ("Woman and Her Text," p. 6). There is a tradition of women writers expressing their own sense of professional restriction by figuring their heroines as trapped in their rooms or houses, but Zayas may instead depict such scenes of entrapment and torture because they appeal to the tastes of her reading public, one that is often looking for lurid details. Both her writing (as reflected in her prologue to part I of the *Novelas*) and her life (witness her fame and prestige among the most important male writers and her status as a best-selling author) attest.

45. On female martyrs and the nature of their complaints against men, see Allison Goddard Elliott, *Roads to Paradise: Reading the Lives of Early Saints* (Hanover, N.H.: University Press of New England, 1987); and Hippolyte Delehaye,

Les Passions des martyrs et les genres littéraires (Brussels: Subsidia Hagiographica, 1921; rpt., 1966).

46. Patricia Grieve, "Embroidering with Saintly Threads," p. 97.

47. Kenneth Stackhouse, "Verisimilitude, Magic, and the Supernatural," p. 69.

48. Marina Warner, *Alone of All Her Sex: The Myth and the Cult of the Virgin Mary* (New York: Random House, 1983), p. 71.

49. Levisi, citing Emile Mâle, recognizes the widespread appeal of sadistic themes (not just of Christian martyrs, but of pagan figures from antiquity as well): "Para subrayar la omnipotencia masculina, la autora exagera lo patético y doloroso de la condición femenina, y este énfasis, aunque con otros fines, es precisamente lo que el arte de la época preconiza, incluso cuando trata temas paganos: 'Il est extremement curieux de voir, au XVIIe siècle, les artistes ne représenter d'ordinaire que les scènes les plus violentes de l'histoire ancienne: Lucrèce se poignardant, Didon et Cléopatre se donnant la mort, Sophonisbe buvant le poison, Sénèque s'ouvrant les veins. Ces figures douloureuses, choisies parfois par des hommes d'Eglise, multipliaent l'image de la mort violente; on voyait le sang ruisseler d'un bout à l'autre de l'histoire.'" Margarita Levisi, "La crueldad en los *Desengaños amorosos* de María de Zayas," p. 455; and Emile Mâle, *L'art religieux de la fin du XVIe siècle, du XVIIe siècle, et du XVIIIe siècle* (Paris: Colin), p. 148. ("In order to underscore the total control exerted by men, [Zayas] exaggerates the pathetic and painful condition of women, and her emphasis, although its goals are somewhat different, is what we find in the art of the period, even when it treats pagan themes: 'It is fascinating to see how seventeenth-century artists favor the most violent scenes from antiquity: Lucretia stabbing herself, Dido and Cleopatra killing themselves, Sophonisbe drinking poison, Seneca slashing his wrists. These painful figures, frequently chosen by men of the Church, multiply the image of violent death; one sees the blood streaming from one end of history to the other'").

For a fascinating study of the essential links between hagiography and Boccaccio's foundational novella project in the *Decameron*, see Julia Reinhard Lupton, *Afterlives of the Saints: Hagiography, Typology, and Renaissance Literature* (Stanford, Calif.: Stanford University Press, 1996).

Chapter 4. In the Labyrinth

Note to epigraph: Maravall, *Culture of the Baroque in Spain*, p. 153.

1. Marcia Welles, "María de Zayas," p. 30.

2. Boyer concludes, for instance, that "the most repeated motif in the twenty novellas is the victimization of an innocent woman sacrificed on the altar of love, or honor, a motif reminiscent of stories of the early Christian martyrs" (*Enchantments*, p. xxx).

3. Allesandra Melloni, *Il sistema narrativo*, p. 95.

4. Alicia Redondo Goicoechea, "La retórica del yo-mujer en tres escritoras españolas: Teresa de Cartagena, Teresa de Jesús, y María de Zayas," *Compás de letras* 1 (1992): 61.

5. María del Pilar Palomo, *La novela cortesana: Forma y estructura* (Barcelona: Planeta, 1976), pp. 68–73.

6. Melveena McKendrick, *Woman and Society*, p. 23.

7. Cesare Segre, et al., *Introduction to the Analysis of the Literary Text*, trans. John Meddemmen (Bloomington: Indiana University Press, 1988), p. 116.

8. *Las Novelas a Marcia Leonarda*, ed. Francisco Rico, p. 28.

9. Peter Coccozella, "María de Zayas y Sotomayor: Writer of the Baroque *Novela Ejemplar*," in *Women Writers of the Seventeenth Century*, ed. Katharina M. Wilson and Frank J. Warnke (Athens: University of Georgia Press, 1989), p. 192.

10. In 1617, the rabidly neo-Aristotelian Torres Rámila published *La spongia* (a work no longer extant), so named because it was designed as "la esponja empleada para borrar o limpiar . . . la obra entera de Lope de Vega." Joaquín de Entrambasaguas, *Estudios sobre Lope de Vega*, 4 vols. (Madrid: Centro Superior de Investigaciones Científicas, 1946–58), 2: 113. See also my *Poetics of Literary Theory*.

11. Emile Benveniste, *Problems in General Linguistics*, trans. Mary Elizabeth Meek (Coral Gables: University of Miami Press, 1971), pp. 206–9.

12. "Volviéndose a los gatos que andaban por el aposento, les tiró muchas cuchilladas; ellos acudieron a la reja, y por allí se salieron, aunque uno, viéndose tan acosado de las cuchilladas de don Quijote, le saltó al rostro y le asió de las narices con las uñas y los dientes, por cuyo dolor don Quijote comenzó a dar los mayores gritos que pudo. Oyendo lo cual el duque y la duquesa, y considerando lo que podía ser, con mucha presteza acudieron a su estancia, y abriendo con llave maestra vieron al pobre caballero pugnando con todas sus fuerzas por arrancar el gato de su rostro." *Don Quijote*, ed. Martín de Riquer, pp. 868–69. [turning round upon the cats, who were running about the room, he dealt them many blows. And all of them rushed to the window and jumped out, except one which, finding itself hard pressed by Don Quixote's sword-thrusts, jumped at his face and dug its claws and teeth into his nose, whereupon Don Quixote began to roar his very loudest in pain. Now when the Duke and Duchess heard him,

realizing the probable cause, they ran in great haste to his room and, opening the door with the master-key, found the poor knight struggling with all his might to tear the cat from his face].

13. *Novelas amorosas y ejemplares*, ed. Pedro Esquer (Zaragoza: Mercaderes del Libro, 1637), p. 125.

14. Lyons, *Exemplum*, p. 34.

15. This poisoning and its outcome recalls, contrastively, the fate of Isabela in Cervantes' *La española inglesa*. After undergoing a monstrous deformation due to the poison administered by a jealous adversary, she regains her stunning beauty.

16. Cervantes' Lotario does the same thing. In I, 32, for example, in drawing a "misappropriated" analogy between the natural inclinations of the ermine and woman: "Cuentan los naturales que el arminio es un animalejo que tiene una piel blanquísima, y que cuando quieren cazarle, los cazadores usan deste artificio: que, sabiendo las partes por donde suele pasar y acudir, las atajan con lodo, y después, ojéandole, le encaminan hacia aquel lugar, y así como el arminio llega al lodo, se está quedo y se deja prender y cautivar, a trueco de no pasar por el cieno y perder y ensuciar su blancura, que la estima en más que la libertad y la vida. La honesta y casta mujer es arminio, y es más que nieve blanca y limpia la virtud de la honestidad; y el que quisiere que no la pierda, antes la guarde y conserve, ha de usar de otro estilo diferente que con el arminio se tiene, porque no le han de poner delante el cieno de los regalos y servicios de los oportunos amantes, porque quizá, y aun sin quizá, no tiene tanta virtud y fuerza natural que pueda por si mesma atropellar y pasar por aquellos embarazos" (335–36). [Naturalists tell us that the ermine is a little animal with a fur of extreme whiteness, and that when hunters wish to catch it they use this trick: they find the places it usually passes and frequents, and stop them up with mud; and then, starting their quarry, they drive it that way. Now, when the ermine reaches the mud it stands still and lets itself be seized and caught rather than pass through the dirt, and soil and lose its whiteness, which it values more than its life and liberty. The chaste and virtuous woman is an ermine, and the virtue of chastity is whiter and purer than snow. If man does not wish her to lose it, but to keep and preserve it instead, he must not treat her like the ermine. He must not put mud in front of her—that is to say the gifts and addresses of importunate lovers—for perhaps—no, certainly—she has insufficient virtue and natural strength to trample down and pass through those obstacles on her own.

17. See Stackhouse for very insightful remarks concerning Zayas's utilization of gossip.

18. See in this connection Joaquín Artiles, "Bibliografía sobre el problema del

honor y la honra en el drama español" in *Filología y crítica hispánica: Homenaje al Profesor Federico Sánchez Escribano*, ed. Alberto Porqueras Mayo and Carlos Rojas (Madrid: Alcalá and Atlanta: Emory University Press, 1969), pp. 235–41; Cesáreo Bandera, "Historias de amor y dramas de honor," in *Approaches to the Theater of Calderón*, ed. Michael McGaha (Washington, D.C.: University Press of America, 1982), pp. 53–63; José María Díez Borque, *Sociología de la comedia española del siglo XVII* (Madrid: Cátedra, 1976); and Melveena McKendrick, "Honour/Vengeance in the Spanish *Comedia*: A Case of Mimetic Transference?" *Modern Language Review* 79 (1984): 313–35.

19. Florentina is not unique in her perfidy directed against other women. In II, 3, Angeliana destroys Roseleta out of jealousy over Juan; in II, 4, once more prompted by jealousy, Elena's maid tells Don Jaime that she has been unfaithful to him; in II, 5, a Celestina-like procuress lies to Diego about Inés; in II, 8, Clavela tells Mencía's brother and father that she is dishonoring the family honor; in II, 10, a mendacious maid tells Dionís that Magdalena is being unfaithful in her wifely virtue. All of these lies by women lead to the deaths of the innocent heroines in question. Lies told by females also abound in part I, thus underscoring the potentially lethal power of gossip in Zayas's world, gossip which is generated by women.

20. In this connection see Mariscal's book, and also his fine article *"Persiles* and the Remaking of Spanish Culture," *Cervantes* 10 (1990), 93–102.

Boyer notes that "*The Ravages of Vice* is . . . a lurid revision of Zayas' own *Just Desserts*, the seventh enchantment narrated by a man. The internal narrator of this tale is again an apparently morally flawed female protagonist, another 'other' woman who takes control over the telling of her story. Hipólita, loved by a good husband, pursued by a lascivious brother-in-law . . . unsuccessfully attempts to have an affair with an unworthy Portuguese lover (whose name, coincidentally, is don Gaspar, the very name of Florentina's rescuer in *The Ravages of Vice*, which takes place in Portugal)." Boyer makes the additional subtextual identification with Lope's *Los comendadores de Córdoba*, which Zayas rewrites in her final tale ("*The Ravages of Vice* and the Vice of Telling Stories." p. 39).

21. By way of demonstrating this inescapable excess, Lyons writes: "A brief story told about Nero to illustrate his cruelty will include details about Nero or about Roman life that are incidental to Nero's cruelty. To account in general terms for these other details, we could add other generalities or rules that apply to Nero (his hypocrisy), to emperors (their authority), or to Romans (their submission or periodic revolts). To make an example of an object is to account for only one limited aspect of that object." *Exemplum*, p. 34.

Epilogue

1. "Bien sé que dirán algunos: '¿Cuáles son las buenas, supuesto hasta en las de alta jerarquía se hallan hoy travesuras embustes?' A eso respondo que ésas son más bestias fieras que las comunes, pues, olvidando las obligaciones, dan motivo a desestimación, pues ya que su mala estrella las inclina a esas travesuras, tuvieran más disculpa si se valieran del recato" (453).

2. See in this connection Alison Weber, *Teresa of Avila and the Rhetoric of Femininity* (Princeton, N.J.: Princeton University Press, 1990), for an interesting discussion of the power wielded by the father confessor, and of Teresa's clever strategies for circumventing his orders and inquisitorial censure. See also Electra Arenal and Stacey Schlau, *Untold Sisters: Hispanic Nuns in Their Own Works*, and Ronald E. Surtz, *Writing Women in Late Medieval and Early Modern Spain* (Philadelphia: University of Pennsylvania Press, 1995).

3. "Conformismo y rebeldía en los conventos femeninos de los siglos XVI y XVII," p. 170. The image of the safe haven as represented, for example, by the convent walls as depicted in the conclusion to Madame de la Fayette's *La princesse de Clèves* can be counterbalanced by Diderot's *La religieuse*, which depicts the convent as a site of lesbian sadism.

4. "María de Zayas determina entrar en un convento, dando así feliz término a la historia de Lisis, que es la suya propia" (*Texto y contexto*, p. 374). Speculation exists about her whereabouts in the latter part of her life, but no conclusive evidence exists.

5. Ruth El Saffar, "Ana/Lisis/Zayas: Reflections on Courtship and Literary Women in María de Zayas' *Enchantments of Love, Indiana Journal of Hispanic Literatures* 2 (1993): 7–28.

6. Michel Foucault, *The Order of Things: An Archeology of the Human Sciences* (New York: Vintage, 1973), p. 67.

Bibliography

Primary Sources

Ariosto, Ludovico. *Orlando furioso*. Ed. Giovanni Nencioni. Florence: Sansoni, 1970.

————. *Orlando furioso*. Trans. Guido Waldman. Oxford: Oxford University Press, 1974.

Boccaccio, Giovanni. *The Decameron*. Trans. G. H. McWilliam. Harmondsworth, England: Penguin, 1972.

Carvajal, Mariana de. "Navidades de Madrid y noches entretenidas, en ocho novelas." Ed. Julio Jiménez. Ph.D. diss., Northwestern University, 1974.

Castillo Solórzano, Alonso de. *La garduña de Sevilla y anzuelo de bolasa*. Ed. Federico Morcuende. Madrid: Espasa Calpe, 1957.

Cervantes Saavedra, Miguel de. *The Adventures of Don Quixote*. Trans. J. M. Cohen. Harmondsworth, England: Penguin Books, 1981.

————. *El ingenioso hidalgo Don Quijote de la Mancha*. Ed. Martín de Riquer. Barcelona: Juventud, 1968.

Espinel, Vicente. *Marcos de Obregón*. 2 vols. Ed. María S. Carrasco Urgoti. Madrid: Castalia, 1972.

Guevara, Antonio de. *Menosprecio de corte y alabanza de aldea*. Ed. Martín de Burgos. Madrid: Clásicos Castellanos, 1928.

Huarte de San Juan, Juan. *Examen de ingenios para las ciencias*. Ed. Guillermo Seres. Madrid: Cátedra, 1989.

Lugo y Dávila, Francisco. *Teatro popular: Novelas morales*. Colección Selecta de Antiguas Novelas Españolas. Madrid: Libreros de la Viuda de Rico, 1906, vol. 1.

Montaigne, Michel de. *The Complete Works of Montaigne*. Trans. Donald Frame. Stanford, Calif.: Stanford University Press, 1967.

————. *Essais*. Ed. Pierre Villey. Paris: Presses Universitaires de France, 1978.

Shakespeare, William. *The Tempest*. In *The Riverside Shakespeare*. Ed. G. Blakemore Evans. Boston: Houghton Mifflin, 1974, pp. 1611–36.

Suárez de Figueroa, Cristóbal. *Plaza universal de todas ciencias y artes*. Madrid, 1615.

———. *Varias noticias importantes a la humana comunicación*.

Vega Carpio, Lope de. *Laurel de Apolo: Colección de obras sueltas, assí en prosa como en verso de Frey Lope Félix de Vega Carpio*. Madrid: Antonio de Sancha, 1776.

———. *El niño inocente de la guardia*. Ed. Anthony J. Farrell. London: Tamesis, 1985.

———. *Novelas a Marcia Leonarda*. Ed. Francisco Rico. Madrid: Alianza, 1968.

Zayas y Sotomayor, María de. *The Disenchantments of Love*. Trans. H. Patsy Boyer. Binghamton: State University of New York Press, 1997.

———. *The Enchantments of Love: Amorous and Exemplary Novels*. Trans. H. Patsy Boyer. Berkeley: University of California Press, 1990.

———. *Novelas completas*. Ed. María Martínez del Portal. Barcelona: Bruguera, 1973.

———. *Novelas amorosas y ejemplares*. Ed. Pedro Esquer. Zaragoza: Mercadores del Libro, 1637.

———. *Novelas amorosas y ejemplares* and *Desengaños amorosos*. 2 vols. Agustín de Amezúa. Madrid: Aldus, 1948, 1950.

———. *Novelas amorosas y ejemplares o "Decameron" español*. Ed. Eduardo Rincón. Madrid: Alianza, 1980.

———. *Parte segunda del sarao y entretenimiento honesto*. Ed. Alicia Yllera. Madrid: Cátedra, 1983.

Secondary Sources

Althusser, Louis. "Ideology and Ideological State Apparatuses (Notes Toward an Investigation)." In *Lenin and Philosophy and Other Essays*. Trans. Ben Brewster. New York: Monthly Review Press, 1971.

Andersen, Benedict. *Imagined Communities: Reflections on the Origin and Spread of Nationalism*. Rev. ed. London: Verso, 1991.

Arenal, Electra, and Stacey Schlau. *Untold Sisters: Hispanic Nuns in Their Own Works*. Trans. Amanda Powell. Albuquerque: University of New Mexico Press, 1989.

Armstrong, Nancy. *Desire and Domestic Fiction: A Political History of the Novel*. Oxford: Oxford University Press, 1987.

Armstrong, Nancy, and Leonard Tennenhouse, eds. *The Violence of Representation*. London: Routledge, 1989.

Artiles, Joaquín. "Bibliografía sobre el problema del honor y la honra en el drama español." In *Filología y crítica hispánica: Homenaje al Profesor Federico Sánchez Escribano*. Ed. Alberto Porqueras Mayo and Carlos Rojas. Madrid: Alcalá and Atlanta: Emory University Press, 1969, pp. 235–41.

Baker, Edward. "Breaking the Frame: Don Quijote's Entertaining Books." *Cervantes* 16 (1996): 12–31.

Bakhtin, Mikhail. *The Dialogic Imagination*. Ed. Michael Holquist. Trans. Caryl Emerson and Michael Holquist. Austin: University of Texas Press, 1981.

Ballaster, Ros. *Seductive Forms: Women's Amatory Fiction from 1684 to 1740*. Oxford: Clarendon Press, 1992.

Bandera, Cesáreo. "Historias de amor y dramas de honor." In *Approaches to the Theater of Calderón*. Ed. Michael McGaha. Washington, D.C.: University Press of America, 1982, pp. 53–63.

Barker, Francis. *The Tremulous Private Body*. Ann Arbor: University of Michigan Press, 1995.

Barthes, Roland. *The Pleasure of the Text*. Trans. Richard Miller. New York: Hill and Wang, 1975.

Bataillon, Marcel. "*La desdicha por la honra*: Génesis y sentido de una novela de Lope." *Nueva revista de filología hispánica* 1 (1947): 13–42.

Benveniste, Emile. *Problems in General Linguistics*. Trans. Mary Elizabeth Meek. Coral Gables: University of Miami Press, 1971.

Bergmann, Emilie. "The Exclusion of the Feminine in the Cultural Discourse of the Golden Age: Juan Luis Vives and Fray Luis de León." In *Religion, Body, and Gender in Early Modern Spain*. Ed. Alain Saint-Saëns. San Francisco: Mellen Research University Press, 1991, pp. 124–36.

Beverley, John. "On the Concept of the Spanish Literary Baroque." In *Culture and Control in Counter-Reformation Spain*. Ed. Anne J. Cruz and Mary Elizabeth Perry. Minneapolis: University of Minnesota Press, 1992, pp. 216–35.

Bouza Alvarez, Fernando. *Del escribano a la biblioteca: La civilización escrita europea en la alta edad moderna (siglos XV–XVII)*. Madrid: Síntesis, 1992.

Boyer, H. Patsy. "La visión artística de María de Zayas." In *Estudios sobre el siglo de oro en homenaje a Raymond R. MacCurdy*. Ed. Alfred Rodríguez. Madrid: Cátedra, 1983, pp. 253–63.

———. "The 'Other' Woman in Cervantes' *Persiles* and Zayas' *Novelas*." *Cervantes* 10 (1990): 59–68.

———. "*The Ravages of Vice* and the Vice of Telling Stories." In *Voces a ti debidas:*

In Honor of Ruth El Saffar. Ed. Marie Court Daniels et al. Colorado Springs: Colorado College Studies no. 29 (1993): 107–27.

———. "Toward a Baroque Reading of 'El verdugo de su esposa.'" In *María de Zayas: The Dynamics of Discourse*. Ed. Amy R. Williamsen and Judith A. Whitenack. Madison, N.J.: Fairleigh Dickinson University Press, 1995, pp. 52–71.

Brown, Laura. "Amazons and Africans: Gender, Race, and Empire in Daniel Defoe." In *Women, "Race," and Writing in the Early Modern Period*. Ed. Margo Hendricks and Patricia Parker. London: Routledge, 1994, pp. 118–37.

Brownlee, Kevin, and Marina S. Brownlee. *Romance: Generic Transformation from Chrétien de Troyes to Cervantes*. Hanover, N.H.: University Press of New England, 1985.

Brownlee, Marina S. "Baroque and Postmodern in María de Zayas." In *Cultural Authority in Golden Age Spain*. Ed. Marina S. Brownlee and Hans Ulrich Gumbrecht. Baltimore: Johns Hopkins University Press, 1995, pp. 107–27.

———. "Elusive Subjectivity in María de Zayas." *Journal of Interdisciplinary Literary Studies* 6 (1994): 163–83.

———. *The Poetics of Literary Theory: Lope de Vega's "Novelas a Marcia Leonarda" and Their Cervantine Context*. Madrid: Porrúa, 1981.

Buci-Glucksmann, Christine. *Baroque Reason: The Aesthetics of Modernity*. Trans. Patrick Camiller. London: Sage, 1994.

Burshatin, Israel. "The Docile Image: The Moor as a Figure of Force, Subservience, and Nobility in the *Poema de mio Cid*." *Romance Quarterly* 31 (1984): 269–80.

———. "The Moor in the Text: Metaphor, Emblem, and Silence." *Critical Inquiry* 12 (1985): 98–118.

Butler, Judith. *Gender Trouble: Feminism and the Subversion of Identity*. New York: Routledge, 1990.

Caro Baroja, Julio. "Witchcraft and Catholic Theology." In *Early Modern European Witchcraft*. Ed. Bengt Ankarloo and Gustav Henningsen. Oxford: Clarendon Press, 1990, pp. 19–43.

Carter, Angela. *The Bloody Chamber*. New York: Penguin Books, 1992.

———. *The Sadeian Woman and the Ideology of Pornography*. New York: Pantheon, 1979.

Cascardi, Anthony J. "The Subject of Control." In *Culture and Control in Counter-Reformation Spain*. Ed. Anne J. Cruz and Mary Elizabeth Perry. Minneapolis: University of Minnesota Press, 1992, pp. 231–54.

———. *The Subject of Modernity*. Cambridge: Cambridge University Press, 1992.

Castro, Américo. *De la edad conflictiva: Crisis de la cultura española en el siglo XVII*. 4th ed. Madrid: Taurus, 1976.

Charnon-Deutsch, Lou. "The Sexual Economy in the Narrative of María de Zayas." *Letras Femeninas* 17 (1991): 15–28.

——. "Locura y forma narrative en *Estragos que causa el vicio.*" In *Actas del IX Congreso de la Asociación Internacional de Hispanistas.* Ed. Sebastián Neumeister et al. Berlin: University of Berlin, 1989. 1: 405–13.

Chartier, Roger. "Leisure and Sociability: Reading Aloud in Early Modern Europe." In *Urban Life in the Renaissance.* Ed. Susan Zimmerman. Newark: University of Delaware Press, 1989, pp. 103–20.

——. "The Practical Impact of Writing." In *A History of Private Life.* Vol. 3, *Passions of the Renaissance.* Ed. Roger Chartier. Cambridge, Mass.: Harvard University Press, 1989, pp. 111–59.

Clamurro, William. "Ideological Contradiction and Imperial Decline: Toward a Reading of Zayas' *Desengaños amorosos.*" *South Central Review* 5 (1988): 43–50.

——. "Madness and Narrative Form in 'Estragos que causa el vicio.'" In *María de Zayas: The Dynamics of Discourse.* Ed. Amy R. Williamson and Judith A. Whitenack. Madison, N.J.: Fairleigh Dickinson University Press, 1995, pp. 219–33.

Coccozzella, Peter. "María de Zayas y Sotomayor: Writer of the Baroque *Novela ejemplar.*" In *Women Writers of the Seventeenth Century.* Ed. Katharina M. Wilson and Frank J. Warnke. Athens: University of Georgia Press, 1989, pp. 189–227.

Covarrubias, Sebastián de. *Tesoro de la lengua española.* Ed. Martín de Riquer. Barcelona: Horta, 1943.

Cruickshank, D. W. "Literature and the Book Trade in Golden Age Spain." *Modern Language Review* 73 (1978): 799–824.

Cruz, Anne. "Feminism, Psychoanalysis, and the Search for the M/Other in Early Modern Spain." *Indiana Journal of Hispanic Literature* 8 (1996): 31–54.

——. "Studying Gender in the Spanish Golden Age." In *Cultural and Historical Groundings for Spanish and Luso Brazilian Feminist Literary Criticism.* Ed. Hernán Vidal. Minneapolis: Institute for the Study of Ideologies and Literature, 1989, pp. 193–222.

Cruz, Anne, and Mary Elizabeth Perry. *Culture and Control in Counter-Reformation Spain.* Minneapolis: University of Minnesota Press, 1992.

Davis, Natalie Zemon. "Boundaries and the Sense of Self in Sixteenth-Century France." In *Reconstructing Individualism: Autonomy, Individuality, and the Self in Western Thought.* Ed. Thomas C. Heller, Morton Sosna, and David Wellberry. Stanford, Calif.: Stanford University Press, 1986, pp. 53–63.

Defourneaux, Marcelin. *Daily Life in Spain in the Golden Age.* Trans. Newton Branch. New York: Praeger, 1971.

de Grazia, Margreta. "The Ideology of Superfluous Things: *King Lear* as Period Piece." In *Subject and Object in Renaissance Culture*, ed. Margreta de Grazia, Maureen Quilligan, and Peter Stallybrass. Cambridge, England: Cambridge University Press, 1996, pp. 17–42.

Delehaye, Hippolyte. *Les Passions des martyrs et les genres littéraires*. Brussels: Subsidia Hagiographica, 1921; rpt. 1966.

Díez Borque, José María. "El feminismo de doña María de Zayas." In *La mujer en el teatro y la novela del siglo XVII: Actas del II° coloquio del Grupo de Estudios sobre teatro español*. Toulouse: Université de Toulouse-Le Mirail, 1979, pp. 61–83.

——. *Sociología de la comedia española del siglo XVII*. Madrid: Cátedra, 1976.

Dolz Blackburn, Ines. "María de Zayas y Sotomayor y sus *Novelas ejemplares y amorosas*." *Explicación de textos literarios* 14 (1985–86): 73–82.

Domínguez Ortiz, A. *El antiguo régimen: Los reyes católicos y los Austrias*. Madrid: Alianza, 1973.

Doob, Penelope. *The Idea of the Labyrinth from Classical Antiquity through the Middle Ages*. Ithaca, N.Y.: Cornell University Press, 1990.

Douglas, Mary. *Purity and Danger: An Analysis of the Concepts of Pollution and Taboo*. London: Routledge, 1966.

Duffy, Maureen. *The Passionate Shepherdess: Aphra Behn, 1640–89*. London: Jonathan Cape, 1977.

Eisenstein, Elizabeth L. *The Printing Press as an Agent of Change: Communications and Cultural Transformation in Early Modern Europe*. 2 vols. New York: Cambridge University Press, 1979.

——. "Some Conjectures About the Impact of Printing on Western Society and Thought." *Journal of Modern History* 40 (1968): 1–56.

Elliott, Allison Goddard. *Roads to Paradise: Reading the Lives of Early Saints*. Hanover, N.H.: University Press of New England, 1987.

Elliott, J. H. *Imperial Spain, 1469–1717*. New York: New American Library, 1966.

——. "Self-Perception and Decline in Early Seventeenth-Century Spain." *Past and Present: A Journal of Historical Studies* 20 (1961): 41–61.

El Saffar, Ruth. "Ana/Lysis/Zayas: Reflections on Courtship and Literary Women in María de Zayas' *Enchantments of Love*." *Indiana Journal of Hispanic Literatures* 2 (1993): 7–28.

Enríquez de Salamanca, Cristina. "Irony, Parody, and the Grotesque in a Baroque Novella: 'Tarde llega el desengaño.'" In *María de Zayas: The Dynamics of Discourse*. Ed. Amy R. Williamsen and Judith A. Whitenack. Madison, N.J.: Fairleigh Dickinson University Press, 1995, 234–53.

Entrambasaguas, Joaquín. *Estudios sobre Lope de Vega*. 4 vols. Madrid: Centro Superior de Investigaciones Científicas, 1946–58.

Ettinghausen, Henry. "The Illustrated Spanish News: Text and Image in the Seventeenth-Century Press." In *Art and Literature in Spain: 1600–1800. Studies in Honor of Nigel Glendinning*. Ed. Charles Davis and Paul Julian Smith. London: Tamesis, 1993, pp. 117–33.

———. "The News in Spain: *Relaciones de sucesos* in the Reigns of Philip III and IV." *European History Quarterly* 14 (1984).

———, ed. *Noticias del siglo XVII: Relaciones españolas de sucesos naturales y sobrenaturales*. Barcelona: Puvill, 1995.

———. "Sexo y violencia: Noticias sensacionalistas en la prensa española del siglo XVII." *Edad de Oro* 12 (1993): 95–107.

Felten, Hans. *María de Zayas y Sotomayor: Zum Zusammenhang zwischen moralistischen Texten und Novellenliteratur*. Frankfurt: Klostermann, 1978.

———. "La mujer disfrazada: Un tópico literario y su función: *Tres ejemplos de Calderón, María de Zayas, y Lope de Vega*." In *Hacia Calderón*. Ed. Hans Flasche. Stuttgart: Franz Steiner, 1988, pp. 77–82.

Foa, Sandra. *Femenismo y forma narrativa: Estudio del tema y las técnicas de María de Zayas y Sotomayor*. Valencia: Albatros, 1979.

Forcione, Alban K. "Afterword: Exemplarity, Modernity, and the Discriminating Games of Reading." In *Cervantes's "Exemplary Novels" and the Adventure of Writing*. Ed. Michael Nerlich and Nicholas Spadaccini. Minneapolis: Prisma, 1989, pp. 49–71.

Formichi, Giovanna. "Saggio sulla bibliografia critica della novella spagnuola seicentesca." In *Lavori ispanistici*, series 3. Florence: Università degli Studi, 1973, pp. 1–105.

Foucault, Michel. *Discipline and Punish*. Trans. Alan Sheridan. New York: Vintage, 1979.

———. *The Order of Things: An Archeology of the Human Sciences*. New York: Vintage, 1973.

———. "The Subject of Power." In *Art after Modernism: Rethinking Representation*. Ed. Brian Wallis. New York: Museum of Contemporary Art, 1984, pp. 417–32.

Friedman, Edward H. *The Antiheroine's Voice: Narrative Discourse and the Transformations of the Picaresque*. Columbia: University of Missouri Press, 1987.

———. "Enemy Territory: The Frontiers of Gender in María de Zayas's *El traidor contra su sangre* and *Mal presagio casar lejos*." In *Ingeniosa Invención: Essays on Golden Age Spanish Literature for Geoffrey L. Stagg in Honor of His Eighty-Fifth Birthday*. Ed. Ellen M. Anderson and Amy R. Williamsen. Newark, Del.; Juan de la Cuesta, 1999, pp. 41–68.

———, ed. *"Otro cantará": Approaches to the Spanish Baroque*. Special issue of *Indiana Journal of Hispanic Literatures* 1 (1992).

Frye, Northrop. *The Secular Scripture: A Study of the Structure of Romance.* Cambridge, Mass.: Harvard University Press, 1976.

Gallagher, Catherine. *Nobody's Story: The Vanishing Acts of Women Writers in the Marketplace, 1670–1820.* Berkeley: University of California Press, 1994.

———. "Who Was That Masked Woman? The Prostitute and the Playwright in the Comedies of Aphra Behn." *Women's Studies* 15 (1988): 23–42.

Gartner, Bruce S. "María de Zayas y Sotomayor: The Poetics of Subversion." Ph.D. diss., Emory University, 1990.

Gilbert, Sandra M., and Susan Gubar. *The Madwoman in the Attic.* New Haven, Conn.: Yale University Press, 1979.

Gorfkle, Laura. "Re-constructing the Feminine in 'Amar sólo por vencer'." In *María de Zayas: The Dynamics of Discourse.* Ed. Amy R. Williamsen and Judith A. Whitenack. Madison, N.J.: Fairleigh Dickinson University Press, 1995, pp. 75–89.

Goulemot, Jean Marie. "Literary Practices: Publicizing the Private." In *A History of Private Life.* Vol. 3, *Passions of the Renaissance.* Ed. Roger Chartier. Cambridge, Mass.: Harvard University Press, 1989, pp. 363–95.

Goytisolo, Juan. "El mundo erótico de María de Zayas." *Cuadernos de Ruedo Ibérico* 39–40 (1972): pp. 63–115.

Grafton, Anthony. "The Importance of Being Printed." *Journal of Interdisciplinary History* 11 (1980): 265–86.

Green, Otis. *España y la tradición occidental.* Trans. C. Sánchez Gil. 4 vols. Madrid: Gredos, 1969.

Greer, Margaret. "The M(Other) Plot: Houses of God, Man, and Mother in María de Zayas." In *María de Zayas: The Dynamics of Discourse.* Ed. Amy R. Williamsen and Judith A. Whitenack. Madison, N.J.: Fairleigh Dickinson University Press, 1995, pp. 90–116.

Grieve, Patricia E. "Embroidering with Saintly Threads: María de Zayas Challenges Cervantes and the Church." *Renaissance Quarterly* 44 (1991): 86–106.

Griswold, Susan. "*Topoi* and Rhetorical Distance: The Feminism of María de Zayas." *Revista canadiense de estudios hispánicos* 14 (1980): 97–116.

Grosz, Elizabeth. *Volatile Bodies: Toward a Corporeal Feminism.* Bloomington: Indiana University Press, 1994.

Gulihem, Claire. "L'inquisition et la devaluation des discours feminins." In *L'inquisition espagnole XVe–XIXe siècles.* Ed. Bartolomé Benassar. Paris: Hachette, 1979, pp. 197–240.

Hassan, Ihab. "The Problem of the Postmodern." *New Literary History* 20 (1988): 1–31.

Hegstrom, Valerie. "The Fallacy of False Dichotomy in María de Zayas' 'La traición en la amistad'." *Bulletin of the Comediantes* 46 (1994): 59–70.

Hegstrom, Valerie, and Amy R. Williamsen. *Engendering the Early Modern Stage.* New Orleans: University of the South Press, 1999.

Hunt, Lynn, ed. *The Invention of Pornography: Obscenity and the Origins of Modernity, 1500–1800.* New York: Zone Books, 1993.

Hutcheon, Linda. *A Poetics of Postmodernism.* New York: Routledge, 1988.

Ife, B. W. *Reading and Fiction in Golden Age Spain.* Cambridge, Mass.: Cambridge University Press, 1985.

Irigaray, Luce. *Speculum de l'autre femme.* Paris: Minuit, 1974.

Jakobson, Roman. "The Metaphoric and Metonymic Poles." In *Fundamentals of Language.* Ed. Morris Halle. Paris: Mouton, 1971, pp. 90–96.

Jardine, Lisa. *Still Harping on Daughters: Women and Drama in the Age of Shakespeare.* Sussex, England: Harvester Press, 1983.

Jauralde Pou, Pablo. "El público y la realidad histórica de la literatura española de los siglos XVI y XVII." *Edad de oro* I (1982): 55–64.

Jauss, Hans Robert. *Toward an Aesthetic of Reception.* Trans. Timothy Bahti. Minneapolis: University of Minnesota Press, 1982.

Jehenson, Yvonne, and Marcia L. Welles. "María de Zayas's Wounded Women: A Semiotics of Violence." In *Gender, Identity, and Representation in Spain's Golden Age.* Ed. Anita K. Stoll. Bucknell, Pa.: Bucknell University Press (forthcoming).

Jencks, Charles. *The Language of Postmodern Architecture.* London: Academy, 1977.

Jiménez, Lourdes Noemi. "La novela corta española en el siglo XVII: María de Zayas y Sotomayor y Mariana de Carvajal." Ph.D. diss., University of Massachusetts, 1991.

Jones, Ann R. "City Women and Their Audiences: Louise Labbé and Veronica Franco." In *Rewriting the Renaissance: The Discourses of Sexual Difference.* Ed. Maureen Ferguson, Maureen Quilligan, and Nancy J. Vickers. Chicago: University of Chicago Press, 1986, pp. 299–316.

Jordan, Constance. *Renaissance Feminism: Literary Texts and Political Models.* Ithaca, N.Y.: Cornell University Press, 1990.

Kahn, Victoria. "Humanism and the Resistance to Theory." In *Literary Theory/ Renaissance Texts.* Ed. Patricia Parker and David Quint. Baltimore: Johns Hopkins University Press, 1986.

Kamen, Henry. *Inquisition and Society in Spain.* New York: Mentor Books, 1965.

———. *The Iron Century.* New York: Praeger, 1971.

Kaplan, Cora. *Sea Changes: Essays on Culture and Feminism.* London: Verso, 1986.

Katz Kaminsky, Amy. "Dress and Redress: Clothing in the *Desengaños amorosos* of María de Zayas y Sotomayor." *Romanic Review* 79 (1988): 377–91.

Kelly-Gadol, Joan. "Did Women Have a Renaissance?" In *Becoming Visible: Women in European History*. Ed. Renate Bridenthal and Claudia Koonz. Chicago: University of Chicago Press, 1984, pp. 19–50.

Kerrigan, William, and Gordon Braden. *The Idea of the Renaissance*. Baltimore: Johns Hopkins University Press, 1989.

King, Margaret. *Women of the Renaissance*. Chicago: University of Chicago Press, 1991.

Krauss, Rosalind. "Poststructuralism and the 'Paraliterary.'" *October* 13 (1980): 36–40.

Krauss, Werner. "Novela-Novella-Roman." In *Gessamelte Aufsatze zur Literatur und Sprachwissenschaft*. Frankfurt: Vittorio Klostermann, 1949.

Kristeva, Julia. *Desire in Language*. Trans. Thomas Gora, Alice Jardine, and Leon S. Roudiez. New York: Columbia University Press, 1980.

Laqueur, Thomas. *Making Sex: Body and Gender from the Greeks to Freud*. Cambridge, Mass.: Harvard University Press, 1990.

Lemaire, Annike, ed. *Jacques Lacan*. Trans. David Macey. London: Routledge, 1977.

Levisi, Margarita. "La crueldad en los *Desengaños amorosos* de María de Zayas." In *Estudios literarios . . . dedicados a Helmut Hatzfeld*. Barcelona: Hispam, 1974, pp. 447–56.

Lupton, Julie Reinhard. *Afterlives of the Saints: Hagiography, Typology, and Renaissance Literature*. Stanford, Calif.: Stanford University Press, 1996.

Lyons, John D. "Belief and Representation in a Renaissance Novella." In *The Dialectics of Discovery: Essays on the Teaching and Interpretation of Literature Presented to Laurence Harvey*. Ed. John D. Lyons and Nancy J. Vickers. Lexington, Ky.: French Forum, 1984, pp. 83–92.

———. *Exemplum: The Rhetoric of Example*. Princeton, N.J.: Princeton University Press, 1989.

McCaffery, Larry. *The Metafictional Muse*. Pittsburgh: University of Pittsburgh Press, 1982.

McKendrick, Melveena. "Honour/Vengeance in the Spanish *Comedia*: A Case of Mimetic Transference?" *Modern Language Review* 79 (1984): 313–35.

———. *Woman and Society in the Spanish Drama of the Golden Age*. Cambridge, England: Cambridge University Press, 1974.

Mâle, Emile. *L'art religieux de la fin du XVIe siècle, du XVIIe siècle, et du XVIIIe siècle*. Paris: Colin, 1951.

Maravall, José Antonio. *Antiguos y modernos: La idea del progreso en el desarrollo inicial de una sociedad*. Madrid: Sociedad de estudios y publicaciones, 1966.

—————. *The Culture of the Baroque in Spain: Analysis of a Historical Structure.* Trans. Terry Cochran. Minneapolis: University of Minnesota Press, 1986.

—————. "La imagen de la sociedad expansiva en la conciencia castellana del siglo XVI." In *Hommage à Fernand Braudel.* Toulouse: Privat, 1973.

—————. "From the Renaissance to the Baroque: The Diphasic Schema of a Social Crisis." In *Literature among Discourses.* Ed. Wlad Godzich and Nicholas Spadaccini. Minneapolis: University of Minnesota Press, 1986, pp. 3–40.

Mariscal, George. *Contradictory Subjects: Quevedo, Cervantes, and Seventeenth-Century Spanish Culture.* Ithaca, N.Y.: Cornell University Press, 1991.

—————. "*Persiles* and the Remaking of Spanish Culture." *Cervantes* 10 (1990): 93–102.

Márquez, Antonio. *Literatura e inquisición (1478–1834).* Madrid: Taurus, 1980.

Melloni, Allesandra. *Il sistema narrativo di Maria de Zayas.* Torino: Quaderni Ibero-americani, 1976.

Mirrer, Louise. "Representing 'Other' Men: Muslims, Jews, and Masculine Ideals in Medieval Castilian Epic and Ballad." In *Medieval Masculinities: Regarding Men in the Middle Ages.* Ed. Clare Lees. Minneapolis: University of Minnesota Press, 1994, pp. 169–86.

—————. *Women, Jews, and Muslims in the Texts of Reconquest Castile.* Ann Arbor: University of Michigan Press, 1996.

Moi, Toril. *Sexual/Textual Politics.* London: Routledge, 1985.

Montesa Pedro, Salvador. *Texto y contexto de la narrativa de María de Zayas.* Madrid: Dirección General de la Juventud y Promoción Sociocultural, 1981.

Neely, Carol. "Constructing the Subject: Feminist Practice and the New Renaissance Discourses." *English Literary Studies* 18 (1988): 5–18.

Nelken, Margarita. *Las escritoras españolas.* Barcelona: Labor, 1930.

Nelson, William. *Fact or Fiction? The Dilemma of the Renaissance Storyteller.* Cambridge, Mass.: Harvard University Press, 1973.

Oltra, José Miguel. "Zelima o el arte narrativo de María de Zayas." In *Formas breves del relato.* Ed. Yves Fonquerne. Zaragoza: Casa de Velázquez, 1986, pp. 177–90.

Ong, Walter. *Orality and Literacy: The Technologizing of the Word.* London: Methuen, 1982.

Ordóñez, Elizabeth. "Woman and Her Text in the Works of María de Zayas and Ana Caro." *Revista de estudios hispánicos* 19 (1985): 3–15.

Pabst, Walter. *La novela corta en la teoría y en la creación literaria.* Madrid: Gredos, 1972.

Palomo, María del Pilar. *La novela cortesana: Forma y estructura.* Barcelona: Planeta, 1976.

Paun de García, Susan. "*Traición en la amistad* de María de Zayas." *Anales de literatura española* 6 (1988): 377–90.

———. "Zayas as Writer: Hell Hath No Fury." In *María de Zayas: The Dynamics of Discourse.* Ed. Amy R. Williamsen and Judith A. Whitenack. Madison, N.J.: Fairleigh Dickinson University Press, 1995, pp. 40–51.

Perry, Mary Elizabeth. "Crisis and Disorder in the World of María de Zayas y Sotomayor." In *María de Zayas: The Dynamics of Discourse.* Ed. Amy R. Williamsen and Judith A. Whitenack. Madison, N.J.: Fairleigh Dickinson University Press, 1995, pp. 23–39.

Perry, Mary Elizabeth, and Anne Cruz, eds. *Cultural Encounters: The Impact of the Inquisition in Spain and the New World.* Los Angeles: University of California Press, 1991.

Peters, Edward. *Inquisition.* New York: Free Press, 1988.

Pfandl, Ludwig. *Historia de la literatura nacional española de la Edad de Oro.* Trans. Jorge Rubió Balaguer. Barcelona: Sucesores de Juan Gili, 1933.

Place, Edwin B. *María de Zayas: An Outstanding Woman Short-Story Writer of Seventeenth-Century Spain.* Boulder: University of Colorado Studies, vol. 13, 1923.

Redondo, Agustin. "Le bandit à travers les *pliegos sueltos* des XVI et XVII siècles." In *El bandolero y su imagen en el siglo de oro.* Ed. Juan Antonio Martínez Comeche. Paris: Presse Universitaire de la Sorbonne, 1991, pp. 123–38.

Redondo Goicoechea, Alicia. "La retórica del yo-mujer en tres escritoras españolas: Teresa de Cartagena, Teresa de Jesús, y María de Zayas." *Compás de letras* 1 (1992): 49–63.

Reed, Walter L. *An Exemplary History of the Novel: The Quixotic versus the Picaresque.* Chicago: University of Chicago Press, 1981.

Rico, Francisco. "Brujería y literatura." In *Brujología: Ponencias y comunicaciones del primer congreso español de brujología, celebrado en San Sebastián, septiembre de 1972.* Madrid: Seminarios, 1975, pp. 97–117.

Riley, E. C. *Cervantes's Theory of the Novel.* Oxford: Clarendon Press, 1962.

Roberts, Josephine. "An Unpublished Literary Quarrel Concerning the Suppression of Mary Wroth's *Urania.*" *Notes and Queries* 222 (1977): 532–35.

Rodríguez, Evangelina. *Novelas amorosas de diversos ingenios del siglo XVII.* Madrid: Castalia, 1987.

Ruggiero, Guido. *Binding Passions: Tales of Magic, Marriage, and Power at the End of the Renaissance.* New York: Oxford University Press, 1993.

Rummel, Erika, ed. *Erasmus on Women.* Toronto: University of Toronto Press, 1996.

Sánchez, Magdalena, and Alain Saint-Saëns, eds. *Spanish Women in the Golden Age: Images and Realities.* Westport, Conn.: Greenwood Press, 1996.

Sánchez Ortiz, María Helena. "Sorcery and Eroticism in Love Magic." In *Cultural Encounters: The Impact of the Inquisition in Spain and in the New World.* Ed. Mary Elizabeth Perry and Anne Cruz. Los Angeles: University of California Press, 1991, pp. 58–92.

Schwartz Lerner, Lía. "La mujer toma la palabra: Voces femeninas en la sátira del siglo XVII." In *Images de la femme en Espagne au XVIe et XVIIe siècles.* Ed. Agustin Redondo. Paris: Presses de la Sorbonne Nouvelle, 1994, pp. 381–90.

Segre, Cesare, et al. *Introduction to the Analysis of the Literary Text.* Trans. John Meddemmen. Bloomington: Indiana University Press, 1988.

Senabre Sempere, Ricardo. "La fuente de una novela de doña María de Zayas." *Revista de filología española* (1963): 163–72.

Sieber, Harry. *Language and Society in "La vida de Lazarillo de Tormes."* Baltimore: Johns Hopkins University Press, 1978.

———. "The Romance of Chivalry in Spain from Rodríguez de Montalvo to Cervantes." In *Romance: Generic Transformation from Chrétien de Troyes to Cervantes.* Ed. Kevin Brownlee and Marina S. Brownlee. Hanover, N.H.: University Press of New England, 1985, pp. 203–19.

Silverman, Joseph. "On Knowing Other People's Lives, Inquisitorially and Artistically." In *Cultural Encounters: The Impact of the Inquisition in Spain and the New World.* Ed. Mary Elizabeth Perry and Anne J. Cruz. Berkeley and Los Angeles: University of California Press, 1991, pp. 157–75.

Smith, Barbara Herrnstein. *On the Margins of Discourse.* Chicago: University of Chicago Press, 1978.

Smith, Paul. *Discerning the Subject.* Minneapolis: University of Minnesota Press, 1988.

Smith, Paul Julian. *The Body Hispanic: Gender and Sexuality in Spanish and Spanish American Literature.* Oxford: Clarendon Press, 1989.

———. *Writing in the Margin: Spanish Literature of the Golden Age.* Oxford: Clarendon Press, 1988.

———. "Writing Women in Golden Age Spain: Saint Teresa and María de Zayas." *Modern Language Notes* 102 (1987): 220–40.

Spacks, Patricia Meyer. *Gossip.* New York: Knopf, 1985.

Stackhouse, Kenneth. "Narrative Roles and Style in the *Novelas* of María de Zayas." Ph.D. diss., University of Florida, 1972.

———. "Verisimilitude, Magic, and the Supernatural in the *Novelas* of María de Zayas y Sotomayor." *Hispanófila* 62 (1978): 65–76.

Steinberg, S. H. *Five Hundred Years of Printing.* Harmondsworth, England: Penguin: 1974.

Stierle, Karlheinz. "L'histoire comme exemple, l'exemple comme histoire." *Poétique* 10 (1972): 176–98.

Stroud, Matthew. "The Demand for Love and the Mediation of Desire in 'La traición en la amistad'." In *María de Zayas: The Dynamics of Discourse.* Ed. Amy R. Williamsen and Judith A. Whitenack. Madison, N.J.: Fairleigh Dickinson University Press, 1995, pp. 55–69.

———. *Fatal Union: A Pluralistic Approach to the Spanish Wife-Murder "Comedias."* Lewisburg, Pa.: Bucknell University Press, 1990.

———. "Love, Friendship, and Deceit in *La traición de la amistad*, by María de Zayas." *Neophilologus* 69 (1985): 539–47.

Surtz, Ronald E. *Writing Women in Late Medieval and Early Modern Spain.* Philadelphia: University of Pennsylvania Press, 1995.

Sylvania, Lena. *Doña María de Zayas y Sotomayor: A Contribution to the Study of Her Works.* New York: Columbia University Press, 1922.

Tomlinson, Janis A., and Marcia Welles. "Picturing the Picaresque: Lazarillo and Murillo's Four Figures on a Step." In *The Picaresque: Tradition and Displacement.* Ed. Giancarlo Maiorino. Minneapolis: University of Minnesota Press, 1996, pp. 66–85.

Traub, Valerie, M. Lindsay Kaplan, and Dympna Callaghan, eds. *Feminist Readings of Early Modern Culture.* Cambridge, England: Cambridge University Press, 1996.

———. "The (In)Significance of 'Lesbian' Desire in Early Modern England." In *Erotic Politics: Desire on the Renaissance Stage.* Ed. Susan Zimmerman. New York: Routledge, 1992, pp. 150–69.

Trevor-Roper, Hugh. *The European Witch Craze of the Sixteenth and Seventeenth Centuries.* New York: Harper and Row, 1967.

Turner, Bryan. Introduction to *Baroque Reason: The Aesthetics of Modernity*, by Christine Buci-Glucksmann. Trans. Patrick Camiller. London: Sage, 1994.

Vasileski, Irma. *María de Zayas y Sotomayor: Su época y su obra.* Madrid: Playor, 1973.

Vigil, Mariló. "Conformismo y rebeldía en los conventos femeninos de los siglos XVI y XVII." In *Religiosidad femenina: Expectativas y realidades (ss. VIII–XVIII).* Madrid: Asociación Cultural Al-Mudayna, 1991, pp. 165–85.

Vollendorf, Lisa. "Fleshing Out Feminism in Early Modern Spain: María de Zayas's Corporeal Politics." *Revista canadiense de estudios hispánicos* 22 (1997): 87–108.

Warner, Marina. *Alone of All Her Sex: The Myth and the Cult of the Virgin Mary.* New York: Random House, 1983.

Weber, Alison. *Teresa of Avila and the Rhetoric of Femininity.* Princeton, N.J.: Princeton University Press, 1990.

Weinberg, Bernard. *A History of Literary Criticism in the Italian Renaissance.* 2 vols. Chicago: Midway Reprints, 1972.

Wellek, René. *Concepts of Criticism.* New Haven, Conn.: Yale University Press, 1963.

Welles, Marcia. "María de Zayas y Sotomayor and Her *Novela Cortesana*: A Re-evaluation." *Bulletin of Hispanic Studies* 55 (1978): 301–10.

Whinnom, Keith. "The Problem of the 'Best-Seller' in Spanish Golden Age Literature." *Bulletin of Hispanic Studies* 57 (1980): 189–98.

Whitenack, Judith. "A Lost Seventeenth-Century Voice: Leonor de Meneses and *El desdeñado más firme.*" *Journal of Hispanic Philology* 17 (1992): 19–42.

———. "'Lo que ha menester': Erotic Enchantment in 'La inocencia castigada'." In *María de Zayas: The Dynamics of Discourse.* Ed. Amy R. Williamsen and Judith A. Whitenack. Madison, N.J.: Fairleigh Dickinson University Press, 1995, pp. 170–91.

Williamsen, Amy R. "Challenging the Code: Honor in María de Zayas." In *María de Zayas: The Dynamics of Discourse.* Ed. Amy R. Williamsen and Judith A. Whitenack. Madison, N.J.: Fairleigh Dickinson University Press, 1995, pp. 133–51.

———. "Engendering Interpretation: Irony as Comic Challenge in María de Zayas." *Romance Languages Annual* 3 (1991): 642–48.

Williamsen, Amy R., and Judith A. Whitenack, eds. *María de Zayas: The Dynamics of Discourse.* Madison, N.J.: Fairleigh Dickinson University Press, 1995.

Wilson, E. M. "Nuevos documentos sobre las controversias teatrales: 1650–81." In *Actas del Segundo Congreso Internacional de Hispanistas.* Nimega: Instituto Español de la Universidad de Nimega, 1967, pp. 155–70.

Index

Coccozella, Peter, 132, 190 n. 9
Comedia, 19, 31
cross-dressing, 18, 66
Cruickshank, D. W., 87, 88, 92, 185 n. 23, 186 n. 30
Cruz, Anne, 12, 170 n. 14, 173 n. 29

Davis, Natalie Zemon, 51, 180 n. 29
De Grazia, Margreta, ix, 167 n. 1
Delahaye, Hippolite, 188–89, n. 45
Díez Borque, José María, 192 n. 17
Domínguez Ortiz, A., 183 n. 51
Doob, Penelope, 168 n. 11
Douglas, Mary, 170 n. 9
Duffy, Maureen, 174–75 n. 35
Dunn, Peter, 178 n. 8

Eisenstein, Elizabeth, 78, 184 n. 12
El Saffar, Ruth, 163, 193 n. 5
Elliott, Allison Goddard, 188, n. 45
Elliott, J. H., 30, 168 n. 2, 173 n. 29, 178 n. 11, 187 n. 38
Erasmus, Desiderius, x
Espinel, Vicente, Marcos de Obregón, 61, 178 n. 9
Ettinghausen, Henry, 78, 181 n. 38, 184 nn. 9, 10, 185 n. 15
Exemplarity, exemplum, 18, 28, 29, 45, 58, 129–59

Felten, Hans, 170 n. 11
feminism, feminist theory, 6, 9, 11, 21, 22, 23, 34, 35, 39, 161
Ferdinand and Isabella, xi, 10, 12, 131
Foa, Sandra, 170 n. 11, 176 n. 53
Forcione, Alban K., 29, 178 n. 7
Formichi, Giovanna, 77, 184 n. 8
Foucault, Michel, 1, 9, 13, 24, 32, 165, 168 n. 1, 172 n. 18, 178 n. 14, 193 n. 6
Franco, Veronica, 16
Friedman, Edward, 26, 175 n. 42, 177 n. 1
Frye, Northrop, 60, 181 n. 37

Gallagher, Catherine, 14, 174 n. 34
García Márquez, Gabriel, ix
Geertz, Clifford, 31
Gender and sexuality, 8, 9, 10, 12, 13, 14, 24, 34, 35, 38, 39, 72, 78, 82, 154

Gilbert, Sandra M., 180–81 n. 31, 188 n. 44
Góngora, Luis de, 33
Gossip and malsín, 3, 4, 5, 6, 22, 23, 58, 93–94, 118, 150
Goulemot, Jean Marie, 76–77, 174 n. 31, 184 n. 6
Goytisolo, Juan, 182 n. 42
Gracián, Baltazar, 31
Green, Otis, 175 n. 44
Grieve, Patricia, 125–26, 176–77 n. 53, 189 n. 46
Griswold, Susan, 23, 177 n. 58
Grosz, Elizabeth, 84, 185 n. 16
Gubar, Susan, 180–81 n. 31, 188 n. 44
Guevara, Antonio de, 2, 169 n. 3

Hassan, Ihab, x, 167 n. 1
Hegel, Friedrich, 78
Hermaphrodite, 14
Histoire and discours, 23
Historia del Abencerraje y la hermosa Jarifa, 66, 69
Homosexuality, 18, 45, 46, 49, 52
Huarte de San Juan, Juan, 168 n. 9
Hunt, Lynn, 13, 174 n. 31, 184 n. 7
Hutcheon, Linda, x, 27, 167 n. 1, 177 n. 3

Inquisition, 2, 12, 96
Irigaray, Luce, 13, 174 n. 33

Jakobson, Roman, 27, 178 n. 6
Jauss, Hans Robert, 23, 177 n. 57
Jencks, Charles, 177 n. 4
Jones, Ann R., 16, 175 n. 38
Jordan, Constance, 34, 178 n. 19

Kamen, Henry, 31, 173 n. 29, 178 n. 11, 187 n. 38
Kaplan, Cora, 172 n. 26
Kaplan, M. Lindsay, 11, 12, 72, 172 n. 24, 183 n. 50
Katz Kaminsky, Amy, 181 n. 35, 183 n. 54
Kelly-Gadol, Joan, 79, 184–85 n. 14
Kerrigan, William, ix
Krauss, Rosalind, x, 167 n. 1
Kristeva, Julia, 23, 179 n. 21

CABRINI COLLEGE LIBRARY
610 KING OF PRUSSIA RD.
RADNOR, PA 19087-3699

DEMCO